Theorizing Archaeological Museum Studies

Theorizing Archaeological Museum Studies works towards reconnecting archaeological practice, the theoretical richness of archaeology and museum studies. The book therefore embraces both the practical aspects of archaeology and empirical studies in museums in order to rethink what happens when an artefact changes into an exhibit.

This study is positioned at the intersection of both history and archaeological theory, and of the history of art and museum studies. The central focus of this book explores the relationship between museums and their dominant paradigms, on the one hand, and new approaches and theories in archaeology, on the other. It thus also illustrates the co-dependencies, relations and tensions that characterize the relationship between academia and museums. This book demonstrates how in becoming exhibits, artefacts have – and continue to – become reflections of the discipline's prevailing paradigms while manifesting the dominant aims and methods of knowledge production pertaining at a given time and place, as well as the desired social interpretations and modes of presenting the past.

Theorizing Archaeological Museum Studies offers important insights for academics and students (archaeology, heritage studies, museum studies) as well as for practitioners (museum employees, heritage practitioners). The book is also intended for scholars from across the humanities interested in museum studies, heritage studies, curatorial studies, cultural studies, cultural geography, material culture, history of archaeology, archaeological theory and the anthropology of things.

Monika Stobiecka is an art historian, archaeologist and assistant professor at the Faculty of Liberal Arts, University of Warsaw, Poland. Her scholarly interests range from digital and theoretical archaeology to critical museum and heritage studies.

Theorizing Archaeological Museum Studies

From Artefact to Exhibit

Monika Stobiecka
Translated by Paul Vickers

Routledge
Taylor & Francis Group

LONDON AND NEW YORK

First published 2023
by Routledge
4 Park Square, Milton Park, Abingdon, Oxon OX14 4RN

and by Routledge
605 Third Avenue, New York, NY 10158

*Routledge is an imprint of the Taylor & Francis Group,
an informa business*

© 2023 Monika Stobiecka

British Library Cataloguing-in-Publication Data
A catalogue record for this book is available from the British Library

ISBN: 978-1-032-35653-2 (hbk)
ISBN: 978-1-032-35654-9 (pbk)
ISBN: 978-1-003-32785-1 (ebk)

DOI: 10.4324/9781003327851

Typeset in Times New Roman
by KnowledgeWorks Global Ltd.

For my parents

Contents

List of Figures

Acknowledgements

This book owes its existence to the kindness, sincerity and intellectual generosity of many people, as well as to the financial support provided by numerous institutions. I would like to thank them all here.

First and foremost, I would like to express my gratitude to Maria Poprzęcka and Ewa Domańska, who at every stage of my research at the Faculty of Artes Liberales, University of Warsaw shared with me their knowledge and experience, offering advice and comments as they helped me to make new intellectual discoveries. They were mentors to me in the truest sense of the word as they encouraged me to follow the academic path, even though I had sometimes lacked the courage to begin such a journey. I would like to thank them for developing my sense of autonomy and my ability to transcend not only my own disciplinary barriers but also those roles that the academic milieu tends to impose on female early career researchers. I am grateful to both women for awakening my sense of rebellion and nonconformity, while sharing with me their openness, enabling me to experience and learn about things that function outside established academic pathways and fields. I will be forever grateful to them for their sincerity and support. I will do my best to continue my mentors' model practices while recognizing what an honour it has been to be able to learn from them both.

I would like to thank several research networks that took me into their fold and thus made important contributions to the findings presented here. First of all, I would like to express my gratitude to the experimental group At the Intersection of Culture and Nature (*Na styku kultury i natury*), which I was part of during my doctoral degree at the Faculty of Artes Liberales. I am particularly grateful to the director of the doctoral programme Jerzy Axer and to the dean of the faculty Robert Sucharski. I would also like to express my thanks to the members of the Unruly Heritage Group, whose remarks and comments on my research provided priceless input to the arguments presented here. I thus thank Torgeir Rinke Bangstad, Levi Bryant, Mats Burström, Denis Byrne, Caitlin DeSilvey, Stein Farstadvoll, Geneviève Godin, Timothy LeCain, Bjørnar Olsen, Þóra Pétursdóttir, Anatolijs Venovcevs and Svetlana Vinogradova. Finally, I would like to thank the Resilience Academic Team (RAT), which was established before the COVID-19 pandemic and formalized during it, so: Ewa Domańska, Gabriela Jarzębowska, Jarosław Jaworek, Joanna Klisz, Piotr Słodkowski, Mikołaj Smykowski, Tomasz Wiśniewski and Małgorzata Wosińska. Their insightful readings of my work and intellectual kinship enabled me to find a way to express in this book ideas that transcend disciplinary boundaries.

For financial support, I am grateful to the Foundation of the Artes Liberales Institute, the De Brzezie Lanckoronski Foundation, the Kościuszko Foundation, the Foundation for Polish Science (FNP) and the University of Warsaw. Research stays, particularly those at Stanford University and the UiT Arctic University of Norway in Tromsø, enabled me to significantly expand my research and develop contacts that proved crucial in shaping this book. Thanks to such funding, I was able to consult drafts of my project with Ian Hodder, Rodney Harrison, Bjørnar Olsen and Michael Shanks. I would also like to thank all of them, as well as other researchers with whom I was in contact as part of seminars and conferences or through e-mail exchanges regarding my book: Doug Bailey, Ewa Bugaj, Michael Carter, Costis Dallas, Kasper Hanus, Cornelius Holtorf, Dawid Kobiałka, Gavin Lucas, Arkadiusz Marciniak, Danuta Minta-Tworzowska, Michał Pawleta, Sara Perry, Włodzimierz Rączkowski, Matusz Salwa, Christopher Witmore, Anna Zalewska and Anna Ziębińska-Witek.

I would like to thank Paul Vickers for reflecting my thoughts so clearly in his fantastic translation of this book.

Last but not least, I express my gratitude to my truly supportive family, friends and loved ones: Benjamin Hanussek, Alicja Bielak, Stanisław Brończyk, Agata Kowalewska, Maja Kozłowska, Marika Magnuszewska, Anka Mrozowska, Rozalia Mazur, Hanna and Marek Niezgódka, Maciek Ostaszewski, Agata Sitarska, Konrad Stępień, Aleksandra Stobiecka, Rafał Stobiecki, Weronika Tomczyk and Joanna Weremijewicz.

Introduction

What is exhibited in archaeological museums? What do the rows of vessels and dishes, tools, pieces of jewellery and figures actually constitute? How are they exhibited and why? What can they tell us? What can we learn from them? In the case of many traditional exhibitions, particularly Mediterranean archaeological collections and large, world-class museums, archaeological objects are reduced to the status of works of art. Regardless of their functions in the past, they are arranged in logical sequences, forming, at best, an aesthetic illustration of progress (Olsen et al. 2012: 42). They are thus admired for their craft, iconography and form, or as ornaments and decorations. My scepticism towards this manner of presenting archaeological objects developed already while I was a student and involved in archaeological excavations. It is unjustified, I would argue, to deny finds' archaeological background, their innate materiality and interpretive context, as established through research-based knowledge, by reducing them to sterilized works of art stripped of diverse connotations (Ting 2010). Presenting impressive unique objects according to typological sequences in display cabinets in museums reinscribes an image of a discipline that is divorced from the materiality of archaeological excavations and the realities of research. Archaeological museums and art galleries are not the same thing.

In this book, I would like to demonstrate how it is possible to develop a different perspective on artefacts, beyond the optics of art. In doing so, I will work towards neutralizing archaeological museums' traditional aesthetic of beauty and the sublime (i.e. projecting aesthetic values onto artefacts) in favour of, firstly, an aesthetics of the abject (Kristeva 1982), which values artefacts' inherent traits: ageing, crumbling and decay, together with the patina, rust and fragmentariness that is associated with these processes; and, secondly, an everyday aesthetics that highlights the value contained in the commonplace, functional, simple objects that, to a great extent, artefacts once were. My critical approach to the dominant paradigm of exhibiting artefacts stems from my position as a researcher located both in the history of art and in archaeology, with knowledge grounded in experiences of archaeological fieldwork. This enables me to approach artefacts "from below", i.e. from a practice-oriented perspective, which in turn informs my

DOI: 10.4324/9781003327851-1

opposition to the reductionism commonplace in archaeological museums whereby artefacts are treated primarily as works of art. Why, then, do we so often encounter artefacts-as-works-of-art rather than artefacts-as-things?

The archaeology of archaeology museums

The intersection of two orders that are usually discussed in isolation – namely archaeological research and museum practices – lays the ground for reflections on things and enables us to work towards an answer to the above question. In their impressive study, *Archaeology: The Discipline of Things*, Bjørnar Olsen, Michael Shanks, Timothy Webmoor and Christopher Witmore connect the birth of archaeology as a discipline with the dawn of the modern museum, highlighting that it was material and tangible objects – concrete, authentic and convincing thanks to the visible traces of the passing of time, exhibited in museums in accordance with the emerging orders of classifying artefacts – that revealed the true object of archaeological research and the focus of its interests (Olsen et al. 2012: 42; see also Olsen and Svestad 1994; Macdonald 1998: 10). Likewise, debates over "authenticity" and "evidence" developed at the same time as the inauguration of the first modern museums (Marstine 2006b: 2). Nineteenth-century museums alongside the emerging scientific apparatus of archaeology thus became a stage for presenting evidence and sources, which provided archaeology with the credentials that enabled it to enter the realm of academia. In the fledgling field of archaeology, artefacts constituted pieces of evidence that unlike unreliable texts simply "do not lie" (Schnapp 1996: 181; Thomas 2004: 13). Treating artefacts as material proof at the time of the formation of both the discipline and archaeological exhibitions, paradoxically, as Yannis Hamilakis suggests, led to archaeology being inscribed into the visual order. Drawing on the Latin etymology of the word "evidence" (Latin *videre* – "to see"), Hamilakis offers a convincing vision according to which even in the early stages of the development of archaeology as an academic discipline, artefacts were divorced from the material realm and situated instead in a system of representation (Hamilakis 2013: 6, 48). Research methods replaced the chaos of cabinets of curiosity, serving the Enlightenment's predilection for classification and categorization (Hamilakis 2013: 48). Visual and educational representations endowed the fledgling discipline with a scientific veneer, thus honouring the Cartesian principle of the realm of ideas dominating the material (Thomas 2004: 130). "Dematerialized" artefacts started functioning as illustrations of scientific hypotheses.[1] Rather than focusing on the tangible, sensory material of artefacts, modern archaeology demonstrated an inclination towards (re)presentation, mostly of fragments extracted from their context and placed on pedestals according to the aesthetic order of science (Hamilakis 2013: 48).

The aesthetic mode of (re)presentation was primarily a product of the traits of historical methodological tools. Typologies, belief in the evolutionary development of technology and stratigraphy all contributed to the formation of the aesthetic paradigm of archaeological exhibitions, which was typified by an approach to objects that laid bare a lack of interest in their materiality (Olsen 2013: 104–112).

In the early nineteenth century, the Danish antiquarian Christian Jürgensen Thomsen proposed a chronology of artefacts that was based on ordering them according to the material they were made of. Thomsen's system was convincing in that it presented large amounts of archaeological "evidence" that endowed his ideas with legitimacy (Olsen et al. 2012: 39). Difficult prehistorical heritage that was open to multiple interpretations, when arranged according to Thomsen's principles and those of his student Worsaae, revealed surprising similarities and guaranteed a sense of "order". Typology proved similarly explicit as it ordered artefacts according to evolutionary principles derived from a biological and Newtonian understanding of the world that strived for scientific classification (Thomas 2004: 23). The order upheld by the typological segregation of objects not only constituted a way of constricting materiality but also offered an illustration of the evolution of forms and the passing of time (Olsen et al. 2012: 42). An outcome of the introduction of methodological tools based on belief in technological progress and cultural evolution was that stratigraphy came to be seen as another way of sequencing artefacts (Thomas 2004: 160). The methodological triad of archaeology – typology, technological evolution and stratigraphy – laid what are still the almost inviolable foundations not only of studying artefacts but also their presentation.

Nineteenth-century archaeology's efforts to seek academic legitimacy by formulating hypotheses and methodologies meant that in museums, typology, stratigraphy and Thomsen's chronology, which were all based on similar evolutionary classification schemes, became the sole mode of presenting archaeological heritage. The impact of introducing the above-mentioned methods to museum spaces was strictly visual. Ordering series of prehistoric and ancient finds in accordance with the evolutionary order guaranteed visitors insight into the "order of things" thus illustrating the "spatial image of time" (Olsen et al. 2012: 42): the ideas of development and progress. This mode of presenting archaeological objects was also evident in the work of Johann Joachim Winckelmann, a pioneer of the academic history of art and one of the founding fathers of Classical archaeology.

Winckelmann gained recognition as the author of the first proper art-historical study of ancient art. His 1764 work *History of the Art of Antiquity* [*Geschichte der Kunst des Alterthums*] not only played a significant role in establishing the history of art as an academic discipline but also exerted notable influence on the practice of Classical archaeology. Drawing on historical and geographical premises, Winckelmann presented a convincing theory of Greek art that was grounded in efforts to establish common stylistic traits. This enabled the determination of particular styles in Ancient Greek art (Preziosi 2009: 14–19). What was revolutionary about Winckelmann's method was that he did not limit himself to studying individual objects and their distinctive features, but instead sought common traits across all the objects, thus making it possible to establish generalizations and evolutionary phases in the development of art (Potts 1994: 14). When his hugely popular ideas were applied to Classical archaeology, they lent legitimacy to historical-cultural descriptions. Nineteenth-century science, with its passion for classifications and an evolutionary order, pushed the seemingly unruly, fragmentary and rather unintelligible archaeological material into the background while at the same time relegating the archaeological imagination to secondary significance (Shanks 2012: 144).

Museums as reflections of a discipline?

In this book I argue that archaeological museum practices are, firstly, connected to the historical models of exposition, as outlined above, and, secondly, largely divorced from contemporary archaeological research. This means that while modern museums of the kind established in the nineteenth century were attempting to provide a platform for emerging academic theories, today's academic and museum institutions are no longer running in parallel when it comes to presenting the latest theoretical concepts.

Still, as far as current practices are concerned, I must disagree with Hedley Swain, who in 2007 claimed that the poor condition of archaeological exhibitions is in general a result of a crisis of archaeology (Swain 2007: 10; see also Skeates 2017b: 43). In contrast to Swain, I would argue that the academic discipline is doing very well as it applies an unprecedented number of diverse theories and methodologies that could also quite successfully be introduced as narrative frameworks in museums. Archaeology is currently the academic discipline that is making the most courageous and successful strides towards trans- and interdisciplinarity, as is evident in developments in archaeometry, landscape and environmental archaeology, bioarchaeology and material culture studies. The discipline is transcending established chronological frameworks as it is concerned not only with the past but also with the present (archaeology of the recent past, archaeology of the contemporary past) and even the future (archaeology of the Anthropocene, space archaeology). It explores the objects of its research through lenses drawn from feminist studies (feminist archaeology, gender archaeology and minority archaeology), postcolonial studies (colonial archaeology, postcolonial archaeology, decolonizing archaeology), the material turn (material culture studies, biography of things, symmetrical archaeology), the digital turn (digital, virtual and cybernetic archaeology), the spatial turn (landscape archaeology and spatial archaeology), the forensic turn (Holocaust archaeology, forensic archaeology), the sensorial turn and the affective turn (archaeology of the senses, archaeoacoustics and archaeomusicology), the ontological turn, flat and relational ontologies (relational archaeology), the non-human turn (multispecies archaeology, social zooarchaeology), new materialism and speculative realism (entanglement theory, symmetrical archaeology).

A more accurate diagnosis of the state of archaeological museum practices came from Susan Pearce, whose writings preceded Swain's. Writing in the 1990s, she ascribed the lack of progress in museums primarily to the failure to adopt problem-oriented thinking (Pearce 1990: 8), arguing that the remedy could be found in in-depth studies of objects. Pearce thus favoured a biographical approach to things, stating that they have been marginalized in museum narratives. Her vision might be seen at least partly as a museum-based precursor to Bjørnar Olsen's manifesto, *In Defense of Things: Archaeology and the Ontology of Objects* (2013). It was this highly resonant and important publication that enabled archaeology to rupture the dominance of text-based approaches, opening up the discipline to completely new research perspectives based in the return to things. Thanks to the project of symmetrical archaeology, things were defended successfully throughout the 2010s. This means that it is not necessary for my book to follow Olsen's call of a decade ago to defend things, something that was echoed by another representative of symmetrical archaeology, Christopher Witmore, who wrote that "to care for things also demands a defense against their further concealment and repression" (Witmore 2014: 14). What I would like to encourage instead is redefining, moving, illustrating and animating things, thus filling them with life. This is the guiding principle of this book, which is all about the shifting, transformation and movement of objects that occurs within the framework of theories located between academia and museums.

This study is positioned at the intersection of both history and the theory of archaeology, and of the history of art and museum studies. The central focus of this book explores the relationship between museums and their dominant paradigms, on the one hand, and new approaches and theories in archaeology, on the other. It thus also illustrates the co-dependencies, relations and tensions that characterize the relationship between academia and museums. I attempt to depict this dynamic situation by observing and analysing the process that produces the transformation of archaeological artefacts into museum exhibits. I am particularly interested in the ontological status of artefacts and exhibits in the context of archaeological museums. The most important task here is to show which definitions and concepts are applied when constructing archaeological exhibitions. My hypothesis, then, is that exhibits, as constituted by prevailing theories, form the basis of the construction of the public image of archaeology as it is presented in museums. I therefore argue that the key objective for archaeological museums today must be finding a place for new archaeological theories, thus becoming open to the polyphony of theories and interpretations.

Key to this study is the conviction that one of the fundamental objectives of any archaeological museum must be achieving the status of a critical museum.[2] What this requires is introducing exhibition narratives that would face up to the challenges of our age while showcasing the latest research trends in archaeology. What would emerge, then, would be a museum that negotiates meanings and promotes a polyphony of interpretations, while engaging with key problems related not only to the past but also the present. It would thus become at the same time a political museum, a contemporary agora and forum that would engender dialogue. Taking up such problems is important, I believe, in relation to current debates regarding the social purpose of academic knowledge. Hence my attempts to show what kind of image of archaeology as an academic discipline is presented to the broader public. These are crucial issues, likewise in the context of theory, as they are connected to the potential for negotiating theories that are then subject to verification, legitimization and mediation as they are put into practice. The issues outlined here also illustrate how museums can generate theories, inspiring discussions among archaeologists.

My research aims at tracing the process whereby artefacts as objects of archaeological research are transformed into exhibits that are part of museum practices. I have attempted to illustrate this process in the context of both the richness of contemporary archaeological theory, and of the agendas of contemporary museum practices. I am interested in ontological exchanges (artefact-exhibit) and epistemological ones (academia-museum). This book thus demonstrates how in becoming exhibits, artefacts have – and continue to – become reflections of the discipline's prevailing paradigms while manifesting the dominant aims and methods of knowledge production pertaining at a given time and place, as well as the desired social interpretations and modes of presenting (in both senses of the word) the past. Particularly instructive in this context is Bjørnar Olsen and Asgeir Svestad's remark that "the role of collections, exhibitions, in short of *museums*, can never be understood in isolation from other statements and practices" (*original emphasis*) (Olsen and Svestad 1994: 18). I also draw attention to narratives that make us aware of the creative scientific and research potential of archaeology and the archaeological imagination (Shanks 2012). Indeed, it is the archaeological imagination that provides the impetus "to recreate a world from ruins", to reanimate the people behind ancient potsherds and other fragments of the past (Shanks 2012: 25). The critical museum is impossible without the archaeological imagination.

Artefacts-exhibits: Museum dialectics

Fundamental to my research is the attempt to transcend existing definitions of archaeological artefacts and to instead develop, from below, a definition that is relevant to this study by applying an autoethnographic method. In doing so, I am seeking to address the challenge posed by Hedley Swain, who wanted to ensure that critiques of or debates about archaeological museums would be based on precise definitions of the aims and tasks of archaeology, as well as its research objects (Swain 2007: 10). Understanding artefacts in the context of the *longue durée*, processes, transformation, movement and dynamics locates my research within the scope of new materialism. Approaching artefacts as someone who has been involved in fieldwork means that they become vibrant matter understood as possessing agency, as active, mobile, dynamic and, above all, living (Bennett 2010). By introducing autoethnographic elements, I refer to my own experiences in the field and understand artefacts in verb-based terms, i.e. in relation to reality and the potential contained in the moods and activities of the present. Adopting such an approach opens up new research perspectives enabling the object to be studied from the inside.

Following Ian Hodder, I am also guided by the principle that on an archaeological site, everything is in flux (Hodder 1997, 1999), thus archaeological objects should not be considered as static, fixed and immobilized. Following these principles, I propose a definition of artefacts in which each component is active: time influences the character and morphology of objects; biological factors transform finds; the people discovering them adapt their working methods to the slowly emerging objects; research methods are selected by way of negotiations; interpretations are debated and updated. There is no room in archaeology for permanence and fixity, and this is something that I aim to draw readers' attention to.

A second central concept guiding this study is the exhibit. As with artefacts, my aim is to refer to prevailing definitions of the term and juxtapose them with archaeological research practices and the realities of museums. I define exhibits by drawing on the etymology of the term: to exhibit means to explain, translate or present. Taking the nominal understanding of the concept as a starting point, I emphasize the fluctuating nature of discourse as well as the verb-based derivation of the term, as this allows us to speak of the process, translation and mediation that occurs in archaeological museums, with particular focus on the transformation of artefacts into exhibits. Tracing the verb-based derivation of "exhibits" foregrounds the polyphony of interpretations, allowing me to illustrate their layers and heterogeneity. My aim, then, is to show that exhibits acquire meanings, are animated and speak to us differently depending on the theoretical frameworks applied to them.

Reflecting on the issues outlined above, I pose the following questions: what does an artefact lose and what does it gain in museums? What theories served, serve and could serve in framing artefacts? And why are certain theories selected and not others? What role do artefacts-as-exhibits play in the visualization process? What opportunities do current archaeological theories provide artefacts-as-exhibits with? What image of archaeology is constructed by museums? What do museums tell us about the realities and conditions of the discipline today? How do museums define the discipline's object of research? What paradigmatic changes are influencing the ontology of artefacts? Do archaeological museums present and explain, or do they also yield opportunities to develop individual visions of the past? Finally, do archaeological museums make it possible to project and conceive the future?

Archaeological museum studies

The heterogenous research object that is the artefact-as-exhibit demands methodological eclecticism and necessarily requires the juxtaposition of highly diverse and disparate theories and approaches to artefacts, exhibits and museums. In this book, I produce research that is based on empirical sources: artefacts, works of contemporary art, exhibits and written sources, including museum leaflets and guidebooks, websites, publications and analyses, as well as archival materials collected during visits to libraries and archives in Europe and the US.

I developed the interpretive lenses applied to artefacts here over the course of many years of studying archaeology and, most importantly, on archaeological excavations. My arguments are thus based on experiences acquired while working between 2010 and 2018 on archaeological sites in Bulgaria, Denmark and Italy. As I was actively involved in fieldwork at various stages of archaeological practice, I was responsible for exploring, documenting and analysing archaeological objects.

My starting point has been to work towards as broad as possible an understanding of artefacts in terms of both the theory and practice of archaeology. Drawing on my own experiences of fieldwork, which I present here in the form of autoethnographic notes, I seek to develop a bottom-up definition of artefacts. In doing so, I refer to objects that I explored in the course of practical fieldwork. My starting point, then, are minor objects of material culture, architectural elements, fragments of objects and archaeobotanical sources; but I do not approach them with the intention of dating them, defining their functions or origins, or classifying them according to type or their mode of preservation. Instead, by emphasizing the multiplicities and heterogeneity that archaeologists encounter in fieldwork, I want to show that these diverse objects are, to paraphrase Claude Lévi-Strauss, "good for thinking with" in that they transcend established analytical and interpretive models. And furthermore, and perhaps most importantly, I want to show that scientific analysis takes place at subsequent stages of archaeological work and it is dependent upon the theoretical frameworks applied. My aim is to present the finds that I encountered in the field in terms of "things for thinking with" rather than as types, practical objects or works of art. This means that I treat them as fluid, mysterious, enigmatic artefacts full of interpretive potential. My study does not feature therefore the traditional archaeological catalogue. Instead, I make the most of my position as a researcher in the history of art and archaeology as this enables me to bring an alternative perspective into archaeological studies that avoids both standard typologies and focusing on the aesthetic aspect of objects. It is for this reason that I abandon what I consider to be reductionist approaches in favour of attempts to comprehend the "nature" of finds and the ontology of artefacts. In constructing such a non-traditional archaeological narrative, I aim to ground my working hypotheses while justifying the choices made as I proceed with reference to the research materials analysed in the study. In the part of the book focused on artefacts, I refer to the rich vein of archaeological theory developed by key thinkers. The most significant inspiration for my efforts to define artefacts comes from approaches situated at the intersection of studies of things, materiality, agency and the theory of practice, such as the work of Matthew Edgeworth, Ian Hodder, Gavin Lucas, Bjørnar Olsen, Michael Shanks and Christopher Witmore.

During my work on exhibits conducted between 2015 and 2019, which was the basis for selecting my case studies, I visited 20 European museums. During these visits, I analysed the arrangement of exhibits (the aesthetics, interiors and lighting), the narrative forms (ways of presenting exhibits, labels and descriptions) and the accompanying exhibition materials (bulletins, leaflets, educations materials and handouts, guidebooks, audioguides, apps and the content of official websites).

The library visits conducted in parallel to the museum-based fieldwork focused primarily on texts referring specifically to museums and archaeological collections. What prevails in such literature are publications on the history of collecting exhibits and the history of particular collections, including monographs on cabinets of curiosities and on Renaissance and Baroque *Kunstkammern*, as well as encyclopaedic studies of large national museums (Impey and MacGregor 1987; Gaimster 1994, 2007; Barkan 1999; Myrone and Peltz 1999; Tsingarida and Kurtz 2002). Archaeological exhibitions are rarely the subject of critical studies. Existing literature directly addressing the central issues of this book includes works from the 1990s and 2000s by Susan Pearce (1990, 2006a, 2006b, 2006c, 2006d), Hedley Swain (2007) and Lynne P. Sullivan and S. Terry Childs (2003). I refer to their works and trace the inspirations often drawn from the realm of New Museology (Vergo 1989a). What I am interested in, though, is getting away from some of the by now less relevant theories whose reach is limited to the UK and US. My aim is to focus instead on contesting established modes of exhibition in order to render exhibits more dynamic. I also refer here, then, to newer literature, primarily Robin Skeates' (2017a) edited volume (Skeates 2017a) that addresses many practical aspects of archaeological museum studies, although it does not cover in as much detail the question of the theory of archaeological museums. Much like the works mentioned above, it is focused largely on British and North American institutions.

My attempt to understand in equal measure the dynamic and the theoretical nature of exhibits is influenced by the works of Eilean Hooper-Greenhill (2005), who in her seminal publication *Museums and the Shaping of Knowledge* convincingly outlined the inextricable connection of the exhibiting institutions with both dominant and alternative approaches to research. Bjørnar Olsen and Asgeir Svestad wrote in a similar vein on archaeological museums, referring to the Foucauldian idea of "disciplinary technology", demonstrating that

> archaeological statements, like books and museum exhibitions, create not only knowledge of the past but, at least to a certain degree, also the very reality they intend to describe. Taking this view seriously, we should be willing to accept that it is the various textual and museological techniques of representation in the present that make the past visible and clear, and that these representations rely upon institutions, traditions, conventions, and agreed- upon codes of understanding the past.
>
> (Olsen and Svestad 1994: 11)

An important remark stressing the need to think about the archaeological museum in its relations to scholarly theories comes from Stephanie Moser who stated that museums are documents tracing the development of the discipline (Moser 2010: 22).

The decisive criteria for the selection of the museums studied in this book were innovation and alternativeness. I was focused on what was new, courageous or unusual. Rather than concentrate on a critique of archaeological exhibition practices, discussing their inadequacy, anachronism and penchant for outdated ideas, I instead searched for exhibitions that went against the grain of prevailing tendencies. The case studies presented in this book primarily seek to draw out alternative forms of archaeological narratives, those that evade traditional definitions and break with dominant exhibition typologies (Swain 2007). My aim, then, was not to offer yet another critique of things that have been criticized numerous times already but to affirm "good practices". In doing so, I follow Ewa Domańska's proposal for an affirmative humanities (Domańska 2018). I have focused, then, on exhibitions presenting what is traditionally described as Classical archaeology, since it is this field that is usually most afflicted by the aestheticization of artefacts. It was my intention to select those museums that present collections linked to local history rather than collections that are an upshot of imperialism. While concentrating on the alternative narratives presented in Mediterranean countries, I consciously avoid the issue of decolonization that is currently the focal point for many experts. Still, I believe that my analyses could also provide them with important arguments supporting claims for further restitutions. The fact that I do not engage directly with decolonization does not mean that my work avoids the political entanglements of heritage, since these are indeed a crucial context of the two cases discussed here in detail.

Things in the field, things in the museum

This book is grounded in the context of the ontological turn and new materialism. The ideas presented here are located within ongoing debates in archaeology and museum studies on matter and materiality. My aim is to contribute to discussions initiated by the return to things and the material turn.

The arguments in this book are influenced significantly by the ideas of the late sociologist and philosopher of science Bruno Latour. They have enjoyed particular popularity in archaeology. His studies on the representation of research findings, his actor-network theory (Latour 2005), as well as the ideas outlined in the book *We Have Never Been Modern* (Latour 2002), have all shaped my thinking about artefacts-as-exhibits. Other formative influences are Graham Harman's speculative realism (Harman 2011), Karen Barad's agential realism (Barad 2007) and the philosophy of new materialism outlined in Jane Bennett's theory (Bennett 2010). Harman's idea has encouraged me to think about the enigmatic nature of things and attempting to discover their essence, while Barad's theoretical proposal provided an impetus to recognize the mysterious material of artefacts. Bennett's seminal work, meanwhile, underlined my conviction to think about things in terms of dynamics, mobility and flux.

An important reference point for all the above-mentioned thinkers is the philosophy of Martin Heidegger. His thought was indeed formative for many of the archaeologists whose ideas I draw on, in particular Julian Thomas, whose works are as associated with a "Heideggerian archaeology", but also Bjørnar Olsen, Gavin Lucas and Matthew Edgeworth. Reading *Being and Time, The Thing,* and *The Question Concerning the Thing* confirmed my view that Thomas is right to state that *Being and Time* ought to be compulsory reading for any archaeologist. My thoughts on artefacts and the process of translating knowledge by putting them on display are inspired to a significant extent reading Heidegger in parallel with the realities of research practices and the latest archaeological theories.

This book is the product of efforts to implement several diverse research methods adapted to the specificities of the research material. In the first part of the book, I use fieldwork-based approaches, drawing primarily on my own observations stemming from archaeological praxis. This is supported by autoethnography in the form of short notes "from the field", which allows me to focus on my personal experiences and, most importantly, to combine practice with theory (Ellis 2004). I am writing the book from the inside out, so from within archaeological practice, which is why I emphasize the constitutive role of self-observation and self-reflection, something that is evidenced by the popularity of archaeological diaries and memoirs from the field as tools of self-reflective research (on the use of memoirs see Mickel 2019). The subsequent section of the book, focused on exhibitions and the interpretation of exhibits, is based on the case study method. In that second part, I describe, discuss and interpret two selected European archaeological exhibitions that have developed over the course of the last 20 years. Above all, though, I turn to things, to material exhibits and their mutual relations. This is why analysis of the inscriptions accompanying exhibits and information boards are of secondary importance here. For too long, I believe, museums have placed their faith in texts (Skeates 2017c: 14, 2017d), rather than in objects. In the final part of the book, where I present potential strategies for archaeological museums, I primarily apply a comparative method and critical analysis. This book is guided by the principles of grounded theory (Glasser and Strauss 2008; Charmaz 2014), which helps to create "bottom-up" interpretive categories grounded in analyses of empirical material, formulate definitions of archaeological objects (as exhibits) and generate generalizations.

Structure of the book

My arguments are focused around three concepts: artefacts, exhibits and museum strategies. The aim is to use archaeological theories and methodologies to outline the process by which artefacts are transformed into exhibits.

In the first part of the book, titled "Artefacts", I discuss the dominant definitions of artefacts (Chapters 1–3). I draw on the prevailing paradigms of contemporary archaeology, which I juxtapose with historical and alternative theoretical models, conservation practices and academic curricula while drawing on conceptual frameworks and explanations pertaining to artefacts that come from both the natural science and laboratory practices. This critical literature review is followed by a chapter titled "The Facets of Artefacts", which is based on a reproducible structure that correlates autoethnography and interpretation. This chapter outlines ten traits of artefacts that emerged from my own fieldwork practice, which I then place in the context of trends in new materialism. Combining a literature review, autoethnography and moves towards new philosophical theories enables me to ground my concept of a definition of artefacts, which is outlined in the third chapter of Part I of this book, "Redefining Artefacts". It also features a model illustrating my ideas, which is close to Michael Shanks' idea of the "life of an artefact" (1998). The definition applied here stems from Heidegger's concept of "past things" supplemented by the findings of the preceding chapters, particularly those on being, temporality, biologism and the transformation of artefacts independent of human factors.

The second part of the book is focused on exhibits (Chapters 4 and 5). I begin this section with a literature review of studies of archaeological museums while also outlining existing typologies of exhibitions. I further develop the etymological conception of the term "exhibit", which guides my study before presenting two case studies that are based on a reproducible structure: I outline the history of a given museum, describe its permanent exhibition and selected two or three particular exhibits, or parts of the exhibition, which I then analyse and interpret in depth. The fourth chapter presents a case study of the Museo dell'Ara Pacis in Rome, focusing on two exhibits: an archaeobotanical reproduction, which I use to develop an argument about archaeology as a life science, and a contemporary artwork, the mosaic *Ara Pacis* by Mimmo Paladino, which provides the impetus for a discussion of artistic interventions in archaeology. In the first part of my interpretation,

I demonstrate the interdisciplinary nature of archaeology and the possibilities for illustrating in graphic form natural science research. I draw attention to the fact that the "science of old things" (Olsen et al. 2012: 3) has the potential to disrupt Cartesian binaries, both in archaeological theory and in exhibition practice. In the second part of my interpretation, I refer to the long-standing relations between art and archaeology, suggesting that contemporary art can help us to understand the past. I show how Mimmo Paladino's mosaic opens up the museum to subjective interpretations of the past. In the fifth chapter, I present another case study, this time of the Acropolis Museum in Athens. I introduce the concept of the "archaeological prosthesis", which I define as a form of exhibit that combines conservation narratives, new technologies and the fragmentary fabric of artefacts. I refer here to studies in the field of conservation biology and chemistry, drawing on the concept of "pastness", while combining these reflections with the latest technological developments in the field of archaeology. I also draw attention to two other strands of the new Acropolis Museum, namely kinaesthetic substitutes, which compensate for gaps in the archaeological site as well as for the inability to gain a sense of scale and actually enter the buildings, and the agency of lighting, with light serving as an often overlooked yet active agent that shapes the experience of a museum, including the one studied here.

The third part of the book, "Artefacts as Exhibits", presents across Chapters 6 to 8 three strategies employed in archaeological museums. In "Prosthetic Archaeology" (Chapter 6), I outline the forms taken by the current trend for introducing multimedia technologies into museums. I mention several critical points while stressing the fairly ad hoc ways that new media are inserted into exhibitions while challenging the position of technoenthusiasts. I show that the best option for archaeological museums is to bring artefacts to life, highlight gaps and supplement losses while avoiding the trend for what I term "digital escapism", which manifests itself in the rather thoughtless application of media technologies. In the seventh chapter, "The Preposterous Art of Archaeology", I engage with the legacies of relations between art and archaeology. I outline a potential alternative mode of mediating art through archaeology and archaeology through art. Drawing on the theories of Frank Ankersmit and Mieke Bal, I propose that in a project of a preposterous art of archaeology, artefacts and works of art alike could become aesthetic materials that encourage visitors to construct their own, subjective visions of the past based in the experiences and references that they carry in them. In a third strategy, outlined in Chapter 8, "The Archaeology of All (Living) Things", I draw attention to the fact that the category of life and the living could provide the basis for a new type of archaeological museum, namely a museum of life. I show how such a museum of life, as a realization of the archaeology of all (living) things, could operate on two registers: the epistemological, where life, as a prevalent category, indicates the existence of problems and phenomena in reality; and the ontological, where the notion of life refers us to the essence and existence of things.

This book ends with a conclusion that is intended to serve to a certain degree as a way of opening up archaeological museum studies, while at the same time inviting ideas and debates on the potential for a critical archaeological museum to emerge. Such a museum would be future-oriented and draw on the opportunities presented by the "theoretical turn" in museums and museum studies while also addressing themes in exhibitions that are relevant to contemporary visitors and, above all, inspiring the archaeological imagination.

Notes

1. This model operated successfully in other museums, too, such as natural history museums; see Thorsen et al. (2013). Nineteenth-century interest in classification, according to Brita Brenna, meant that the encyclopaedic presentation of objects became the ideal standard, with exhibits effectively expected to provide illustrations of textbook cases; see Brenna (2013).
2. The critical museum is a concept and project developed by Piotr Piotrowski, who was a Polish art historian and art critic. He served as director of the National Museum in Warsaw in 2009–2010. In his vision, the critical museum provides an open platform for discussion becoming a kind of contemporary agora or forum that is open towards the intellectual spirit of the age while negotiating and mediating theories. Piotrowski shows that throughout their long history, museums have faced epochal challenges and dealt with the problems posed by political, social, cultural and, above all, scientific realities. In his view, "museums must change if they are to retain – paradoxically – their traditionally important social status", see Piotrowski (2011).

Part I

Artefacts

As outlined in the introduction, the central aim of this book is to trace the transformation of artefacts into exhibits. I will begin my discussion with a definition of artefacts, while also outlining their facets and qualities, before going on to show which features are emphasized or, alternatively, effaced in exhibitions. I start this section by citing and exploring the etymology of the term artefact as provided in dictionaries as well as the definitions evident in leading archaeology textbooks and publications on archaeological theory. I will also present some interpretive pointers that draw on this term and its applications in the natural sciences while suggesting an alternative reading of such dictionary and textbook definitions by making a disruptive etymological move.

Further on, I will present ten factors shaping the ontological status of artefacts. I derive the proposed terms from my own archaeological practice. Hence why I have opted to include with each subchapter a short note that provides a *post factum* record of my engagements with diverse archaeological material. My work is guided by Sophie Woodward whose outline of a method for studying things reveals the complex path that the researcher must conquer in order to orient herself to things (Woodward 2020). I have made the conscious decision to adopt colloquial, non-academic language in these naïve and often anecdotal introductions. These fragmentary and noncontinuous autoethnographic "memoirs" (Ellis 2004) provide preludes to arguments that are strongly based on empirical research. This approach allows me to maintain my openness towards things while giving me an opportunity to constantly attune myself to them (Pétursdóttir and Olsen 2018: 105; see also Stewart 2008). I follow Olsen and Witmore who believe that "being open-minded and curiously naive in our engagement with things and the world may indeed be more helpful than theoretical regimes where everything important is decided in advance" (2015: 191). At the same time, by stressing the empirical nature of my research, I want to demonstrate that I am writing from the position of a then-practicing archaeologist, rather than from the standpoint of a desk-based researcher who is divorced from material and haptic contact with archaeological objects. The ten proposed facets of artefacts will assist me in presenting further on in the book a complementary definition of artefacts grounded in the realities of research practices.

DOI: 10.4324/9781003327851-2

Concentrating on the ontology of finds, I move away from discussing what the object had been before it became an archaeological artefact. In light of the current flood of studies on material culture,[1] I see no need for further in-depth reflection on the functions or production techniques of objects from the past. Such reflections are of little significance to my efforts to develop a definition of archaeological artefacts. For similar reasons, I have avoided drawing on the classical catalogue of artefacts typical of archaeological publications. By treating the objects referred to here as "things that are good for thinking with", I move further away from the conviction that a traditional list of artefacts could be capable of shedding new light on the themes discussed here.

The following part of the book is inspired by theories of vital materialism, speculative realism and agentic realism, correlating these approaches with the horizon of what is known in the discipline of "old things" as Heideggerian archaeology. In what follows, I explore the relevance of prevailing definitions to the realities of research practice and the current tendency in the humanities to transcend binaries (human/non-human, culture/nature, material/spiritual). My main aim in this chapter is to construct an updated and complex empirically grounded definition of artefacts that is also based on new paradigms in the humanities that emphasize much more strongly the nature of archaeology as a discipline positioned at the intersection of nature and culture. Guided by the principles of the ontological turn in the humanities, I enquire not into the "how" of thinking about artefacts but rather into "what" they are in essence. I do so in order to then analyse what they become as part of museum exhibitions.

Note

1. British and American approaches, and primarily the former, apply the concept of material culture in broad studies focusing on the technical production and functions of objects from the past; see Gould and Schiffer (1981); Hicks and Beaudry (2010). A highly complex approach to this can be found in Allison (1999). It is also necessary to highlight those studies of materiality that have abandoned the concept of "material culture" altogether given its associations with traditional archaeology; see Tilley (2004); Ingold (2013); Miller (2013).

1   Artefacts in Archaeological Terminology

Artefacts in archaeological terminology

At the outset of my reflections on artefacts, I refer to dictionary definitions to highlight, first and foremost, the ambiguity and sematic wealth of the term. However, this is something that also stems from reflections on its colloquial use. The word artefact often appears in journalism, everyday language and is common in art criticism, particularly where writers are avoiding the term "work of art". The word artefact suggests "making" (Ingold 2013), revealing the weaknesses of the vocabulary of the history of art, as the term stands in for everything that is material and unnameable. Etymologically, artefact describes an object that is created artificially (Latin: *arte factum*). According to the Merriam-Webster Online Dictionary, an artefact is

> 1 a: a usually simple object (such as a tool or ornament) showing human workmanship or modification as distinguished from a natural object especially: an object remaining from a particular period
> 1 b: something characteristic of or resulting from a particular human institution, period, trend, or individual
> 1 c: something or someone arising from or associated with an earlier time especially when regarded as no longer appropriate, relevant, or important
> 2 a: a product of artificial character (as in a scientific test) due usually to extraneous (such as human) agency
>   b: an electrocardiographic and electroencephalographic wave that arises from sources other than the heart or brain
>   c: a defect in an image (such as a digital photograph) that appears as a result of the technology and methods used to create and process the image[1]

The above definitions might be marked by only minor differences, but they are nevertheless indicative of a certain terminological impasse that reveals, generally speaking, how artefacts should be understood, first and foremost, as human-made objects that are bound up in culture, in contrast to natural

DOI: 10.4324/9781003327851-3

ecofacts or geofacts. Interestingly, the first explanation (which is specifically archaeological) of what an artefact is includes a definition suggesting that it does not have to be entirely human-made but might bear the marks of having been worked on or transformed by human hands. Such a nuance, perhaps imperceptible to non-archaeologist readers, is for those involved in fieldwork the essential difference that means that clean-cut stones, an arbitrarily carved animal bone, a clod of burned clay or waste products resulting from iron production can be termed artefacts. This difference is what actually determines the essence of artefacts as objects whose intentional and deliberate production might be questioned without ruling out the possibility of defining such finds as archaeological artefacts. The traces of human activity that distinguish artefacts from ecofacts also mean that chance plays a role in what defines archaeological artefacts. They do not necessarily have to be human-made objects that have ceased to circulate and subsequently entered archaeological contexts. Indeed, archaeological artefacts might be elements of flora or fauna that have survived in the archaeological layer and serve as carriers of information, just like things made by humans.

In one of the world's most popular textbooks, *Archaeology: Theories, methods and practice* by Colin Renfrew and Paul Bahn, artefacts are defined as "humanly made or modified portable objects, such as stone tools, pottery, and metal weapons (...) artifacts provide evidence to help us answer all the key questions – not just technological ones (...)" (Renfrew and Bahn 2012: 49). Renfrew and Bahn show that artefacts are subject to a variety of specific investigative approaches – material, typological, environmental and social, to name just a few. The authors indicate that artefacts are to be understood much more broadly than as mere material traces. Some scholars use the term to mean "all humanly modified components of a site or landscape, such as hearths, postholes, and storage pits" (Renfrew and Bahn 2012: 50). Renfrew and Bahn suggest that such traces should be defined as non-portable artefacts. They distinguish "non-artifactual organic and environmental remains", which include "human skeletons, animal bones, and plant remains, but also soils and sediments" (Renfrew and Bahn 2012: 50).

The generally accepted definition is partially an upshot of theoretical debates on artefacts ongoing since the founding of the discipline. In the early twentieth century, archaeology was bound up in evolutionistic models that were a legacy of Thomsen's division of time into three epochs. The historical-cultural paradigm that dominated for half a century viewed artefacts primarily in cultural terms and as a source providing access to past societies, their structures, the technologies used in them, their economies and their ideologies. Categorizations, norms and descriptions served primarily to indicate cultural differences and similarities (Childe 1951), which is why in this model the term artefact possessed purely epistemological meaning.

Transformations in the discipline stemming from methods drawn from the natural sciences and interest in the social theory of evolution, ecology and adaptation led to challenges to historical-cultural archaeology.

New Archaeology was inaugurated by Lewis Binford in 1962 (Binford 1962). He differentiated three kinds of artefacts: technomic – emerging from technological systems; socio-technic – reflecting social organization; and ideo-technic artefacts – reflecting ideologies and the cognitive realm. However, Binford's distinctions were only of epistemic significance.

The term artefact was applied less often by representatives of processual archaeology, with "material culture" and "archaeological data" preferred. The reduction of tangible artefacts to immaterial data offers, I argue, the clearest illustration of one of the aims of the processual paradigm, namely, to create laws, systems, models and generalizations. New Archaeology served, then, as a way of discovering not artefacts as individual object but rather, to use language typical of the time, the "Indian behind the artifact" (Flannery 1967) and developing systematic solutions based less on resear- ching particular "types" of objects, as was the case in historical-cultural archaeology, and more on generalization, the aim of which was to assist the construction of a holistic, objectivized image of the past (Flannery 1967).

New Archaeology was far from being a theoretical monolith, though. Michael Schiffer's perspective differed from that of Binford or Flannery as he focused on archaeological finds that in the course of being used, deposited and discovered were subjected to cultural (*C-transforms*) and non-cultural (*N-transforms*) factors (Schiffer 1976). Introducing correlates, i.e. factors influencing the behaviour of objects during deposition (Schiffer 1976: 13–14), and the "manufacture-use-reuse-abandonment" scheme that is close to the *chaîne opératoire* proposed slightly earlier by the French archaeologist André Leroi-Gourhan (1993), shed new, ontological light on artefacts.

The post-processual revolution in archaeology, inspired by structuralist and post-structuralist humanities, used hermeneutics to promote reading archaeological sources as texts (Hodder 2005), providing a platform for interpretive polyphony while breaking with the positivist approach of the processualists. Inspired by the theories of praxis of Pierre Bourdieu and Anthony Giddens, the post-processualists endowed artefacts with agency. No less significant than these sociological influences were thing studies and biographical approaches (Kopytoff 1987). From the post-processualist view, artefacts were "animated" by agency and appreciated as objects that were experiencing their own "life".

Tensions between the processual and post-processual schools in archae- ology remain evident to this day. The clash of approaches bound up in the positivism of the natural sciences, on the one hand, and those that were once associated with poststructuralism and postmodernism and now with the posthumanities, on the other, resonates with the ways in which artefacts are designed as objects of archaeological interest. It is not possible here to outline all the ways in which artefacts are understood in all archaeological subdis- ciplines. However, it is necessary to draw attention to the fact that artefacts are viewed primarily through epistemic lenses, meaning they are treated as a means of posing questions asking: "in what way?", "how?" and "why?". Even some pioneering studies that gave rise to new subdisciplines are indicative of the role epistemic dimensions of theory play in understanding artefacts.[2]

A different conception of artefacts is evident in research connected to the ontological turn. Here archaeologists focus on questions asking: "what are we researching?" rather than "how are we doing research?". Among the recent theories in archaeology, it is worth highlighting above all studies that have taken a turn to things and the symmetrical archaeology proposed by Bjørnar Olsen and Christopher Witmore that stresses the ontological dimension of artefacts (Olsen 2013). Ian Hodder's concept of entanglement, which values the natural-cultural dimension of artefacts as well as their inherent, non-human temporality and constant movement and dynamics, also offers an answer to what are archaeologists researching, in an approach marked by the influence of new materialism (Hodder 2012, 2016).

The concept of the archaeological find is still the subject of theoretical investigation and general studies. Gavin Lucas' book *Understanding the Archaeological Record* is, I believe, the most comprehensive source outlining what has been and remains of interest to archaeologists. He introduced the concept of the *archaeological record*, suggesting that the term's value can be traced back to its Latin etymology, stemming from the word "remember" and a long-forgotten French meaning of the term as "testimony committed to writing" (Lucas 2012). Lucas recognizes that his central framing concept possesses a great deal of ambiguity, as a record could refer to a fossil whose description, a certain kind of self-archive, is contained in the material itself; but it could also be applied successfully to objects that are verified through reference to texts. Lucas' theory, then, has its origins in post-processual archaeology, which is associated with attempts to understand material culture as a text (Hodder 2005).

Closer to current theoretical tendencies in archaeology and to my own position is Michael Shanks' work on "the life of an artifact", which was actually published in the 1990s. Here he introduced a definition of artefacts "as a multiplicity, a historical and heterogeneous *assemblage*" (original emphasis) (Shanks 1998: 24), linking the material and the human (Shanks 1998: 27). An artefact thus contains a "multitude of data points, an infinity of possible attributes and measurements" (Shanks 1998: 24). These can all be revealed today thanks to the application of research methods and posing appropriate research questions. Shanks' definition is thus close to the ideas of new materialism, whose chief proponent in archaeology has been Christopher Witmore (Witmore 2014).

In order to comprehend the semantic load of the term artefact, I have turned not only to dictionaries, archaeology textbooks, historical texts, theoretical works and overviews but also to the field of artefact studies, especially its academic curricula. The field is most prominent in the UK, with study programmes offering interesting insight into how artefacts are conceptualized generally. University College London (UCL) offers a master's module in Working with Artefacts and Assemblages, with students taking courses with a practical profile where they learn to identify, describe, document, catalogue and analyse artefacts and artefact assemblages, as well as practice the description of ceramic, lithic and metal objects. At Durham University, artefact studies are based at the intersection of museum studies and material studies, too. There the aim is to prepare graduates for work in museums while developing both students' analytical skills, in relation to objects' provenance, material and dating, as well as their potential for exhibition, and students' ability to conduct research on artefacts, i.e. working with theoretical models. Such forms of teaching programmes have much in common with Fleming E. McClung's (1974) model for analysing artefacts, which was based on positioning artefact studies clearly within the realm of materiality (material analysis, provenance and dating), as this, he argued, would enable a given object to be placed in further interpretive contexts, including the cultural and social, as well as within institutional contexts, thus reflecting on the potential for exhibition (McClung 1974).

Laboratory work is a crucial element of artefact studies, while at Leiden University it constitutes the central component of the curriculum. I have therefore turned to a publication from the field of artefact conservation in order to see how archaeologist-conservators who supposedly seek to "sterilize the past" (Shanks 1998: 17) actually define artefacts. In the handbook *Conservation Practices on Archaeological Excavations: Principles and Methods*, an artefact is an object made from either organic materials (wood, fabric, bones) or non/organic materials (ceramic, stone, metals). The authors note that artefacts made of organic material burn, are photosensitive, hygroscopic, are transformed by water and attract microorganisms that provide a source of nutrition; by contrast, artefacts made of non-organic materials do not burn, are not photosensitive, but are subject to salt salinification and corrosion. This definition does not contradict those contained in strictly archaeological textbooks, nor does it contrast with what is contained in dictionaries or in theoretical works. What it does reveal, however, are some completely different traits of artefacts that I will seek to incorporate into a holistic definition.

Turning again to the natural sciences, it is worthwhile, I believe, to explore how other disciplines understand artefacts. Biologists use the term artefact to define the structures of a cell or tissue that is typical of microscopic specimens that emerge when developing preparations that do not exist in any organism. Similarly, in psychology and medicine artefacts are artificial products emerging from research methods, rather than elements that exist in nature. Artefacts are created in laboratories; they are artificial and a side-effect of research, meaning that they "occur" even unexpectedly (Lynch 1985: 84–85). In laboratories, artefacts function as constructions that are of no particular interest to researchers, as intrusions or distortions (Lynch 1985: 82). In his analysis of laboratory artefacts, Michael Lynch indicates that these non-natural forms have a different meaning to archaeological artefacts. For Lynch, archaeologists treat objects used and transformed by humans as artefacts, with analysis of such objects providing information on

artistic, practical or ceremonial customs (Lynch 1985: 82). He draws attention to the disciplinary discussions on how ordinary stones, bone fragments
or pieces of wood that have not been subject to human intervention can be
differentiated from artefacts. Lynch finds, then, that in archaeology, artefacts serve as "positive evidence" (Lynch 1985: 82), while in biology they
are generally troubling, confounding issues (Lynch 1985: 84), the equivalent of what archaeologists would treat as post-exploration traces on a find.
Lynch's definition of archaeological artefacts is somewhat limited, as shown
by the fact that he limits their significance to artistic or ritual aspects, or by
his assumption that they necessarily yield positive evidence. Drawing on
the example from biology, I would stress the possibility of negative artefacts
existing likewise in archaeology, i.e. unexpected objects that undermine
existing hypotheses and lack any analogies, with scientific explanations
unable to account for their presence. I would therefore like to take from the
biological definition of an artefact this element of chance, thus enriching the
humanities' traditional concepts of archaeological artefacts.

At this juncture, I would propose one further reading of the term artefact,
one that involves deconstructing the word. The part *arte-* suggests artificial
construction, while the second part *-factum* indicates that the word is to
be defined in terms of what has occurred or is occurring in reality, i.e. an
event, phenomenon or particular state.[3] The origins of this part of the word,
however, are to be found in the Latin term *factum*, meaning "made" or
"done". This approach leads me to understand artefacts as objects that have
undergone material transformation over the course of time. "Fact" is of key
significance in understanding archaeological artefacts. As the dictionary
definition suggests, facts are "an actual occurrence" or constitute "a thing
done", albeit not limited to singular events; instead, there is the possibility
of "hav[ing] actual existence" over time, as part of a process and by way of
gradual becoming. In the case of artefacts, then, this brings us closer to the
notion of the *longue durée*. Archaeological artefacts are in a long-term process of becoming. The moment of being discarded, deposited and leaving
active circulation initiates a process of transformation that moves towards
potentially becoming an archaeological artefact, an element of an excavated
site and then a find. The transformation process determines the nature of
archaeological artefacts and distinguishes it from discarded things, broken
parts and imperceptible everyday objects.

A key question for me though is: what is the relationship between the *arte-*
part and the *-factum* part? *Arte-* points towards understanding the *longue
durée* as a creative process in which objects are autonomous and completely
independent of humans as they undergo various transformations resulting
from post-deposition factors,[4] namely the geological substratum, soil type,
the presence of salts, the ability to hold or filter water, oxygen levels, the
extent to which soil is frozen, the depth at which the object was deposited and
the effects of microorganisms, plants, animals and other objects. My aim,
then, is to demonstrate that the essential aspect of artefacts is not that they

were created by humans but that they were **discarded** by them, either being thrown away, lost, hidden or intentionally placed underwater or underground, where they were left to face the actions of non-human agents. This event is the most significant in determining what format subsequent investigations are to take. The state of the artefact – has it been chipped, broken, eroded, damaged, fragmented – determines which research methods will be applied in the analysis, interpretation and conservation of the find, while it will also be of crucial significance in determining its fate as an exhibit.

This literature review has enabled me to outline the various conceptions of artefacts. The boundary conditions of definitions of the term artefact (biological approaches and the semantic deconstruction of the elements of the word) will be applied throughout this study as I work towards a holistic definition. It is worthwhile, I suggest, to supplement the established conceptions as outlined above with reflections on the state of artefacts when they are first encountered, thus laying the foundations for a redefinition of the concept based on the terminological framework emerging here. In order to ground the definition of artefacts that is emerging here, namely as objects that are independent of humans for the majority of their existence, I will now present ten facets of artefacts that archaeologists encounter when uncovering and investigating them. Most factors shaping the nature of artefacts result from non-human actors, a condition that is of massive significance to the subsequent analysis, interpretation and exhibition of finds in museums.

Notes

1. *Artifact*, https://www.merriam-webster.com/dictionary/artifact [accessed 28 October 2022].
2. An example of this are the pioneering studies by Rodney Harrison and John Schofield (2010), which outline the programmatic principles of the archaeology of the contemporary past. The authors treat as artefacts an abandoned Ford Transit, an Ikea Billy bookshelf and everyday domestic goods. They highlight the complexity of objects, their microhistories and contemporary distribution. In the archaeology of the contemporary past, artefacts can be material, imperceptible and ephemeral mass-produced objects. Even though Harrison and Schofield break with the objects from the ancient past that are traditionally of interest to archaeology, their works do not seem to add a great deal of depth to reflections on the essence of artefacts.
3. *Fact*, https://www.merriam-webster.com/dictionary/fact [accessed 23 October 2022].
4. I focus primarily on underground deposits since I have no experience in underwater research. However, as existing literature shows, watery environments have a much more noticeable impact on the formation of artefacts; see Rich (2019).

2   The Facets of Artefacts

Fragments

Bone

At the archaeological site where I completed my student internship, during one single excavation season alone, several hundred bone pins were discovered. These hairpins were made of animal bone that was usually smoothed, while the more exquisitely crafted ones were also polished. We found some complete exemplars, while others were fragmented with only the pinheads, stems or sharp ends preserved. The pinheads were of greatest interest to those finding them as they were often decorated.

How many pins did I find during that season? I am not sure, perhaps around twenty in various states. What I do remember clearly, however, is the day I discovered one particular pin. We were removing a carelessly erected Late Roman wall. First, we would "shift" the heavy stones with a pick then turn them on their side. At one point, we saw the flash of a long, thin object. Expecting it to be a pin, we started removing a layer of the wall more quickly and soon we had managed to gain hold of the bone "baby". The pin was broken, though. After closer inspection, we realized that the cut was fresh, meaning that the pin must have been broken just a few moments previously. Further exploration and searches of the piles of earth enabled us to locate the missing fragment. The pin had broken exactly in half. After being washed and dried, the two halves could be put back together.

The case of the bone pins offers a perfect introduction to two themes that are inherent to the nature of archaeological finds: mass quantities and fragmentariness. Returning to my fieldwork diary, I will focus here on the second of these two facets because of all the hundreds of pins discovered, explored and described, only one has become etched in my memory and for reasons that have nothing to do with decorations or exquisite craftsmanship. The pin that was broken during our excavations provides the basis for a contribution to debates on fragments. I begin this chapter with fragments because I believe that without them, whether literal or figurative, there can be no archaeology.

DOI: 10.4324/9781003327851-4

Fragments understood in the spirit of German Romanticism, following Schlegel, constitute at the same time both a closed whole and parts of chaotic reality (Lacoue-Labarthe and Nancy 1988: 44). Friedrich Schlegel and other representatives of the Jena School defined fragments as something that was broken off or separated, straight and pure, bearing traces of being chipped. However, this approach does not provide an answer to the question of what constitutes the beginning, middle or end (Lacoue-Labarthe and Nancy 1988: 42). The German Romanticist understanding of fragments was also of philological significance as it was connected to the fragmentariness of Classical texts. The term itself was seen as indicative of affinities with the popular eighteenth-century motif of ruins. The origins of this connection can be traced back to Diderot's elevation of ruins' significance. Like ruins, fragments function as an evocation and memorial, marked by absence and yet present (Lacoue-Labarthe and Nancy 1988; see also Diderot 2011: 22). This internal paradox of the ontology of fragments possesses creative potential that was recognized not only German Romanticists but also by antiquarians, opening up perspectives for constructing scientific theories that lent legitimacy to archaeology as an academic discipline. The Romanticist fascination with fragments understood as part of a forgotten whole symbolizing a lost past, namely the genius of late lamented Antiquity, metamorphosed into a scholarly urge to reconstruct, classify and segregate that could guarantee the effect of "closed" and complete wholes.

In his text *Fragments as Something More: Archaeological Experience and Reflection*, Mats Burström explicitly addresses the significance of fragments in the vocabulary of contemporary archaeologists:

> For an archaeologist, fragments are the normal order of things. We meet them all the time, in many different shapes and contexts; we meet them during field surveys, in excavation trenches, in museum collections and in scholarly publications. Fragments are by definition pieces that once belonged to a larger whole, one now lost forever either in part or entirely. The question is, what should we do with all these fragments, and, indeed, what do they do with us?
>
> (Burström 2013: 311)

Burström recognizes the commonplace nature of fragments, with objects encountered constantly in this form by archaeologists at every stage of their work.

Fragments are found and created, likewise in the course of excavation. But what happens to them after that? The case of the pin that was destroyed and then rendered whole again is indicative of a not uncommon scenario, with the object being put back together while still in the field. However, should reconstruction fail, then the fragment becomes a victim of the ongoing archaeological process during which missing parts are hidden. The desire to find a missing element of a whole dominates the ambition of the archaeologist, who would like to view him/herself in the role of a detective or forensic scientist (Holtorf 2006: 75–83). The reality of archaeological excavations, meanwhile, is rather different than the idealized depictions that appear in scholarly publications, where the act of completing wholes prevails. The process of recreation and reconstruction is hindered by the fragmentariness, scrappiness and incoherence of the material.

Gavin Lucas refers to fragments, contrasting them with relics. Linking the latter to temporality and belonging to another epoch and being temporally unfamiliar, the former always refers back to a whole, although its power in fact "lies in evoking or underlining an absence or loss and, as such, initiates a discourse or poetics on the relation between the fragment and the missing parts or between the fragment and the whole" (Lucas 2014: 314). Michael Shanks views fragments in a similar fashion: "(...) the fragment of the past evokes. We can work on the archaeological fragment to reveal what is missing; the shattered remnant invites us to reconstruct, to suppose that which is no longer there. The fragment refers us to the rediscovery of what was lost" (Shanks 1998: 19). For Shanks, fragments play a key role in archaeologists' arguments and in inspiring the archaeological imagination. For him, it is the fragmentary nature of the artefact that leads to questions about what has been lost and neglected, with the answers leading to a fuller reconstruction of the past as fragments provide the link between the material and the human (Shanks 1998: 24). Both Shanks and Lucas thus propose a metonymic reading of fragments where the part stands for the whole. This is an alternative to thinking in terms of cause-and-effect relationships.

Fragments are, I would argue, not only metaphors for archaeological finds in general but also metaphors of archaeology as a discipline. Fragments serve as reminders of incompleteness and the attempts to transcend this state with the help of various paradigms and perspectives in archaeology. Incompleteness together with the resulting insecurities that historical-cultural, processual and post-processual archaeology have sought to counter by applying typologies, generalizations and an interpretative focus, respectively, in fact create conditions for theorizing and putting the archaeological imagination into practice (Burström 2013). In this respect, I would agree with Bjørnar Olsen, who writes that it is worthwhile

> to let this 'record' be fragmented and incomplete, to let things also be trivial and banal, in short, to let them be things – and allow their otherness to affect and be part of the archaeology we produce. This is an archaeology that sacrifices historical narratives in favour of a trust in its own ruined things, things that emerge from and bring forth a different past.
>
> (Olsen 2012b: 25)

Fragments serve as reminders of the material dimension of archaeology, of the incompleteness of the past and the infinite possibilities of investigation and reconstruction, while at the same time making us sensitive to the uncertainty and powerlessness felt in the face of encounters with rather oblique pieces and elements of the past. Since fragments cannot be inscribed into fixed theoretical frameworks, they demand that we constantly attune ourselves to them, they demand attention, care and patience. This is why they are "things for thinking with" that encourage us to theorize (see Olsen and Witmore 2021: 71).

Mass

Ceramics

> During the first excavations that I was involved in in the Mediterranean region, I was excited by every single find. The tiniest ceramic fragment brought me great joy. But over time, my emotions changed. Halfway through my time there, I was already averse to looking at potsherds. After each day in the field, they had to be cleaned extensively with a brush in order to be able to establish if any fragment could be matched to its "other half". The leaders of the excavations had a soft spot for large fragments of amphorae, with only the diagnostic ones stuck together and analysed because they enabled the dating of vessels. What happened to the rest? The superfluous, individual potsherds, large and small, were simply dumped on a heap. Together with all the useless soil that had been dug up.

Several hundred fragments of ceramics, several dozen small objects made of bone or bronze, several unique objects, including many that barely differed in form: this list is illustrative of the mass of material that archaeologists encounter when working on many archaeological sites. All the objects that they discover must be recorded – so drawn, photographed and described. Even if they appear in such amounts that they almost constitute a mass of material, each individual thing should be given at least a moment of attention to avoid overlooking any factors that refute standardization. When publications and museums present images of unique objects and singular specimens, the scale of such finds seems disproportionate to the way in which they are represented (Lucas 2012). Contrary to widespread opinion that is often based in pop-cultural representations (Holtorf 2006), archaeologists do not set out to search for unique objects and nor do they find them. They excavate masses of ceramics, bones, coins, toppled stones, damaged tools and even masses of objects that in museum spaces are presented as unique.

While working on the material, its quantity is reduced. As in the natural sciences, types are selected that serve as the basis for classification, most commonly in the form of typologies that restrict individual objects to the role of signs stationed along the developmental path of forms (Olsen 2013: 111). Masses of material are transformed into singular representations that come to serve as "circulating references" that travel between scientific publications (Latour 1999: 24–79). The idea behind the process that prepares objects for further scientific analysis or indeed their presentation in exhibition has much in common with the notion of transubstantiation, as

Latour suggested in his essay "Circulating Reference: Sampling the soil in the Amazon Forest" (Latour 1999: 24–79). Here Latour discusses the knowledge production process, analysing the stages of pedological research in South America. Like archaeologists, a group of specialist scholars, in this case comprising botanists, pedologists and geographers, work on acquiring data to be used in the laboratory research that follows fieldwork. The research process begins with direct contact with the tangible matter forming the centre of the researchers' interests and it ends with publications presenting research findings in the form of statistics and diagrams. The data acquired during fieldwork in the forest undergo a metamorphosis that is so radical that Latour describes it as a transubstantiation. For Latour, this involves reducing the tangible material to textual form, a form of compression that takes place at the boundaries of reality, research practices and academic discourse. The non-material data concerning samples of material start to function as scientific representations, whose form means that they can be transformed in any way and reused in subsequent research. Studying the case of the Amazon Forest, Latour began by asking the question: "how do we pack the world into words?" (Latour 1999: 24).

The reference to Latour's work highlights just how far removed the objects presented in academic publications or exhibited in museums are from their state at the time of their discovery. Scholarly objectivity determines the nature of publications, while Kantian aesthetics of beauty dictate the reductionist direction adopted in exhibitions to ensure the presentation of "beautiful types". In the field, however, the truth of material can be read primarily through the lens of the aesthetics of the abject and destruction. The realities of the discipline and the truth of the material do not overlap in well-preserved unique specimens but rather in the materiality of damaged fragments that pass through the hands of archaeologists during excavations.

The renowned archaeological theorist Gavin Lucas has also drawn attention to the analogy between Latour's idea of the "circulating reference"[1] and the practices involved in representing archaeological reality in significantly simplified form in exhibitions (Lucas 2012: 245). Lucas, furthermore, emphasizes another important aspect emerging from the similarities between the practices outlined by Latour and the presence of artefacts in museums, namely that when objects find their way into exhibitions, they do not become exhibits endowed with meaning that is given once and for all; rather, they remain of interest to archaeologists who continue to study them and thus potentially disrupt any apparent definitive meanings. In *The Archaeology of Time*, Lucas also addresses the theme of the representation of archaeological practices in museums, presenting a somewhat different perspective. He argues that a typical feature of archaeological exhibitions is that they are marked by completeness and a veneer of perfection that is derived from creating an impression of "timelessness" (Lucas 2005: 127). Lucas considers this to be a rather ironically perverse depiction of archaeology because it denies the reality of archaeological practice as something that involves revealing dirty, fragmentary, damaged remains of the past that are strongly marked by the passing of time (Lucas 2005: 127). He goes on to show that archaeologists approach the material rather meekly, denying its truth and the genuine forms that constitute the basis of archaeological thought. The popular image of archaeologists as detectives reconstructing the past on the basis of fragmentary and incoherent material is also partly responsible for the current state of archaeological museums. Lucas draws attention to the fact that discarding fragments, which are typical and mass archaeological objects, is something that resonates in the scholarly literature, with academic publications full of "ideal" whole unique objects. This is indicative of the archaeological tendency towards totalization (Lucas 2005: 127).

As fragmented, damaged objects that are discovered en masse at archaeological sites are piled high in the field and in storehouses, artefacts do indeed inspire new materialist readings while at the same time revealing quite perfectly the nature of archaeology as the study of old, mundane things. Yet the early stages of research practice, which involve enquiries into resistant matter and dealing with its mass and fragmentary nature, rarely find their way into either publications or exhibitions.

Mystery

Stone

At the outset of my student internship on archaeological excavations, I had very little knowledge of Greco-Roman artefacts. Many times I had to ask the excavation leader, "what is this?" The head of the mission always gave highly detailed answers.

One day, one of the students found a regular, polished round stone. It was difficult to say at first glance what it might be … The employees of the archaeological park happened to be present, as they had come to observe us at work, and they took an interest in the find. After a brief examination of the object, they started to giggle, saying 'pesca' (which in Italian means peach). A man indicated the indentation in the stone and suggested that it had a vaginal form.

One weekend, I was assigned to wash registered finds, with the abovementioned mysterious item among them. Using a lightly-moistened toothbrush, I delicately cleaned the stone object of clay. Suddenly, my eyes picked out a pigment. The stone was orange! After cleaning it very carefully, it turned out that the stone was indeed covered in an orange pigment, while the indentation that had proven so humorous to the Italian man indeed looked like the stone of a fruit. Ultimately, the object was revealed to be a realistic stone carving of a peach. Since it was made of stone, it might have served as a grinder. There was also a suggestion that it should be classified as an artificial fruit, something akin to those that are today made of plastic.

> To recognize a common object is mainly to know how to use it. [...]
> But to know how to use a thing is to sketch out the movements which
> adapt themselves to it [...].
>
> (Bergson 1991: 93)

The attractive thing about stone objects is that they are most often encountered whole[2] with details preserved and in unchanged form; they thus are,
to put it in Heideggerian terms, present-at-hand (*vorhanden*), ready to be
reflected upon, as well as being ready-to-hand (*zuhanden*), thus available
to be used in a practical sense. Fully preserved marble mortars and stone
pestles encourage us to grind the mixture of cheese and herbs that Virgil
describes in his epic poem, *Moretum*. But what happens when we don't
know what we have before us?

The stone peach provides the basis for discussing artefacts as unexpected
events. Unlike the laboratory artefact that I referred to in Chapter 1 when
outlining the definition of artefacts applied in the natural sciences, however,
it does not have a negative impact. There I presented a view that depicted the
negative artefact as an unexpected outcome or process that can undermine
hypotheses, something that has no analogies and even defies scientific explanation. In discussing the stone peach here, I apply the same term, "negative
artefact", albeit as something that does not in itself undermine general hypotheses regarding the archaeological site, certain groups or types of artefacts, or
stratigraphical dating. The stone peach will not alter dating, nor will it form
a missing piece in reconstructing a landscape. It seemingly lacks any scientific significance whatsoever. Indeed, it is rather quaint, perhaps irritating, and
undoubtedly intriguing. But what meaning does it possess as something that
we cannot give any name to other than the rather infantile "stone peach"?

This stone curio manifests in a nutshell, I would argue, the Romantic
vision of archaeology: as the science of old things that are no longer in use
and thus apparently useless because it is not clear what function they might
have had. The stone peach offers a perfect illustration of the reasons why I
am not interested here in material cultural studies as applied in archaeology.
This perspective, which began gaining immense popularity in the 1980s,
restored archaeologists' interest in mundane items that had been used in
the past after years of focusing on systemic theories. Having discredited the
paradigm of processual archaeology, researchers again turned to studies
of materials and production techniques, to functions performed in the past
and to symbols and social significance. Few archaeologists, however, opted
to follow the path strewn with things that defy typologies, analogies and
classifications, things that cannot be studied using the methods of experimental archaeology and where ethnology offers little help in understanding
them. They are, then, those things that Bjørnar Olsen describes as

> things discarded, lost, and forgotten but which stubbornly remain, things
> that object to that persistent image of the past as gone; things which in

their assembly, gathering, and bonding resist temporal ordering and chronological sequencing; things which defy completeness and system and which constantly affect us by their sheer physiognomy and raw bulk.
(Olsen 2012b: 21)

According to Lynn Meskell, archaeologists do not want to get caught up in the complexity of matter, in its settings and countless connections (Meskell 2013: 92). It is difficult to disagree with Meskell when thinking about the stone peach. Although it is an individual artefact, preserved in an ideal state, it nevertheless does not constitute an object that could radically transform the facets of the site, a culture or epoch. What is interesting, though, is that in other times, outside the age of contemporary archaeology, it would have been a fascinating and unique find, one that would have quickly been given a prominent place in a cabinet of curiosities. Today, though, it lacks any scientific significance whatsoever, unless it were to be reduced to the status of a symbol[3] or transformed into a source of theoretical speculation.

As a find that is difficult to interpret, the stone peach demonstrates that certain objects remain unnameable and their functions cannot be established without skirting the realm of the absurd. In considering this object, which most certainly must be described as an artefact rather than as a specific and familiar object from the past, I will turn to Karen Barad's theory of agential realism (Barad 2007; see also Jones 2014). Barad presents a convincing theoretical framework that breaks with the principles of constructivism. They (Barad's chosen pronoun) dedicate a significant amount of attention to a critique of the role of language in the binary structuring of reality. They note that we have become accustomed to attaching great importance to naming things while at the same time assuming representation of an object through a word will cement its status (Barad 2007: 132–138). Following Niels Bohr, they restate that objects do not possess fixed and immutable traits and limits, just as words do not possess a meaning that is fixed forever (Barad 2007: 138).

The exclusion of the stone peach and other curios from the realm of contemporary archaeological research stems primarily from the inability to either ascribe a name to them or to recreate how they were used. I recall my haptic contact with the material it is made from as it was this that most probably dictated that I applied a crushing motion to it. Others wanted to see in the stone peach something static and aesthetic to be positioned in a bowl, as if it were the equivalent of the plastic fruits we are familiar with today. Others, meanwhile, would seek in it a kind of symbolic explanation of a peach as an ancient fertility symbol by, for example, intimating that it must have served a religious or ritual function. Perhaps somebody else would try to set the peach in motion, like a ball in a game of boules. It would also be necessary to consider whether the object might not perhaps have served all of these functions, leaving behind its previous use before entering another functional register. The various ways of interacting with this mysterious object made me aware just how little novelty phenomenology can bring archaeologists in the field (Tilley 1994; but see

Olsen 2013). Each of us can use an artefact as an object in a hundred different ways, but would even one of them be close to the functions ascribed to it in the past? What, then, is to be done with this strange orange stone?

The powerlessness of language and the lack of analogies ensure that as this artefact cannot fit traditional typologies, it will be excluded from scientific circulation. The reasons for this can be found in what Walter Benjamin diagnosed as the human urge to control things through language (Benjamin 1979). According to Barad, meanwhile, this undefined object could be treated as a material mystery that, like other things, might prove capable of repeatedly surprising researchers. When an object cannot be associated with others, ordered according to an established category, dated precisely (which is particularly difficult in the case of stone objects; see Stobiecka 2018), or even named, then it falls out of scientific circulation, becoming a negative artefact: an unusual surprise lacking any analogies located on the existing horizon of identifiable objects. The difference between the stone peach and a laboratory sample lies in the stubborn material existence of the former, an impression that is strengthened by the sense that it possesses functionality and handiness and could be ready to use precisely because of the material it is made of. The stone peach becomes a nameless witness to non-human existence. In a museum store or even in an exhibition, it would serve the role of a "portable artefact" that distorts and disrupts reality. Indeed, this is precisely the nature of archaeological exhibitions which are composed of the mysteries and surprises that in fact do not occur that often in excavations.

Secrecy

Stone

> During one period of archaeological fieldwork, I excavated a demar-
> cated space that was most probably part of an ancient house. The room
> I was responsible for was small and unfortunately rather inaccessible.
> As a result of the fact that it was located far below the present-day soil
> level, I tried to avoid leaving it unless absolutely necessary. What was
> particularly difficult was removing the soil that had been dug out. I usu-
> ally placed buckets full of soil on the walls of the space then stepped on a
> perfectly flat block of stone, and then from this space I passed them up to
> the "porter" on duty that day. The block was large, but it was positioned
> on an "island of earth" that would also need to be excavated in order to
> level the ground in the space. Towards the end of the dig season, a few
> strongmen took on the difficult challenge. After removing the object and
> putting it at the edge of the trench, it turned out that for two months I had
> been standing on a beautifully made element that was part of a frieze.
> The block had been laying "on its belly" rather than "on its back" …

In his book *The Quadruple Object*, the speculative realist Graham Harman writes that objects lie dormant and do not reveal their true nature to us as they "both display and conceal a multitude of traits" (Harman 2011: 17). Drawing on Harman's theory, I would stress that it is often the case that artefacts only slowly liberate their particular qualities and reveal their essence to us completely by chance.

The story presented above shows that even when having an object present-at-hand (*Vorhandenheit*), we might not notice its essence. For a month, the building block was for me just an ordinary flat, stone block that I placed buckets full of earth on. For four months, I used this object as a step without considering whether it might be decorated, whether it might come from the space that I was excavating, without considering how it got there and where it might have fallen from. My attitude towards it was in some ways close to that which Harman writes of in his critique of Heidegger's real objects: "yet the basic opposition in the tool-analysis is not between conscious and unconscious. Instead, the truly important rift lies between the withdrawn reality of any object and the distortion of that object by way of both theory *and* practice" (Harman 2011: 90).

As far as "discovering" the essence of an artefact is concerned, in contrast to Harman, I would rather place the emphasis on conscious, rather than unconscious, actions. In doing so, I am close to Heideggerian philosophy, to which Harman referred.

Being and Time, The Thing, or *The Question Concerning the Thing* remain for many authorities in the field (Thomas 1996; Olsen 2012b: 23; Burström 2013; Edgeworth 2013; Andersson 2014) some of the most important philosophical references for archaeologists. According to one of the leading figures of Heideggerian archaeology, Julian Thomas (1996), *Being and Time* should even be treated as a textbook for trainee archaeologists. Indeed, I am convinced that no other philosophical treatise has had as much of an influence on how I think about artefacts, things from the past (Heidegger 1996: 348), as *Being and Time*.

Harman performs a rather substantial reduction of Heidegger's idea of things, as in *The Quadruple Object*, he "forgets" time even though the process of discovering hidden traits takes place in time, just as Harman's concept of the dormancy of objects, something that I treat as a useful metaphor here, is temporal (see also Edgeworth 2016). The building block described above was most probably brought to the Greco-Roman house from one of the public buildings located in another part of the ancient city. Already then, one of its qualities had been withdrawn – namely its artistic craftsmanship. It ceased to serve as a decoration but instead became a *spolium*, a reused element that strengthens or completes a wall. Then, once the house had been abandoned, the building block underwent non-human dormancy, in that it ceased to be a useful object with qualities used by humans while at the same time entering the register of the effects of post-deposition factors. Following Heidegger, it could be that the object had been abandoned (*gelassen*), which for him was the equivalent of allowing it to "be as it is" (Andersson 2014: 39).

In the course of the excavations, the object revealed itself to the archaeologist, even though its initial traits remained dormant. In relation to Heidegger's writings on defining the essence of past things, the building block became a historiological object and a tool, albeit in a certain time and world that no longer existed (Heidegger 1996: 348–349). To me, the object revealed itself as a simple, unremarkable block of stone to which I then ascribed a new function. It was only upon closer examination of it that I realized the block's original predestination as an object without "reawakening" it. Indeed, the building block could never return to its original function, meaning that one of its qualities was at the moment of deposition – or perhaps even sooner, so when being transferred – withdrawn forever.

Nevertheless, I risk a return to Harman at this juncture and put object-oriented ontology into practice. If the block were to be treated as what Harman calls a real object (RO), then to reach it, I would first need to attune myself to its sensual qualities (SQ). For Harman, the sensual is always bound to experience. I experienced the block as a stone, a step, a piece of decoration, a part of an archaeological site and a piece of reality. I am not convinced that I exhausted the potential ways of experiencing or indeed naming it. Indeed, there is no response to this endlessness, to the undefined margins of not knowing. To Heraclitus' classical statement, which Heidegger often repeated and which Harman also seems to have appreciated, I would add, with reference to archaeology, that the "nature (of things) likes to hide". Nevertheless, the revelation of the hidden nature of things beyond their sensual qualities takes place in time, during excavations and conservation, in scholarly analysis and, finally, in the context of museums, too, where objects continue to be able to surprise us while at the same time eluding us.

Biology

Ceramics

> As a student participating in archaeological excavations, I was summoned to clean potsherds that were discovered during a previous dig season. Together with my female colleagues, we were expected to clean fragments of an amphora. We were given bowls and brushes. We scrubbed each of the fragments extensively, but the deposits were full of calcium and would not budge. Cleaning the contents of one bucket full of potsherds took us about three hours and the results were disappointing. When the professor saw the fruits of our labours, he was disgruntled, to say the least. He suggested that we tidy up our workplaces and pour away the water from cleaning the ceramics in a very specific place that he had indicated. A few days later, we learned that the professor

was attempting to grow mushrooms and he believed that the water full of clay would be perfect for speeding up growth. The mushrooms did indeed grow.

I present this anecdote in order to demonstrate the biological potential of artefacts, although certainly not in the sense of nineteenth-century British reports that powdered mummies supposedly provided the perfect vegetable fertilizer (Elliott 2017). Often, objects that are of interest to humanities scholars are seen in terms of being fixed, stable and unchanging (Thomas 2004), yet for archaeological artefacts this conviction radically diverges from the truth. Artefacts only appear to stabilize in the course of conservation or even in museums, where any transformations are closely controlled (Pye 2017), while before this stage they undergo a whole series of changes of a biophysical and chemical nature.

Jane Bennett laid the foundations of the theory of vital materialism with her hypothesis on vibrant matter, which shifted agency and autonomy from humans to matter (Bennett 2010). I would argue that there is no theory more profound and no theory of more constitutive significance to ideas regarding the nature of archaeological artefacts than hers. Abandoning anthropocentrism and the glorification of the role of humans as shapers of matter seems to me to be crucial in redefining finds.

The ceramics that I presented at the outset of this subchapter were made by people in the first centuries of the CE. Having ceased to be used, perhaps as a result of a vessel being smashed, the fragments were deposited. For over a dozen centuries, they remained underground, independent of human influence, before being excavated by archaeologists. Covered in sticky clay, they found their way into a large bucket. Perhaps they were discovered towards the end of the excavation season and there was no time left to clean them or perhaps that season yielded particularly many finds and the ceramics were forgotten. A year on, the ancient matter was covered in a calcified deposit that even intensive scrubbing could not remove from the potsherds.

Over time, artefacts are transformed by various biophysical and chemical factors. In the case of the ceramics discussed here, an important role is played by the way the vessels were manufactured (how intensively they were burnt) as well as by external factors linked to environmental conditions, so the soil type, geological substratum, presence of salts, the ability to retain or pass water, the oxygenation levels of the soil, whether the soil was frozen and to what degree and the activities of microorganisms. Artefacts can also be transformed by the vitality of plants and animals; worms, ants and mites decompose artefacts, while the microbiological environment causes further damage.

Given the vast extent of transformations, how is it possible to believe that what archaeologists encounter is dead and static matter? The absence of deeper reflection in archaeological theory on the factors transforming artefacts is rather striking. While delving into cultural and social meanings, what is overlooked is the fact that what archaeologists have at hand is a shifting, impermanent object that even when apparently forgotten – like the potsherds in a bucket – can continue to change. Such ignorance of the biology of artefacts is strengthened by the "sterilization of the past" (Shanks 1998), i.e. the series of conservation activities that seem to fossilize an object, stop time and thus also halt the natural processes occurring at the level of an object's material composition.

What has become commonplace is an image of dead, instrumentalized matter with no potential for metamorphosis (Bennett 2010: IX). As Bennett notes, there is an observable consistent and powerful tendency to understand all material changes as being a result of human agency, with this perception of things given impetus by the cultural, linguistic and historical constructivism that ensures that we perceive "thing-power" or "the force of things" to be a result of the work of culture, which in turn constitutes an act of violence towards the work of nature (Bennett 2010: 17). I consider the constructivism that Bennett describes to be of crucial significance to the system of purging and negating the impact of nature on artefacts while consistently locating artefacts within the cultural realm (Nativ et al. 2018). Archaeologists focus on the past dimensions of objects, investigating functions, the time and place where they emerged, and the people who made and used them, albeit without always noticing that the objects studied are constantly changing before seemingly being fossilized by conservation, which eternalizes a mere moment of its life (Shanks 1998: 17).

In attempting to draw attention away from human agency, Bennett cites an archaeological anecdote indicating that worms also "make history". She writes about the ways in which worms assist in preserving human-made artefacts that are in the ground, jokingly suggesting that archaeologists should express gratitude towards worms (Bennett 2010: 96). In this particular case, archaeologists should indeed be grateful, though not necessarily towards worms but rather towards heterotrophic microorganisms such as fungi and bacteria, which in fact often perfectly preserve non-organic material, such as ceramics, glass or stone. The presence of life in things from the past is of enormous significance in determining what object will be encountered during excavations.

The non-human factors that vitalize artefacts possess the potential, I would argue, to disrupt the dichotomy of nature and culture. Bennett suggests a possible direction that developments in vital materialism could take, noting that in a world of "lively matter" we are starting to recognize the force of biochemical processes that can develop in unexpected directions, countering deterministic causality (Bennett 2010: 112). I believe that in order to develop a deeper understanding of the essence of an artefact as an object co-constituted by a series of human and non-human factors, it is necessary to disrupt the constructivism of nature and culture and instead bring them together again as nature-culture.

Colour

Metal

Working on excavations does not only involve digging, of course. When I was learning to describe artefacts as part of documenting excavations, what I least enjoyed was working on metal objects. Initially, every piece of green bronze caused me difficulties; when the standardized form required me to enter the material, my pen came to a halt. Small green discs with sharp edges did not look like fragments of bronze mirrors, while long, ruddy fragments with rough edges did not resemble iron tools at all.

A key role in interpreting artefacts is played by field documentation produced during excavations. Archaeological missions use standardized object cards that require accuracy and complete focus on the object being described from the person producing the inventory. The documentation card should include information on the type of object, the material it is made from, its dimensions, its stratigraphic context and exact details of where and when it was discovered, etc. The card should also feature a precise description of the object, a drawing and a photograph.

The documentary demands are determined by the fact that researchers most often analyse material once it is generally no longer physically accessible, such as when, for example, it has been deposited in museum or in a remote or foreign storehouse. Such descriptions are also significant with respect to the transforming matter of the object, which could be damaged either in the course of conservation or even in supposedly safe museum stores. For this reason, descriptions of artefacts should be as full as possible because these documents record its condition, appearance and traits at the moment just after excavation. Each detail contained in this initial description is significant in future interpretations.

As I have shown above, an artefact is not a fixed object but rather something that is subject to various factors and undergoes transformation both during its deposition and after excavation (Pye 2017). The nature and speed of changes are above all dependent upon the material it is made from. Metal artefacts are rather specific in this respect. As the conservator of the Polish State Archaeological Museum in Warsaw stated:

the existence of each human-made metal object forms a fragment of a closed and irreversible cycle of material transformations that begins the moment the raw material (in this case, metal ore) is extracted and ends when the abandoned and damaged object again becomes a variety of chemical substances, namely minerals, due to oxygenation (corrosion). People use the elements contained in minerals (ore) and as part of a sequence of intentional actions, they bring about the creation of the final product, namely the planned article. Nature, though, stakes its claim to its property, thus it slowly and systematically reclaims the processed material, turning the metal object back into a more stable form of matter: minerals. The cycle is thus brought to a close.

(Weker 1998: 47)

In this brief paragraph, Władysław Weker presents a summary of the life of an artefact that ends with a "return to nature" while the same time leaving a material trace, a vestige or *vestigium* (Domańska 2017: 264–269) in the form of a negative that is left behind by the material in exactly the same place (Haber 2013: 79). In the description opening this subchapter, what is striking are two other crucial aspects of the ontology of the changing artefact: the timing of the transformations and their impact. The metamorphosis of the bronze mirror into a green disc or the iron bar into a shapeless, brick-coloured lump takes place in the register of the *longue durée*.[4] In the course of deposition, the object is transformed from a functional everyday tool into a form that is not conducive to identifying exactly its function. The form that this deformation, operating on the register of non-human scale,[5] takes is influenced by a series of factors that are independent of human activities. As chemists and conservators have noted, being located alongside organic substances in the soil accelerates the corrosion of metal artefacts. Beyond corrosion, salination also poses a threat (Pedeli and Pulga 2013: 21). The speed at which corrosion occurs can also increase when following deposition metal objects are in contact with organic material, such as textiles, skin, wood and bone, as such matter attracts microorganisms. This occurs rather often, particularly in the case of metal tools with wooden handles. Excavated metal objects that are then left without conservation for an extended period are subject to oxygenation and mineralization (Pedeli and Pulga 2013: 13–20). The "sense of wholeness" achieved through ad hoc conservation at the archaeological site is often momentary, since small and delicate objects made, for example, from thin metal plates soon start to crumble. The fleeting nature of the initial form that is subsequently restored during conservation work indicates how, despite all human endeavours, matter will in any case "return to nature" (Ingold 2011: 27).

One outcome of the transformation described by Weker is, in the case of the bronze mirror, a change in colour. The artefact acquires its "new colour" after several dozen years, when the surface is covered in a patina that emerges during the last stage of passivation. The patina forms a protective and waterproof covering on the metal that is formed of layers of oxides, carbonates and basic carbonates (Dornieden et al. 2000). As a typical property of very old objects, patinas are regularly brought up in debates relating to the authenticity or aura of archaeological artefacts (Holtorf 2013; Jeffrey 2015; Jones 2017; Jones et al. 2017). In an article on the concept of "pastness",

Cornelius Holtorf indicates that one condition determining the authenticity of an object is visible changes to its composition (Holtorf 2013). He develops a definition of authenticity focused not on the age of artefacts but on how they appear to accumulate time, with the condition of objects from the past expressed visibly in matter that is marked by loss, damage, cracks, fading and patina. Such traces, which mean that an object loses its original texture and colour, are traditionally treated as proof of its authenticity.

What is the significance, then, of the loss or transformation of the original colour? As Michael Taussig rightly argued, colour enables the form to thrive (Taussig 2006). In the case of artefacts, all changes in colour are indicative of the biological vitality of matter. Green bronze is thus a point of encounter for two crucial and mutually entangled qualities of an artefact: the *longue durée* and naturally occurring, long-term transformations whose impact is often visible only for a fleeting moment, namely at the point of excavation.

Spectre

Negative

> How should objects be treated that leave only traces, outlines and impressions in the ground? This is a question that I had to ask myself when participating in excavations at prehistoric sites. We explored a neolithic hut or, rather, what was left of it. The soil had not preserved its wooden constructions, so all that I could see when it turned out that we had reached the object were dark contours suggesting a rather regular outline of a building.

> "So it would be necessary to learn spirits. Even and especially
> if this, the spectral, is *not*. Even and especially if this,
> which is neither substance, nor essence, nor existence,
> *is never present as such.*" (original emphasis)
> (Derrida 2006: XVII)

We have become accustomed to stating that archaeologists examine "traces of the past". This claim is entirely accurate when it comes to negatives, such as hollows, hearths and postholes, whose "spectral" presence indicates that something had been there in the past. The categorization of such archaeological spectres raises less doubts among archaeologists than, for example, recognizing objects of relatively natural origins as artefacts.

Derrida writes that "a classical scholar would not be able to speak to the ghost" (Derrida 2006: 12). Yet, archaeologists do follow spectres, staking them out, tracing them and seeking to give meaning to "non-sensuous sensuous" (Derrida 2006: 6) objects. The spectre constitutes a *vestigium* – a trace that remains left over from matter in exactly the same place (Haber

2013: 79). The negative, the vestige, the spectral presence, in contrast to fragments, fuels the imagination. While fragments can be supplemented and reconstructed, negatives are merely a trace that can liberate much greater speculative potential. Traces fall apart, evade, disappear, get lost and cannot be held. Material traces remain in place owing to the oxygenation of carbon, which is why the vast majority of artefacts made of organic matter, but not only those, are destined to face the same fate. I remember the faint, green traces on the dry ground that indicated the presence of metal in this layer; but upon contact with a tool or hand they disappeared, like a spectre.[6] In the context of archaeological research, this was the ghost of an artefact that had returned to earth and is decomposed into minerals; a trace of a trace that had survived and haunts the researcher. It is worthwhile posing here Derrida's question: "what does it mean to follow a ghost?" (Derrida 2006: 10).

Tracing spectres at archaeological excavations requires patience and attentiveness. The archaeological negative constitutes material momentum, as something impermanent and fleeting, the only possible trace of what had been. At the same time, it is predictable momentum, just like the spectral moment that is inscribed with impatience, uncertainty and fascination. Therefore, as Derrida writes, "this, the thing ('this thing') will end up coming" (Derrida 2006: 2). This archaeological-spectral moment is not subordinated to time, just as spectral materiality is insubordinate: crumbling in researchers' hands and frustrating them. Although hauntology has in archaeology usually been applied in reference to reflections on exhumations (Shepherd 2013; González-Ruibal 2016; but see Rich 2019), I would like to draw attention to the potential contained in a literal reading of Derrida's spectral object. This could enrich subsequent discussions on the dichotomies in which artefacts are often located. The spectrality of things operates between materiality and immateriality, time and timelessness, nature and culture; thus, in order to come closer to comprehending this spectrality, it is necessary to recognize, rather than suspend, such oppositions. The spectral object is always liminal: it has form, contours and shape, but it cannot be grasped as if it were an object that is ready-to-hand; it comes from the past, but when it took the form in which we encounter it is not known; such objects are often made and used by humans, yet they are transformed by nature.

In contrast to the mysterious stone peach, which was a kind of negative artefact seemingly deprived of meaning, the fleeting appearance of the spectral object can transform the reading of an entire archaeological site. Despite its impermanence and fleetingness, it has the potential to give solid foundations to the entire interpretation process. As I now recall one of the excavation spectres, the bronze object that almost immediately decomposed into the soil, I remember the feeling of frustration, excitement and growing awareness of loss. Regardless of how I would use my trowel, the trace would disappear anyway.

Dynamics

Plaster

During one excavation season, I explored a section that formed part of a house. While the space might not have been overflowing with finds, it did become a genuine mystery as I discovered white plaster on a fragment of wall. It is no secret that in Antiquity, people did whitewash their walls and even less of a secret, of course, is that they decorated them. I was therefore particularly cautious in uncovering flakes of plaster that looked as if they had "fallen" off the wall. That plaster could slip – particularly if it had been applied poorly and all the more so given that the wall was located in an area of seismic activity – comes as no surprise. Yet as work proceeded, this hypothesis seemed increasingly less likely. The large, smooth flake of plaster indeed proved to be a fragment of floor but the impression that it had fallen from the wall was strengthened by the plaster element resembling a contemporary skirting board.

> "On an archaeological site, everything is in flux."
> (Hodder 1997, 1999, after Edgeworth 2012: 86)

Working on excavations demands constant negotiations or, as Matthew Edgeworth noted, constant adaptation to the object being explored (Edgeworth 2012: 78). Its form, dimensions and material dictate how it will be uncovered. This process, however, has more in common with the work of natural scientists than humanities scholars, according to Renfrew and Bahn (2012: 13). Applying a template drawn from the natural sciences, which begins with collecting data then conducting experiments, formulating hypotheses and attempting verification, before finally presenting a model, Renfrew and Bahn recognize that "[t]he archaeologist has to develop a picture of the past, just as the scientist has to develop a coherent view of the natural world" (Renfrew and Bahn 2012: 13).

Excavations thus have more in common with laboratory work than might appear to be the case at first sight. Matthew Egdeworth has encouraged comparisons of archaeological sites to wet labs, pointing out that through tactile and close contact with matter that is being sieved, washed, cleaned and conserved – so generally being set in motion – the work of archaeologists reveals many similarities to that of chemists and biologists (Edgeworth 2015: 44). So, what is the source of such motion or dynamics?

I am deeply convinced that the driving force and impetus that generates motion is the essence of the artefact: i.e. what it imposes upon us by the way that it is. Form, dimensions, weight, its condition and the location of its deposition are all indicators of how we should enter into contact with it, while a genuine assessment of the object causes us to take decisions dictating to how we should excavate it, photograph it and draw it. Artefacts force us into making a move likewise during excavation. This move can be understood both literally (a change in the mode of excavation entails a change in movements) and metaphorically (a change of assumptions, negotiation of meanings and hypotheses, as well as generating a form of intellectual stimulation). Particularly significant in this dynamic process of discovery is the method of excavation. While excavating the piece of plaster described in the introduction to this subchapter, I upheld the principles of classical stratigraphic excavation, which involves uncovering systematically the layers that are located above the object without digging trenches that could damage the artefact under investigation. The object is revealed slowly, layer by layer. There is a great deal of uncertainty in this movement – does the object continue into the subsequent layer? Will it turn out that it is positioned even deeper? Will it require mechanical excavation involving a trowel or can it be done through the rather more delicate movements of a brush that will not damage its structure?

Matthew Edgeworth gives a succinct answer to this question: follow the material, follow the cut, follow the rhythm (Edgeworth 2012). At the same time, he draws attention to the fact that we have become accustomed to ascribing a profound role in discovering the past to theory, yet in reality, theoretical aspects are relatively unimportant in the face of the process of negotiating movements and in relation to steps taken in the course of haptic contact with excavated matter. In this sense, archaeological work does not begin with posing hypotheses but "at the trowel's edge" (Edgeworth 2012: 77; see also Hodder 2005, 2012). The story cited above offers a perfect illustration of this moment, with the object under investigation seeming to me to be, at first, a piece of wall plaster, but the further the work progressed with layers slowly being uncovered by my trowel and then my brush, it emerged as a piece of whitewashed flooring.

In this context, the artefact determined movement, co-creating our approach to it, demanding responses to it as an unexpected object (Edgeworth 2012: 77), thus evading our assumptions and presuppositions.

Context

Glass

After weeks of preparation, I entered the depths of a Roman cistern. The work was especially difficult because of the temperature, the lack of fresh air and limited room for manoeuvre. The excavation method involved digging out as much soil as possible, pulling up buckets of soil to the exit where the contents were checked both manually and with metal detectors. Cisterns usually promise a wealth of objects. The first week of excavations, however, proved highly disappointing. The objects discovered were fragmentary and not particularly unique. In the third week, however, the situation changed. How surprised I was to find in the wet, clay earth, glass vessels preserved almost in their entirety! The closed context and intact stratigraphy offered the ideal conditions for preserving glass.

Fragmentary, broken, damaged and deformed are the adjectives usually associated with archaeological artefacts. Their condition is dependent upon the post-deposition factors that I have mentioned extensively already. I have also drawn attention to how far-removed museum exhibits are from fragmentary objects. This does not mean, of course, that all artefacts presented in museums are reconstructions of damaged or destroyed objects. On the contrary: museums most often opt to display those objects that were discovered whole.

In this subchapter, I will use the introductory anecdote to highlight the role of archaeological context in ensuring that an object can be preserved in the state it was in at the moment it was created or as it was when in use in the past. In their now classic archaeology textbook, Renfrew and Bahn stress the significance of the context of a find, defining it as the sum of three elements: the immediate layer of material in which the artefact is located; the object's provenance, i.e. whether it is positioned horizontally or vertically within this layer; and its relations to other objects co-existing within the same layer (Renfrew and Bahn 2012: 50). The concept of archaeological stratigraphy is thus complex. Ian Hodder, who has drawn attention to the role of archaeological context as the foundation for constructing complex and in-depth interpretations, is guided by the term's etymology, which stems from the Latin *contextere*, meaning "to weave, join together, connect" (Hodder 2005: 170). Artefacts are woven together, the archaeological context joins them together, thus enabling their connection in the course of interpretation.

What is the significance of this term drawn from archaeological methodology for the story presented at the outset of this subchapter? At the moment of discovery, the entrance to the cistern was covered with a large rock, which had sealed it for centuries. This means that the contents being excavated were part of a closed context. A closed context is not a common phenomenon, especially given the centuries-long tradition of pilfering from archaeological sites. Excavating a space that you can be completely certain had not been touched by human-hand since ancient times is highly thrilling. It is one of those moments when archaeologists feel a shiver of excitement that stems from knowing that you are entering a space where none of your contemporaries has been and from being able to extract from the earth artefacts that have been preserved whole.

Among the ancient objects I excavated during that dig, what stands out most in my memory are glass vessels. What you usually find are glass shards. But this time, I was coming across complete objects. Covered in sticky clay, the delicate objects in the cistern were safe from mechanical damage and weathering, meaning that their form was almost completely intact even as I removed the wet deposit. The moist cistern that had been cut into the rock did attract fungi and other microorganisms, but they posed no serious threat to the inorganic glass matter. Thus, the context proved responsible for the specific "fossilization" process that the objects that were conserved in barely altered form underwent. This shows that the approach that I have opted for, namely searching for the essence of an artefact and shifting attention away from the role of humans in order to instead highlight the significance of non-human factors could, *de facto*, most closely resemble practices in the field. Context destroys and context preserves: there is no room here for moves by humans. Why we encounter an object in a particular condition is an outcome of a whole series of factors that have no connection whatsoever with human activities.

Extraction

Pit

> Flotation is a typical method used to capture small remnants that could be overlooked when employing standard, mechanical excavation. When using floatation, each and every particle, right down to the tiniest one, is studied. After several minutes of pouring water through a sieve holding a portion of soil, even the smallest stone attracts suspicion. But attention must be maintained at all times! During such precise investigations, I together with two other people involved in the excavations came across an olive pit! The stone was rather small and unremarkable, but its almond shape immediately caught our attention. Along with a host of archaeobotanical and bone matter, it formed part of our further studies of the ancient landscape.

What does the olive pit that I together with other archaeological apprentices extracted from among the pebbles and tiny fragments of shells constitute? Is it an ecofact? Or perhaps a natural object that can be differentiated from cultural objects, i.e. artefacts? And what does an olive pit mean to an archaeologist?

The olive stone that we discovered is certainly a find. It was indeed dug up together with soil and then extracted from sediment in the course of wet work (Edgeworth 2015: 47). The pit is also an archaeological record, to use Gavin Lucas' term. It records the fact that the people living in a particular archaeological period that can be dated by stratigraphy and the objects found in it had access to olives. The pit is certainly an archaeological source, as it provides information connected to a specific archaeological context, with this information in turn proving useful to studies of the archaeological landscape or environment.

The olive pit, according to the perspective applied here, is also an archaeological artefact. This conviction stems partly from the fact that I am keen on new materialist approaches in archaeology and I agree with the view that there is no dichotomy in archaeology between the human and non-human, the natural and cultural. Therefore, everything that is discovered, whether through the lens of archaeological context or by studying material facets, functions as an object. I am also aware that the division between artefacts and ecofacts is a by-product of nineteenth-century archaeology, whose theories were Cartesian in spirit and thus also featured the dichotomy of nature and culture (Thomas 2006; Olsen et al. 2012). As Matthew Edgeworth, the much-cited field researcher and archaeological representative in the Anthropocene Working Group, has noted, the concept of ecofacts has never attracted much interest among archaeologists, meaning that it has been cast into the margins of theory, since the focus of researchers' interests has always been tied up with human agency. For this reason, "artefact" has for decades been the central concept (Edgeworth et al. 2014: 83).

Given the ongoing debates regarding archaeological objects, things and artefacts, I would like to stress that I side with new materialism. This perspective, in my view, offers a response adequate to experiences in the field: it recognizes that a host of natural processes constantly impact and thus transform objects that are traditionally seen as cultural and/or social. Archaeologists in the field enter into close, haptic contact with vibrant matter. In contrast to what desk-based researchers might claim as they solve the mysteries of culture in the silence of sterile libraries, the object of archaeology is neither cultural nor social, nor even scientific – to refer to archaeometric analyses of samples acquired in the field.

In light of current debates on deconstructing the dichotomy of nature and culture, and also in light of proposals to adopt new perspectives on artefacts, things and archaeological objects, I would argue that, firstly, the category of ecofacts is becoming increasingly less useful and more reductive as it upholds the above-mentioned binary opposition. Objects that have thus far been termed ecofacts, I would instead include as part of definitions of artefacts, although, as indicated in the introduction, I would point to completely different boundary conditions in understanding this definition. Secondly, I would like to return to the etymological deconstruction of the term artefact that I proposed at the outset of this chapter while drawing on the above note relating to flotation. Since *factum* relates to being and *arte* to making, with neither of these words offering a direct indication of the role of humans, it could be argued, then, that the artefactuality of the extracted olive pit is based on the fact that it underwent transformation as it existed alongside other objects in an archaeological layer and was shaped by post-depositional factors that deprived it of its initial qualities (the ability to take on water, sprout and grow). As an artefact, the olive pit is something that will never return to its original function, just like the corroded bronze mirror, the fragment of a stone pin and the building block. The pit lost its initial qualities and abilities when it became a deposit before later being discovered as an artefact.

Notes

1. It is worth mentioning at this point that Latour has inspired archaeologists to reflect on the nature of archaeological labour and the collectives of things that are involved in the collection and analysis of data. Furthermore, he encouraged thinking about the social and agentic role of things. The archaeologists who have turned most intensively to Latour's ideas, including actor-network-theory and concepts related to the philosophy of science include Jones (2002); Lucas (2005, 2012); Olsen (2013); Edgeworth (2015).
2. This does not mean, of course, that they are in no danger of being damaged or destroyed by, say chemical, physical, mechanical or biological factors; indeed, these factors might become more significant in, for example, polluted environments. See Scheerer et al. (2009).
3. A peach as a symbol of fertility and life, as well as sensuality.
4. For more on Fernand Braudel's concept of the *longue durée* and the reception of the French Annales school in archaeology, see Lucas (2008).
5. Processes taking place on the non-human scale are currently the subject of many interesting discussions in the context of the geological turn and studies of the Anthropocene. An interesting perspective on non-human time is offered by Jeffrey J. Cohen's studies of stone; see Cohen (2015). Among those writing on the non-human scale of time are archaeologists investigating the Anthropocene; see Edgeworth et al. (2014).
6. It is worth recalling at this juncture Heidegger's reflections on the subject of crushed chalk – not the kind that is familiar from school and used for writing on blackboards, but the crushed powder that can no longer perform its original function; see Heidegger (1970).

3   Redefining Artefacts

When writing about the various facets of artefacts, I quickly became aware that many of them are interconnected and mutually constitutive, while many also cooperate and interact, as Ian Hodder has outlined in his theory of entanglement. His notion of "entanglement" is grounded in an etymological perspective on the term "context"; hence, it does not concern artefacts as individual beings but entire sites, structures and archaeological assemblages.

Artefacts are unruly, unstable beings that possess their own temporality; they become entangled with each other and with the archaeological context, with the site, with past makers and users, as well as with the people later discovering them. In *Entangled: An Archaeology of the Relationships between Humans and Things*, Hodder writes that all "things are just stages in the process of the transformation of matter" (Hodder 2012: 4–5), but we do not see them in motion because they operate in a different temporal register (Hodder 2012: 6). We also forget about the spatial relations and mutual connections of objects when we attempt to study them as isolated existences – we describe, photograph and categorize them in isolation from their broader context or connections with other objects (Hodder 2012: 9). Above all, though, we view them primarily as cultural constructs. By refusing to theorize on archaeometry and treating the natural sciences as mere tools, rather than as full and complementary perspectives contributing to the study of artefacts (Hodder 2012: 14, 24, 41), we are guilty of a certain ontological reduction.

Archaeology "after interpretation" returns to matter and aims to realize a horizontal model of sciences (Jones and Alberti: 2015). Today's archaeology has the potential to enliven matter in the way that Jane Bennett indicated, namely by transcending binaries and working towards a synergetic combination of the social sciences and natural sciences (Lucas 2015: 378). The movement away from material symbols and towards vibrant materials, to use Bennett's terms, requires an updated definition of artefacts, one based in viewing through the lens of the newer approaches that I have referred to while theorizing on the basis of my own experiences of archaeological excavations.

For the purposes of the analyses of museums presented in the following part of this book, I propose a definition of artefacts that incorporates within

DOI: 10.4324/9781003327851-5

its boundaries both ecofacts and also the rather understated geofacts, while also forging new connections between things that are entangled within a given archaeological context. However, the boundary condition of artefacts according to my definition involves shifting the vector of the creator or maker away from the human beings who made objects used in the past towards nature, which has co-created a given object from the moment it was abandoned.

Particularly inspiring for my redefinition of the concept of the artefact is Heidegger's proposed definition of the term in *Being and Time*, with artefacts being historical historiological objects and pieces of equipment or tools, but always from a particular time and world that no longer exists (Heidegger 1996: 341–350). I thus understand artefacts to be objects that were made and used in the past (in past worlds) but their past functions and intended use are no longer applicable today. Artefacts are objects that ceased to be used and were abandoned, hidden, lost or intentionally deposited. Why, though, are artefacts unsuitable as "historiological objects"?

It is the moment of "breaking off", "disconnecting" and "withdrawing from" relations with human beings that I consider to be the constitutive event in the life of an artefact. In turn, this influences the fact that objects cannot return to the functions once ascribed to them. Abandoned, an object enters the archaeological context alongside other objects. They can mutually influence each other, which, as I have shown, can condition the state they are in at the moment of excavation. The iron elements of tools can corrode, with this process potentially accelerated by the wooden handles that attract microorganisms. Such damaged or abandoned objects that no longer serve their intended purpose can undergo transformations in the *longue durée*. In the time they are independent of human beings, they are affected by a series of post-depositional factors that constantly change their form. As I have demonstrated, context can destroy and context can preserve. Everything that occurs underground or underwater is independent of humans. An abandoned object becomes an artefact, i.e. "something created in the course of the *longue durée*", with other, non-human actors inscribed into this temporal frame. Objects do not emerge, then, as archaeological artefacts; they become them as a result of being abandoned: being cast aside and suspended from culture; this is the moment that they also acquire autonomy.

Artefacts can be preserved whole, as we saw in the case of the glass vessels; they can be fragmentary, as was the case with the bone pins; they can be negatives, as with the corroded bronze. The condition that we find them in during excavations is a result of processes taking place in the register of the *longue durée* over centuries of deposition and in the environment that the artefact was discovered in. At the moment of discovery, an artefact can seem mysterious, a "negative artefact" (Lynch 1985) that we are unable to define precisely and recognize. Sometimes, the inability to name something is a result of the fact that it is a tool from the past whose users are long since dead. This was the case with the stone peach. In other cases, the form of an object might be so distorted that it is difficult to establish what its function might have been, while at other times we have at hand whole objects or parts of them, as was the case with metal objects. Artefacts can just as easily transform before our very eyes, as happened with the ceramics, which ultimately crumbled and remained only as traces of information lacking any material body, as happened with the postholes. Artefacts can remain hidden in plain sight for a time, which was the case with the stone block, until we change our movements. Finally, artefacts can be discovered as large-scale elements during standard stratigraphic excavation, as happened with the plaster, or as almost imperceptible miniscule objects that are washed up through floatation, as was the case with the olive pit.

The aim of this summary is to emphasize how I could have given a different title to each of the above-mentioned cases precisely because a series of factors impacts the materiality of objects. The example of the plaster could have been used to discuss fragments, as the plaster was fragmentary, while the history of the vibrant ceramics might have served to illustrate context, as the change of context resulted in a sudden transformation. At this point, I would again like to recall the words of Ian Hodder: "on an archaeological site, everything is in flux" (Hodder 1997, 1999, after: Edgeworth 2012: 86). In flux are active matter, people and tools. But also the meanings that are negotiated first and foremost in the field.

I understand an artefact to be the sum of the above-mentioned facets and factors that are contained within something made of organic or non-organic matter that has then ceased to circulate and lost its original traits and meaning, but without being deprived of its material vibrancy. In this book, I therefore define artefacts as objects of archaeological interest that are marked by instability, the ability to change, the *longue durée* and a tendency to be susceptible to factors stemming both from human activity and factors of a biophysical and chemical nature that are independent of humans. As such, artefacts transcend human temporal scales and the dichotomy of nature and culture. Artefacts are not the same as objects as they cannot be reconciled with their original use; they do not return to their past historical functions. Artefacts are proof, traces, sources and archaeological records. Artefacts are long-term, dynamic matter operating outside the realm of human agency. Artefacts are open and open-ended in terms of their ontological existence. We will never be in a position to exhaust the meaning of an artefact since it will remain capable of surprising us, depending on the relations we enter into with it (Figure 3.1).

An illustration of such an understanding of artefacts is provided by Figure 3.1, "Artefacts: interventions and bottlenecks", which is inspired by Shanks' biological outline of the "life" of an artefact (Shanks 1998). At the same time, my model is influenced by Julian Thomas' proposal that the study of artefacts should focus on tracing life processes (Thomas 2015: 1294). I treat models as heuristic tools that can help us to think and conceptualize the factors that influence the status and/or condition of an artefact. Interventions, marked by the incoming arrows, point to the diverse factors impacting an

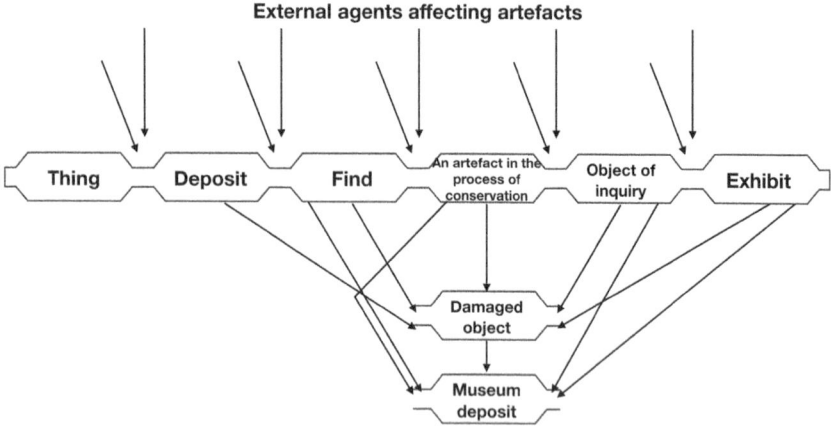

Figure 3.1 Artefacts: interventions and bottlenecks, author: Monika Stobiecka.

artefact and shaping human and non-humans in the realm of both culture and nature. The bottlenecks are intended to indicate transitory states, "holding" the artefact within a particular phase for a period of time whose extent is determined by the factors exerting an influence on it. The history, or life story, of an artefact includes a chapter when it functions as a "thing". This stage is broken by an "intervention" that might involve being abandoned, damaged or accidentally lost. As an event, an intervention causes a bottleneck, a moment when the artefact escapes human agency. The first "bottleneck" guides the artefact into the state of deposition, leaving the artefact/deposit to face the impact of non-human timescales, as well as the impact of biological, physical and chemical factors. The next intervention occurs with the moment of discovery. At this stage of "life", the artefact/find can be influenced by the circumstances in which it was discovered and by the excavation methods employed. The object can also become a damaged or destroyed artefact due to inaccurate excavation. The bottleneck that appears between the find and the research object depends, for example, on conservation processes, conditions in storehouses and the preparations for research analysis. The artefact/object of research is impacted by theories, research methods and modes of analysis and interpretation that later transport the object into the state of "exhibit". Artefacts can become damaged goods during transportation, due to conservation or unsuitable modes of exhibition, while they can also become abandoned deposits in museum stores. The model presented here illustrates the movement and the changes of state and status of an artefact, pointing towards its impermanence and susceptibility to various actions by human and non-human actors. In each transition phase, new qualities and abilities are ascribed to the artefact relating to its functions (as a thing), its life (as a deposit), its independence and autonomy (as a deposit and, in part, as a find), its being (as an object of conservation practices), its constitution (as an object of research) and its representation (as an exhibit). Artefacts are constituted by vibrant matter that transforms both materially and in terms of meaning in the course of events taking place on the human and non-human temporal axes.

I consider the vibrancy of an artefact to be an invitation to theorize. While the *arte-* element indicates "making", the *-factum* element points to "events and action", so the "fact" can also be treated as the act of creating theory from matter, or to put it another way: theorizing the thing. In doing so, the aim is not only to construct a coherent theory but to construct a practice of theorization (Lucas and Olsen 2022), one that would be open, flexible and encourage discussion. This was the guiding principle behind my attempts to illustrate the facets of artefacts: rather than presenting dogmatic ideas, my aim was "thinking with", juxtaposing, negotiating, moving and creating theory grounded in the material nature of things.

By shedding light on artefacts, I have sought to offer as clear as possible an outline of the realities of practices in the field and of the role of empirical experiences, which I have then correlated with the postulates of new materialism in archaeology. My observations and reflections have led me to pose the following questions, which I will attempt to answer in the following chapters: what is the relationship between artefact and exhibit? How can such unstable, material and often dysfunctional damaged objects from the past become museum exhibits? What do artefacts lose and what do they gain when placed in museums? What do artefacts and exhibits have in common? Are exhibits merely representations of dynamic objects? Which principles guide the selection of the dominant and, according to curators, important attributes of artefacts? And, finally, what can artefacts-as-museum-exhibits tell us about archaeology?

Part II

Exhibits

Contemporary archaeological exhibitions are rarely the subject of extensive and systematic problem-based studies.[1] The scope of existing research is most often limited to British and US-American museums, while most researchers who study archaeological museums primarily come from, or are based in, the UK and US (Skeates 2017a). The available literature has successfully addressed a series of practical aspects of museum activities (Sullivan and Childs 2003; Skeates 2017a), yet the dearth of comprehensive theoretical reflection on the essence of archaeological exhibits is troubling, especially given the far-reaching transformations affecting the discipline today. It might seem that archaeological museums have hardly changed to a significant degree since the emergence of New Museology (Skeates 2017c). As Bjørnar Olsen and Asgeir Svestad argued in the 1990s already, the role of museums "can never be understood in isolation from other statements and practices" (Olsen and Svestad 1994: 18), since both museums and archaeological discourse more broadly "create not only knowledge of the past but, at least to a certain degree, also the very reality they intend to describe" (Olsen and Svestad 1994: 11). Yet, since the mid-1990s, archaeological museum studies have continued to be conducted by and large in isolation from archaeological theory (but see Hamilakis 2013).

As the eminent British archaeologist and museologist Susan Pearce noted in the 1990s, the lack of progress in archaeological museums results from a lack of clearly formulated objectives for exhibitions (Pearce 1990). The dominance of traditional exhibition models, Pearce argued, was connected to the absence of problem-oriented thinking that could transcend nineteenth-century ideas (Pearce 1990: 7–9). She noted that while archaeological objects should be central to curators' interests, especially small, fragmentary pieces, they were in fact omitted in museum narratives. Pearce concluded that rethinking the idea of the archaeological artefact could lead to a transformation of museum practices (Pearce 2006d: 9–11). Favouring a biographical approach to things, she stated that for archaeological exhibitions to succeed, a series of questions to be posed of objects should be prepared from the outset (Pearce 2006b: 126).

DOI: 10.4324/9781003327851-6

Hedley Swain has made similar arguments in his contributions to debates on the state of archaeological museums. In 2007, he argued that the main problem with archaeological exhibitions was that archaeology as a discipline was in crisis (Swain 2007: 10). He believed that the powerlessness of the discipline was evident in its methodological failings that meant it was unable to construct definitions either of archaeology or artefacts, a situation that was then projected onto ways of thinking about exhibits. Clear definitions, according to Swain, provide the key to producing attractive exhibitions. In his critical introduction to archaeological museum studies, Swain drew on Peter Vergo's model, presented in the 1989 volume *The New Museology* (Vergo 1989a), that posited the existence of two dominant types of exhibitions: the aesthetic and the contextual. Even though over 30 years have passed since the publication of that seminal work, Vergo's classification of exhibition types, at least with regard to continental European archaeological museums, seems to have lost none of its relevance.

Aesthetic archaeological exhibitions remain highly popular as they constitute an established and traditional form whose origins can be traced back to the nineteenth-century aestheticized gaze on museum objects (Bennett 1998; Macdonald 1998; Classen and Howes 2006: 207). It was at this time that archaeology was emerging as a discipline and developing its research apparatus, most notably the typological method that has been described as providing a "spatial image of time" that reveals "the order of things" (Thomas 2006: 13–27; Hamilakis 2013 39–53; Olsen et al. 2012: 27–42; Olsen 2013: 111). Today, this model is manifested by presenting objects in sealed glass cabinets according to typological groups. Exhibits are rarely accompanied by detailed descriptions, meaning that it is difficult to establish their past functions, while any information is often provided on labels employing hermetic specialist language. This presentation model treats exhibits as if they were always highly valuable jewels, foregrounding objects' aesthetic value and focusing viewers' attention on the visual sphere.

Aesthetic archaeological exhibitions create numerous problems. Reducing objects to visual signs as if they were encyclopaedic illustrations of evolutionary development ensures that artefacts cannot be seen as ordinary objects, tools from the past or finds discovered in the particular archaeological context that had shaped them, let alone as things that might enable subjective interpretations of time, history and the past. Viewers instinctively seek out aesthetic values in accordance with Kantian categories. What becomes evident, then, is just how extensive the unfamiliarity with the excavation process, as well as with the functions, usefulness and ontology of objects that were created as things and tools, and not necessarily as works of art, is. Aesthetic exhibitions are, furthermore, aimed at educated visitors already possessing a degree of factual knowledge, as indicated by the use of specialist language in the brief descriptions accompanying exhibits (Lea 2017: 477; Skeates 2017d: 348). Even though such exhibitions are anachronistic, they continue to set the trend in exhibitions,

Figure II.1 Louvre, fragment of the exhibition, photo: Monika Stobiecka, 2017, by courtesy of the Louvre.

particularly those in institutions focused on Mediterranean archaeology and in large national museums. As Hedley Swain has emphasized, such "Über-Museums" are the places where people generally have their first encounters with archaeology (Swain 2007: 35). The aesthetic model of presenting archaeology is perfectly illustrated by the British Museum in London, the Pergamon Museum in Berlin and the Louvre in Paris (Figure II.1), as well as in smaller regional institutions.

The second type of exhibition noted by Vergo are contextual exhibitions. This model of exhibition is rooted in structuralism, thus artefacts function as signs pointing to other materials. In this type of exhibition, archaeological objects are accompanied by a significant number of educational aids, most often texts. Contextual exhibitions are currently being developed in many museums, likewise in those where multimedia are being introduced on a mass scale. The surfeit of materials, including new technologies and films alongside texts, can result in the material evidence of the past, the archaeological artefact, becoming lost.

Both types of exhibition outlined by Vergo fail to offer visitors anything that would go beyond either an aesthetic experience or an opportunity to acquire and/or deepen knowledge. Museums that today seek to address the challenges presented by Pearce and Swain need to engage visitors, creating a space for them to develop experiences based on contact with artefacts (Pearce 2006c: 28), while also granting a certain sense of empowerment that would enable visitors to understand and appreciate what contemporary archaeology has to offer (Chan 2017: 522; see also Nash and O'Malley 2012: 100). Michael Shanks' and Christopher Tilley's critical remarks were already pointing in this direction in the 1990s (Shanks and Tilley 1992). Based on an analysis of British archaeological museums, they found that artefacts are presented as chronological objects, objects of academic study, specimens, raw data, objective substances, ikons, solitary fetishes, signs in our present, signifiers of the past and objects for possession and consumption. As a result, they argued, museums reduce the significance of artefacts to their aesthetics or their objectivity, which again confirms the validity of applying Vergo's typology to archaeological exhibitions. Shanks and Tilley did not simply offer critique but also provided five recommendations, setting out an alternative route that archaeological museums could take. They argued that it is necessary to: (1) introduce political content into conventional displays; (2) disconnect artefacts from fixed chronological narratives and their traditional context by juxtaposing them with contemporary objects; (3) introduce exaggeration, irony, humour and absurdity; (4) avoid permanent displays and instead emphasize authorship and changing perceptions of the past; (5) encourage the (community) use of artefacts outside the museum in order to allow people to present their own versions of the past (Shanks and Tilley 1992: 98).

Interestingly, these ideas from the 1990s largely correlate with the proposal to redefine museums presented at the 2019 ICOM (International Council of Museums) Congress in Kyoto and the latest version finally accepted in 2022 at the Extraordinary Assembly of ICOM. It is worth drawing attention to the fact that archaeological theorists were highlighting 20 years previously issues that have gained acceptance only recently. Indeed, museums are still in a state of transformation. The question remains, though, as to how relevant Shanks and Tilley's observations are for today's archaeological museums and their transformative potential.

Right now I would reject Hedley Swain's view that archaeology is in crisis, but I nevertheless agree with his argument that there is still an unwillingness to construct definitions, whether of archaeology or artefacts, and this contributes to the stagnation of archaeological museum practices. Drawing on the etymology of the term exhibit, which comes from the Latin *exhibeo*, meaning "to present", "show" or "display", I emphasize the crucial role of exhibits in presenting and appropriating theory. At the same time, my work is also shaped by the etymology of the Polish term for exhibit, namely *eksponat*, meaning "to present", "explain" and "translate". Reflections on translating this term expose, then, the fruitful multiple positionality that has shaped my thinking about exhibits and artefacts. My understanding of "exhibits" is thus inflected by the etymology of *eksponat*, with the prefix "ex" meaning to "bring forth", while *ponere* means "to place", "to lay" or "to locate". An *eksponat*, then, can be considered a foundation that is laid in the course of excavating or "revealing" and "presenting" the essence of artefacts, archaeology, the past, materiality and time.

Etymological approaches thus come close to Heidegger's method of revealing the meaning of things. Nevertheless, Heidegger himself points to a different word that is often applied in studies of representations (Llewelyn 2001). The German term *Vorstellung* offers interesting insights into exhibition processes (Heidegger 2004). Heidegger used the word when developing his concept of *Weltbild*, as *Vorstellung* means an idea, an image and presentation. However, he deconstructed the term, pointing to the root word *stellen*, which means to "place", while the prefix *vor* indicates a position, namely before. *Vorstellen* thus means to "place something before something else or to move forwards", which offers a pointer towards representation, meaning and introduction. Such an understanding of the verb *vorstellen* is also encouraged by the reflexive form, *sich vorstellen*, which means to introduce oneself, while the infinitive *vorstellen* means both to present or introduce something or someone, or to imagine something. The noun *Vorstellung* means a performance, presentation of something or an introduction, while also pointing to notions of an "idea, conception or imagination".

The etymological approach applied here yields an image of exhibits as means of presenting and explaining what is evident to us, namely material reality. This reality is made familiar through archaeological practices and theories. Exhibits are, then, material, evident elements of the reality of museums, that through scientific framing emerge as the foundation of the process of presenting knowledge. As such, they possess the potential to inspire the imagination. I believe that such an understanding of exhibits is a crucial element in presenting the current state of research, developments in the field and its dominant theories.

Guided by the etymology of the term *eksponat*, I have selected two case studies for this book. Both museums break with long-standing traditions in exhibition practices, they avoid the dichotomous division of aesthetic and contextual exhibitions presented by Vergo and accepted by Swain and, above all, they problematize the contents of exhibits by applying the latest archaeological theories while also suggesting completely new formats for archaeological exhibition practices. Selected from among 20 institutions that I have analysed, the Acropolis Museum in Athens and the Museo dell'Ara Pacis in Rome were both founded in the 2000s and they are examples of site-specific museums based in Southern European capital cities. The exhibitions focus on what is traditionally understood as Classical archaeology, something that historically has been most notably afflicted by reductionist approaches, with artefacts displayed, first and foremost, as works of art. The two institutions are connected not only by the weight of Mediterranean archaeology but also by common motifs. Particularly significant in this context is the notion of the fragment as it shapes today's artistic sensibilities towards archaeological matter. Equally important in my reading of both institutions is the entanglement of archaeology in debates over new media, visual studies and the history of art. Also significant to my analyses are political issues, both postcolonial resonances and the politicization of heritage. Both case studies take the following form: a justification for choosing the particular museum, a history of the institution, a description of the exhibition and, finally, interpretations of selected exhibits. The aim of my analyses is to show that it is possible to view Classical archaeology through a different lens, beyond Kantian aesthetics, while also highlighting that finds from the Mediterranean region are archaeological artefacts as they, too, are damaged, fragmentary, sometimes mysterious and hidden, things that are experienced temporally.

Tracing the path of artefacts leading from excavations to museums, I highlight the role of theoretical frameworks in bringing forth the diverse meanings of objects while also shaping the form they take as exhibits. Inspired by the critical remarks of all the above-mentioned researchers, in my two case studies I will focus on artefacts as they remain the central type of exhibit presented in archaeological museums while pointing to the relationship of artefacts to current trends in archaeological theory and methodology. I will show that the exhibits currently on display transcend the meanings of archaeological artefacts presented by Shanks and Tilley. In the next two chapters, then, I will concentrate on two exhibitions that visibly reflect current theoretical trends in archaeology and respond to transformations in the discipline while at the same time contributing to the enrichment of the narratives relating to the exhibited artefacts, thus breaking with traditional exhibition models.

Note

1. Some works on archaeological museology, however, are available as part of general studies in the field of museum studies; see Macdonald and Fyfe (1999); Gosden et al. (2006); Marstine (2006b); Dudley (2010a, 2012); MacLeod et al. (2012).

4   The Acropolis Museum

Artefacts between Reconstruction and Experience

At a time of far-reaching transformations of the discipline, contemporary arch-aeological museums have not remained indifferent to resonant theories and new paradigms. While the visualization and mobilization of unconventional ideas does not seem too difficult in smaller and local archaeological museums that use diverse artefacts that are not burdened by traditional exhibition practices, in the case of emblematic institutions, on the other hand, positioned on the difficult yet rich terrain at the intersection of archaeology and art, revising archaeolog-ical practices and giving museums a modern makeover that would align them with contemporary approaches in the discipline pose bigger challenges.

The Acropolis Museum is a specific case, burdened as it is both by a dif-ficult history inscribed with colonial debates and identity issues, and by the monumental symbol of European culture, the eponymous Acropolis. As a relatively new institution, it could be presented as a spectacular fail-ure housed in a concrete pavilion. This is certainly how it has been viewed by numerous critics.[1] My analysis of this museum, however, distances itself from such critiques. As I have made clear from the outset here, my focus on affirmative examples of exhibitions is intended to highlight that criticism alone does not offer a productive basis for archaeological museum studies.

The exhibition at the Acropolis Museum sets a precedent for discussing archaeological museums in general as fully fledged substitutes for a visit to an archaeological site rather than as mere supplements. In this case study, I will discuss how artefacts are the central pillars upon which the compensatory sub-stitute of the Acropolis Museum is founded. The outline of the exhibition in the Athenian museum is grounded in an interest in matter, technology, conserva-tion, space and light, which, when taken together and set in motion, generate an experience of the past and mould the exhibits on show by placing them in con-texts that expand the existing tendentious and narrow understandings of them.

History and architecture

The Acropolis Museum (gr. Μουσείο Ακρόπολης; Figure 4.1) is located at the foot of the Acropolis in Athens and the contemporary museum building, designed by Bernard Tschumi, opened in 2009. It is impossible to discuss

DOI: 10.4324/9781003327851-7

Figure 4.1 Acropolis Museum, view of the building, photo: Monika Stobiecka, 2016, by courtesy of the Acropolis Museum.

the exhibition without at least briefly outlining the tempestuous history of the institution and its ongoing repercussions that resonate in the extensive literature addressing, firstly, the restitution of objects plundered during various waves of colonialism, secondly, political-ethical debates and, thirdly, the perception of exhibits whose status as archaeological objects or works of art is ambiguous.[2]

The history of the museum at the Acropolis can be traced back to 1874, when the first building dedicated to putting on show artefacts found on the hill and its slopes opened. This first museum presented remains of decorations from the Parthenon that were carved by the most outstanding Ancient Greek sculptor, Phidias. Part of the fragments were removed from Athens in the early nineteenth century already and transported to London by Thomas Bruce (Lord Elgin). From 1802, the British aristocrat acquired for his London collection a total of 56 panels of the Parthenon frieze, 15 metopes,

17 carved figures and the caryatides from another temple on the Acropolis, the Erechtheion. How Elgin acquired the artefacts remains controversial to this day, as Thomas Bruce was awarded a *firman* from the Ottoman Sultan that permitted documentation, excavation and partial removal of inscribed blocks and figures from the Acropolis. While being removed, the Parthenon frieze suffered significant damage. The objects that Elgin acquired were not immediately put on display in London. The public had to wait until the 1960s to see them.

The history of the remaining objects on the site is connected to the activities of Greek conservators that were involved in repair work on the Acropolis from the 1830s. Some of the fragments were subject to anastylosis and reinstated on the Parthenon, the Erechtheion and the Temple of Nike, while others were collected in the museum on the hill, whose collections grew as archaeological work progressed.

The dispersal of artefacts between the British Museum and their original location in Athens over two centuries has been a bone of contention in British-Greek relations. Debates on restitution, which came and went in waves, flared up again notably in the 1980s, fuelled by the charismatic Greek minister of culture Melina Mercouri, who served between 1981 and 1989 and again in 1993 (Hitchens 2008: XII). Mercouri took steps towards recovering the Parthenon decorations that were plundered by Elgin. However, her policies did not lead to a rational discussion that might have brought the controversy to a mutually beneficial conclusion. In response to the Greek minister's demands, there came tough, political declarations that often lacked any rational argument. This was evident, for example, in a claim from the then director of the British Museum Sir David Wilson, who compared the desire to transfer the marbles to Greece with an act of "cultural fascism" (Hitchens 2008: 98). In her struggle for restitution, Mercouri opted for a pragmatic approach. In response to British claims focused primarily on the lack of suitable conditions for displaying valuable Greek heritage in the old museum building, in 1989 the minister of culture announced a call for designs for a new Acropolis Museum in Athens (Hitchens 2008: 80).

Following much political turbulence as well as complications resulting from the discovery of further archaeological sites at the site earmarked for construction, it was the design of the world-famous Swiss architect Bernard Tschumi that was commissioned in the fourth call and he set to work. His building was completed in 2009, although the inauguration did not pass without difficulties. During the construction phase already, there were protests from residents of the historical Makrygianni district, where the museum is located.[3] For the local community, the monumental concrete-and-glass design created by Tschumi, who is considered an architectural deconstructionist, was an all too drastic intervention in the historic fabric of the city. There were also unfavourable responses to the museum from the British side, as is evident in some scathing comments on its architecture[4] as well as in rather bitter remarks relating to its financing (Carassava 2009).

The subject was also addressed by representatives of the British Museum. Jonathan Williams, the curator of its European section, issued a democratic and defensive statement declaring that the Acropolis Museum building was indeed impressive, but on the unavoidable issue of the marbles he said that the value of presenting them in two locations was that museums at two different ends of Europe could use the same objects to tell a different history (Hitchens 2008: XVI). For Christopher R. Marshall, these two stories are presented in a "temple", the Duveen Gallery at the British Museum, and in an "archaeological pavilion", the Acropolis Museum (Marshall 2012).

Marshall's terms provide a metaphorical summary of the debates over the marbles. Many British critics glorified the gallery in the British Museum while proclaiming their disdain not so much for the exhibition itself but for Tschumi's "decon" design, focusing their ire on poor lighting, the concrete walls and the sheer scale of the place. Yet this piece of deconstructivist architecture has earned prizes in numerous competitions[5] and is admired by architecture scholars and critics (Jakobsen 2012; Lending 2018). Reviewers' radically divided opinions are driven by several factors located at the boundaries of architectural, political and indeed museological and archaeological debates.

Tschumi's controversial design should certainly be commented upon. Deconstructivism as an architectural trend emerged in 1988 in an exhibition at the Museum of Modern Art in New York (Newhouse 1998; Merkel 2002). Peter Eisenman, Frank O. Gehry, Zaha Hadid, Rem Koolhaas, Daniel Libeskind and Bernard Tschumi were all invited by Philip Johnson to present their deconstructivist designs. And for years now they have been commissioned to create prestigious museum buildings showcasing avantgarde architecture. Tschumi himself has designed two archaeological museums, the Acropolis Museum, of course, and also MuséoParc Alésia in Alise-Sainte-Reine, France. The key terms accompanying his works are "movement" and "events" (Bernard Tschumi Architects 2011b), words that in the context of apparently static structures are suggestive of the deconstructionist nature of designs where the architect produces "ruptures" in traditional perceptions of architecture.

The immense concrete-and-glass museum in Athens, with interiors partly finished in marble, was intended as a counterpart to the Parthenon that dominates the Acropolis hill. The angle of the slope of the museum's upper gallery, the Parthenon Gallery, is identical to the angle at which the temple stands in relation to the Acropolis. The monumental museum thus constitutes a contemporary, concrete revision of the sacred hill. In Tschumi's design, the museum at the foot of the Acropolis juxtaposes fragile archaeological finds, the present-day city and its urban fabric, and, of course, the presence of the Parthenon, one of the most influential buildings of western civilization (Bernard Tschumi Architects 2011a). The architect's aim was to create a multi-layered dialogue between the architecture, the archaeological site and the contemporary city. Such an understanding of architecture resounds with the Derridean concept of the parergon,[6] which as something that is neither internal nor external forms a bridge onto a bank (Derrida 1979). In my view, Tschumi's museum constitutes a bridge connecting both current reality, the contemporary city, and the reality of the past, namely the ancient ruins on the Acropolis. This aspect is stressed by Annette Svaneklink Jakobsen in her analysis of the Acropolis Museum, in which she employs Deleuze's concept of signaletic material.

> For the experiencing visitor the architecture creates a conditional field of possible connections between the building, the exhibited archaeological artefacts, the adjacent hill, and the body and mind of the visitor. The character of these possible connections is experienced both spatially and temporally, because it is experienced here-and-now in Athens, in the twenty-first century and yet points towards the historic past, to ancient Greek culture.
>
> (Jakobsen 2012: 4)

As the central motif of Tschumi's architecture, movement occurs on the level of both how the structure is positioned in two dimensions and how visitors position themselves within its interiors. Thanks to the large number of glass windows, visitors are given the opportunity to constantly orient themselves towards the heart of ancient Athens, which is another element of the deconstruction, as it encourages moving away from traditional conceptions of museums as closed "temples of art", illuminated by spotlights that guide the visitors towards things that are "worth looking at". Tschumi's idea is based on using natural light to illuminate the museum so that the light wanders across the Greek sculptures while evading standard ideas of what a museum should be. In terms of the new museum housing some of the Parthenon marbles, Tschumi actually managed to achieve an architectonic-archaeological reconstruction that restored the Acropolis frieze to its original position in the exhibition while also restoring the forgotten archaeological context.

Description of the exhibition

The exhibition in the Acropolis Museum presents collections from the Archaic and Classical times, as well as from the period of early Christianity in Athens. The encounter with Athenian artefacts from the Acropolis hill and its slopes begins even before passing through the threshold of the museum. The path towards the main entrance leads across an open viewing platform, below which the archaeological remnants of a dwelling dated from the period of Antiquity or early Christianity can be seen. While in the queue for the ticket offices – which owing to the popularity of the museum often stretches beyond the foyer – visitors have a chance to view ruins indicative of the ancient urban fabric, including houses and bathhouses.

The excavation site, which was uncovered in 1997, can today only be viewed from above and has been intentionally left open to the public in this form.

After entering the museum, it is possible to proceed immediately to the permanent exhibition or alternatively head towards an open space located behind the ticket offices, where there is an information board introducing the exhibition themes. In this space, there is a model depicting the development of the Acropolis from the most ancient times until the period of Ottoman rule in Greece. The exhibits are accompanied by a film about the techniques involved in building temples. The space serves as a prelude that brings together two strands that are not addressed in depth in the main exhibition yet are integral elements of the construction and functioning of the Acropolis, namely urban development and ancient building methods.

The journey through the intricacies of the history and material culture of the Acropolis begins with a slightly tilted platform, whose base features artefacts presented in reconstructed archaeological contexts. The first part of the exhibition presents finds from sanctuaries and houses located on the slopes of the hill. Upon entering the first gallery, visitors to the museum are indeed surrounded by artefacts – beyond the objects beneath their feet, there are showcases on the wall filled with ancient pieces grouped thematically (for example, a section featuring women's accessories, including pins, spatulas, unguentaria and spindles, another displaying vessels arranged according to iconographic themes, for example wedding gifts), while above their heads loom Archaic sculptures that can be reached via a platform resembling the form of the Propylaea, the gateway to the Acropolis.

The exhibition on the first floor is focused on two themes. Glass cabinets on the walls present small pieces of material culture that are arranged according to the material they are made from (for example, bronze), the techniques involved in making them (for example, types of marble presented alongside the tools used for working on the material), their origin (a nymph's sanctuary, the Sanctuary of Asklepios or the theatre and sanctuary of Dionysius) or a leitmotif (animals and mythical creatures, for example). These are supplemented by technical diagrams and reconstructive archaeological drawings that offer an accurate indication of key elements of archaeologists' skillset. In the open spaces, perfectly illuminated by natural light coming through the glass panels in the walls, there are Archaic Greek sculptures found on the site of the Acropolis that had initially been displayed in the old museum building located on the hill itself. The presentation of these sculptures diverges notably from the conventional and traditional approach adopted in the previous museum. The famous *Moschophoros* is presented in a "semi-conservational" state in the Acropolis Museum as the screws that hold it upright are clearly visible, while the conservation processes applied to the sculpture are presented in an accompanying film. The Archaic sculptures are arranged in a way that draws attention to the restoration and reconstruction that working on archaeological material entails, thus ensuring that the display is positioned within the realm of exhibitions that address conservation.[7] The reconstruction of sculptures forms a key strand running broadly through the exhibition, with the ornaments and colours of many objects being recreated. Some of them are accompanied by copies that can be touched. The narrative on the first floor is fluid, despite the duality of the questions addressed. Narrative continuity is guaranteed by the spatial forms that are open, both to light – something that is of crucial significance for the reconstruction aspect of the sculptures on show – and to dialogue, which is understood here not only metaphorically but also literally. It is worth mentioning that a multilingual archaeologist is present at the exhibition, ready to help and answer questions that visitors might have.

The second floor of the building features service infrastructure, including a souvenir shop, restaurant and library. The restaurant leads out onto a spacious terrace that offers a view onto the entire range of Athenian hills as well as onto the contemporary city. The terrace fulfils one of the three intentions shared by the architect and the people responsible for selecting the location for the museum: it provides a continuous reference point between the building and the genuine remnants of ancient architecture on the hill (Pandermalis et al. 2015: 18).

The third floor of the museum is dedicated entirely to the Parthenon. Many tourists' primary goal is to view the Parthenon Gallery, which is preceded by an educational area featuring film materials and models referring to specific objects at the Acropolis. The darkened space, reached via an escalator from the floor below, forms the heart of the reconstruction of the Parthenon Temple. Visitors viewing the models and films are positioned in the naos of the temple and they can then take a corridor leading around the space where the Parthenon frieze and tympana carved by Phidias are presented. The temple's decorations are reconstructed directly in the location they were first displayed in in ancient times. The panels of the frieze are located above visitors' eyelines, precisely at the level they were positioned at some 20 centuries ago. Where elements are missing, because they are currently exhibited in the British Museum, there are brilliant white copies that contrast perfectly with the grey originals marked by the passage of time (Figure 4.2). The authenticity of each fragment of the frieze is indicated by a label with an inscription, ensuring that the exhibition is positioned within political debates on the restitution of the marbles to Greece.

The third-floor exhibition is not solely focused on the temple. The realistic reconstruction of the space not only recreates the layout and design of the building and its decorations but also features materials commenting on the strands linking the exhibits. There are screens, located directly below the originals, showing reconstructions of the polychrome that adorned the Parthenon frieze. This gives visitors an opportunity to verify the state of preservation against what conservators propose.

The route through the exhibition is accompanied by an extensive view out of the floor-to-ceiling windows. As is the case on the first floor, light plays a

Figure 4.2 Acropolis Museum, Parthenon Gallery, copy of a tympanum held in the collections of the British Museum. In the background: original metopes from the Parthenon, photo: Monika Stobiecka, 2016, courtesy of the Acropolis Museum.

crucial role in creating the impression of a total reconstruction: the marble decorations of the Parthenon can be viewed in the same light that illuminated them when the temple was in use, rather than in the rather different light provided by museum spotlights. Furthermore, visitors can constantly

Figure 4.3 Acropolis Museum, Parthenon Gallery, view of the Acropolis, © Acropolis Museum, 2009, photo: Nikos Daniilidis.

refer the exhibits back to the realities outside the windows, namely the emblematic ruins on the Athenian hill (Figure 4.3).

After leaving the third floor, visitors to the museum return to the level below, where there are exhibits and films on ancient building techniques. Heading towards the exit, visitors pass through the first floor again, where, as in the Parthenon Gallery, objects are arranged to evoke the spatial impressions left by the remaining buildings erected on the Acropolis. When viewed from afar from the museum, the Temple of Nike and the Erechtheion, out of bounds to visitors to the archaeological site, seem to invite people to enter them and become symbolically, at least, acquainted with the structures' volume and layout. Devices employed in the museum, such as depicting the outline of the Temple of Nike on the ground, the arrangement of the walls and reproducing the scale of this building, allow visitors to experience its dimensions. While it might appear monumental on slides and plates, it is actually relatively small. The Erechtheion is treated in a similar fashion, with the heritage site presented in such a manner so as to reproduce the layout of a temple that was rather unusual for Ancient Greeks. As is the case with the missing elements of the Parthenon frieze, a political narrative is subtly introduced here, too. All that remains in place of the caryatid pilfered by Lord Elgin is an empty space. The exhibit is also accompanied by a film on the conservation of caryatids.

Archaeological prostheses

As part of a series of deconstructivist acts, the Acropolis Museum seeks
to revise established traditions – and not only on the architectural level.
Some critics of the Athens museum accused its initiators and architect
of lacking ideas and imagination when forming the exhibition narrative
and lacking awareness of the artistic aspects of the Parthenon decorations. Other critics, meanwhile, emphasized the apparent ignorance of the
archaeological context, something they felt had been sacrificed in favour
of an aesthetic presentation.[8] The radically divergent opinions in these
debates encourage us to consider the ways in which the contested marbles
are presented in the Acropolis Museum.

In my view, the Acropolis Museum gives the sculptures and other decorations from the Athenian hill a decidedly archaeological character by
recreating their original contexts and by emphasizing the traces of damage together with the passage of time.[9] Such an approach to the objects,
and not only to Phidias' works of art but also to archaeological artefacts,
marks a break with the traditional cult of the fragment that has continued
to dominate many exhibitions. By presenting the famous *Moschophoros*
on a supporting frame in the Archaic Acropolis Gallery or the *Euthydikos
Kore* complete with a bolt that holds up the construction, as well as visualizations of the polychrome of the apparently brilliant white marble of
the Parthenon frieze in the Parthenon Gallery, the Acropolis Museum
formulates a new approach to sculptures that at the same time serve as
archaeological artefacts.

The conservational-reconstructive procedures presented in the exhibition juxtapose the material, virtual and technological orders, reflecting the
contemporary zeitgeist that seeks completeness and attempts to produce
wholes (Stiegler 1998), with these procedures at the same time departing
from the sentimental aesthetics of the fragment. What I propose is catego-
rizing this deconstructive move in relation to traditions of archaeological
museum practices as an archaeological prosthesis that could bring together
strands positioned at the intersection of studies of materiality, practical
conservation guidelines and digital archaeology. I understand archaeological prostheses to be substitutes and artificial supplements that stand in
for losses or lack.[10] I use the term to mark a transcendence of the visual
dimension of digital media in archaeology, while at the same time forming
a conservational procedure that has a tangible effect. The concept will enable me to further consider how reconstructive-conservational exhibitions
can go beyond the "soft" humanities of archaeology and enter the realm
of "hard" science that exists in the domain of virtual media and conservational interventions on material.

The objects that have been supplemented by archaeological prostheses
are primarily the anthropomorphic and zoomorphic sculptures presented
in the Archaic Acropolis Gallery, the marble decorations in the Parthenon

Figure 4.4 Acropolis Museum, Archaic Acropolis Gallery, prosthetic figures, © Acropolis Museum, 2013, photo: Socratis Mavrommatis.

Gallery and exhibits relating to the Erechtheion and the Temple of Nike. I apply the notion of the archaeological prostheses to a variety of objects, both in relation to material supplements (construction bolts, supporting frames, three-dimensional print outs and plaster cast models of missing elements) and to digital aids (film reconstructions presenting the exhibited artefacts, such as those showing the original polychrome or those documenting the laboratory work of conservators) (Figure 4.4).

Archaeological prostheses could not exist without the damaged archaeological material that is marked by the passage of time. In this context, it is worth drawing on a concept proposed by the heritage scholar Cornelius Holtorf (2013). Analysing the debates between materialist and constructivist archaeology, Holtorf suggested applying the category of "pastness" in reflections on artefacts, as this term brings together the issues of the authenticity of objects, the construction of meanings and matter. In order to increase the precision of the concept of pastness, Holtorf develops a definition of authenticity that does not focus on the age of artefacts but on how they accumulate time and on conditions marking objects as being from the past that are expressed in visible traces on their material, namely in chips, damage, patina and being smashed or faded. Holtorf emphasizes that these traces were acquired in the past but are visible today. Pastness, then, is defined through the perception and experience of an object, with these aspects being located in a particular cultural context. Holtorf notes that museum exhibits can indeed be perceived through the framework of pastness because labels indicate that they come from the past;

the pastness of a medieval church is expressed in an architectural style that we associate with a particular construction period; pastness also applies to ruins as the damage they have incurred and thus the passage of time is immediately evident. Holtorf suggests that the category of pastness can be used to differentiate archaeological authenticity from the material constituting an object. He outlines the conditions that an object must meet in order for the concept of pastness to be applicable to it. For Holtorf, such an object must bear material traces of pastness, for example patina; it must be perceived by those viewing it as being from the past; and it must have an engaging, meaningful history that combines past and present.

The facets of pastness inherent to the archaeological objects displayed in the Acropolis Museum are clearly expressed and openly revealed. Furthermore, the sculptures that are accompanied by a variety of construction supports, together with the film material commenting on conservation and restoration procedures, reveal the pastness of the damaged and destroyed elements. Material traces of the passing of time – damage, chips or remnants of polychrome – are left visible to visitors to the Acropolis Museum. The silver bolts holding up the *Moschophoros* and the *Euthydikos Kore* create clear contrasts between the old and new, the present and the past. The material traces that time leaves on archaeological finds are for museum visitors visible evidence of the authenticity of the objects on display.

Reading the exhibition through the lens of Holtorf's concept of pastness, however, leads me towards a traditional understanding of archaeological exhibitions, with emphasis placed on the materiality of damage and destruction as well as on the possibilities of compensating for it today. Indeed, the approach remains caught up in the aesthetics of the fragment. Fragments and ruins experienced through the passing of time have traditionally formed the quintessential object of archaeological research, the "science of old things" (Olsen et al. 2012: 3). Furthermore, the traces and signs of damage on the objects point towards the category of authenticity, which started to emerge as a concept in the eighteenth century, in parallel to the dawn of museums (Marstine 2006b: 2). As products of a materialist reading of what is accented in exhibitions, fragmentariness and authenticity offer pointers, admittedly rather attractive ones, towards a highly traditional reading of archaeological exhibits.

My reading of the narrative of conservation and reconstruction in the Acropolis Museum, however, finds that it actually breaks with the traditional exhibition model. This is possible because my interpretation also employs concepts stemming from preservation science. What is striking about this field is the prevalence of medical terminology, with words such as "treatment" and "medicine" highly prominent (Pedeli and Pulga 2013; Rouba 2012). The translation of language usually applied with reference to people and animals acquires suggestive meaning in the context of (non-)living matter, particularly when considering the nature of publications on conservation as they typically employ the condensed, concise scientific format of academic texts. The medical terminology used by praxis-oriented conservators represents a legitimization of the concept of archaeological prostheses, as they signify compensatory supplements resulting from the care and attention currently lavished on artefacts as if they were sick patients.

The treatment of artefacts is depicted in films shown in the Acropolis Museum. Reading them through the prism of the medical metaphors used in the scientific language of conservators provides insight into the materiality and autonomy of artefacts, as well as the potential to view artefacts as the "cyborgs" of archaeology and museums. Paths guiding interpretation in such a direction are set out by concepts including "patina", which is a familiar element of the biochemical vocabulary of conservation. The same applies to Holtorf's use of "trace" to signify material expressions of pastness and ageing.

From the biophysical and chemical perspective, patina is a layer of oxides, carbonates and base carbonates that appear on the surface of an object, thus endowing it with a desirable tint that also has protective properties. Patina is formed over time and has a different chemical composition and different physical qualities to the object it appears on (Dornieden et al. 2000). There are two well-known forms of patina – acquired and applied. Acquired patina emerges organically and gives stone, for example, hardness and protection while at the same time weakening its deeper layers by allowing water to penetrate inside and weaken it. What poses a serious threat to stone or other non-organic material, however, is applied patina, a deposit that emerges in polluted environments, significantly weakening the condition of the material. The definition of patina used in the natural sciences is primarily aesthetic, rather than technical, which unwittingly guides us towards understanding patina as a dignified trace of passing time.

Patina, then, is what enables a belief in the *longue durée* of an object, seeing it as an expression of the accumulation of time, something that in turn lends legitimacy to the concept of authenticity. Patina constitutes an essential, protective layer that, on the one hand, indicates the archaeological nature of an object, while on the other hand making its "return" to an original state impossible. The Acropolis Museum seeks a solution to the irresolvable dilemma that has haunted efforts to protect and care for heritage from the outset – to preserve or restore (Scott 2015) – in the form of accompanying films. These documents presenting the reconstruction of polychrome do not come into contact with the ancient patina and manage, at the same time, to fulfil the educational mission of museums, thus supplementing the artefact. The films therefore depict a different embodiment of the "old" artefact without interfering with its structure in the way that invasive reconstructions would.[11] At the same time, the films make it possible to care for the artefact's materiality using a series of conservation methods (Pye 2017: 121). An advantage of films, and not only for epistemic reasons, is that they permit the step-by-step presentation of conservation processes. The "treatment" of the priceless Acropolis sculptures requires many stages, involving the implementation of a series of procedures adapted to the individual "patients". The range of methods, from the mechanical (piercing, scraping, sanding, using abrasive sponges, brushing, using higher temperatures, and oiling) to the chemical and physicochemical (ultrasound and lasers), demonstrates just how far-removed from its original state the object's fragile material presented on monitors and in colour reproductions is, even if it might appear to be a resilient, unfaltering piece of marble that has accumulated centuries of experience.

Together, the series of conservation procedures and the introduction of digital materials into the exhibition reveal how mistaken the arguments about the destructive dimension of archaeologists' work appear today.[12] The new opportunities presented by digital archaeology also go beyond the dimension of pure reproduction and visualization, which has been the usual focus, and cross the boundaries between the epistemology and ontology of objects. In the case of the Acropolis Museum, the interactive panels and films depicting reconstructions that are alive with a riot of colours are directly juxtaposed with the original, faded grey objects, thus undermining the way artefacts are reduced exclusively to their historical matter. The digital supplements form an "extension" of the object as a prosthesis, reproducing its original appearance to which a return is impossible without damaging the authentic material of the artefact. Virtual models and digital reconstructions as non-invasive supplements to artefacts possess an epistemological dimension as they permit the visualization of the "unimaginable", such as object's colourful polychrome or complex patterns on sculptures. This epistemic value is of crucial significance as an embodiment of the goal of democratizing museums (Kidd 2014) so that they have the potential to teach everyone something, although this same principle is also the embodiment of the didactic museum.[13] Technology is not limited here to satisfying the desire for entertainment through "tourist products". The Acropolis Museum exhibition, where the use of technology is limited to the presentation of short films and visualizations, offers a perfect illustration of how current technologies should not be associated only with tablets and games, which often distract visitors from the artefacts. Instead, the new possibilities that are applied could be seen as having the potential to enable deeper insights into the essence of artefacts, their past, matter and meanings. On the ontological level, digital supplements come close to embodying the archaeological "cyborgs", figures that transcend the boundaries between reality and virtuality. Digital technologies guarantee compensation, with what has gone before and the past being restored without interfering in the fragile essence of artefacts, thus maintaining the valuable sense of "authenticity". The potential for creating supplements and historical "cyborgs" correlates with the contemporary desire for "wholeness", seeking completion in a form that differs significantly from the nineteenth-century cult of nostalgic fragments.

Archaeological prostheses understood as substitutes for losses or lack that appear as part of fragmentary artefacts engender a re-evaluation of ways of thinking about the role of technology and conservation in archae-ology. Virtual and material prostheses, as a response to a reality stripped of colour and to fragmentary sculptures, become a Heideggerian enframing (*Ge-stell*), which

> means the gathering together of that setting-upon which sets upon man, i.e., challenges him forth, to reveal the real, in the mode of ordering, as standing-reserve. Enframing means that way of revealing which holds sway in the essence of modern technology and which is itself nothing technological.
>
> (Heidegger 1977: 20)

Virtual aids and conservational interventions thus function as the technical scaffolding that expands the possibilities for discovering an artefact. Such approaches to archaeologicals objects distance them further from the artis-tically entangled aesthetics of the fragment and enable the revelation of the essential nature of archaeological prostheses. The idea of archaeological prostheses automatically gives rise to the question of what are artefacts if they are no longer that which they had been? What was an artefact when it was not an artefact?

Kinaesthetic substitutes and the agency of light

Continuing to address the theme of substitution, I will discuss the spatial dimensions of experiencing the past in the Acropolis Museum. This man-ifests itself in a series of exhibits beyond those discussed previously, so in arrangements that reproduce the dimensions of Athenian temples. I will therefore consider whether spatial exhibits are an attempt at bringing to life the idea of a total reconstruction, or whether they perhaps function as yet another multidimensional substitute for reality. Realistic architectural reconstructions guarantee a certain "translocation effect" from museum galleries into the once accessible interiors of temples. However, the proxim-ity of the actual ruins suggests that the recreated spaces are compensatory substitutes for genuinely experiencing archaeological remains. In consider-ing this question, I would like to emphasize from the outset just how closely the museum is positioned in relation to the archaeological site whose history it tells. The unmistakable outline of the Acropolis, visible from each floor of the exhibition, seems central to solving the problem I am addressing here. Equally crucial is the position of autonomous artefacts as actors within a network of full-sized (re)constructions. In attempting to respond to the questions relating to the spatial nature of exhibits, I will use the concept of kinaesthesis, which comes from physiological studies but has also been applied in human geography and spatial studies. I will also outline the role of light in creating impressions of space and in (re)constructing kinaesthetic experiencing of the site.

When applied in physiological studies, the concept of kinaesthesis describes information derived from structures associated with movement, or more precisely speaking, from the receptors located in skeletal muscles, tendons, joint capsules and the bony labyrinth of the inner ear. Kinaesthesis refers to the flow of stimuli without eye activity, so the ability to move limbs without looking at them. Kinaesthesis forms one of the elements of proprioception, which is responsible for the flow of information between the central nervous system and the osteoarticular and muscular system, meaning that it is responsible for the movement of the entire body. It also includes the sense of balance. Thus, kinaesthesis [gr. *kinéō* "I move", *aisthēsis* "feeling"] is defined as the sensing of the position and movement of body parts in relation to each other.

As a physiological concept describing the sense of position and movement, kinaesthesis has become one of the fundamental pillars of sensory strands of human geography, namely haptic geographies and the project of sensuous geography. Human geographers exploit the potential contained in this to rethink space (MacCormack 2010: 208). According to theories of haptic geographies, grounded in human "sensory dispositions", the body forms a research tool that operates by employing kinaesthesis, understood not in terms of an individualized sense, but as a series of perceptual dispositions that expand the perspectives for sensing space (Paterson 2009: 767–769). Paul Rodaway's earlier idea of sensuous geography defined its research tools in a similar way but without using the term kinaesthesis (Rodaway 1994). Sensuous geography is grounded in the tactile or haptic potential of the body, especially the skin, which assists in gaining insight into relations between humans and the environment in a given time and place. Sensuous geography addresses issues of sensuality and reality, which are particularly crucial to Western culture given the continuous transformation of this particular sense. The idea of sensuous geography opened the way for human geography to address the question of movement and positionality in, and in relation to, space (Paterson 2009).

What is missing from human geography approaches that use the term kinaesthesis is sensorial engagement with matter, something that is essential to my study of the Acropolis Museum exhibition. Complementary to the theories and ideas presented here, however, are Tim Ingold's concepts grounded in materialist discourse. Ingold uses the term kinaesthesis when attempting to demonstrate the role of objects as transducers of our activities (Ingold 2013: 91–108). He writes that we are as equally aware of the movement of objects, such as gliding kites, as we are of our own movements performed through kinaesthesis. Ingold sees the potential form transforming humans' kinaesthetic movements into the "bodies" of objects. Immaterial movement would thus be materialized and transformed, or transduced, into another form, namely the kinaesthetic movement of objects, for example a cello that emits a sound as a result of human movement.

In relation to the exhibition of the Acropolis Museum, I would like to incorporate into my interpretation of the artefacts on display both Ingold's concept of transducers and the term kinaesthesis, referring the latter back to how exhibits are experienced. However, in order to discuss the spatial relations of exhibits, I require an actor, one that we cannot see and without which we cannot see – light. As Ingold puts it "though we do not see light, we do see in light" (Ingold 2011: 96). Light plays a huge part in creating meanings in the exhibition at the foot of the Acropolis.

Associated with sight, one of the human senses, there is a long philosophical tradition of seeing light as the "primary" form of perception and as something that enables engagement between humans and things (Steane 2011: 2; see also Bille and Sørensen 2007). As I noted when describing the architecture and exhibition of the Acropolis Museum, light serves an important function in visitors' experiences. Derek Phillips' extensive study *Daylighting: Natural Light in Architecture* outlines a series of reasons why the relationship between light and surroundings should be emphasized. He stresses that light enables the contextualization of architecture in relation to its surroundings, it realizes the human need for change, facilitates orientation, makes it possible to experience the landscape and guarantees a sense of natural colour (Phillips 2004: 5–6). "Bad" lighting in a building, or indeed the absence of light or only experiencing brief periods of sunlight, is a factor contributing to what architecture scholars call "bad building syndrome". This can then lead to serious health problems, such as dry eye, migraines and pain (Phillips 2004: 19; Steane 2011: 2). The effects that unsuitable lighting can have on people draw our attention to the agency of light (Bille and Sørensen 2007: 273). As emphasized by the authors of *An Anthropology of Luminosity: The Agency of Light*, it is possible to manipulate nature when creating culture through skilled "use" of light.

Conscious application of light is the key to constructing an attractive exhibition as light contours exhibits, bringing out their assets while hiding faults. Like architecture, it serves as a framework for experiencing a museum (Marstine 2006b: 4). *The Manual of Museum Exhibitions* offers practical advice on lighting in museums. The author of a chapter on light writes that the only suitable form of museum lighting is illumination from above while advising strongly against lights coming from the side, as this generates reflections and a phototropic effect, meaning that people's gaze is directed towards the most brightly illuminated elements, namely the light source (Hahn 2002: 167–170). Hahn draws attention to the fact that natural light, so important in domestic architecture (see also Steane 2011), is supposedly highly undesirable in museum galleries because it generally contributes to damaging valuable artefacts (Hahn 2002: 168). There are though, as Hahn highlights, certain groups of artefacts that are not threatened by natural light, naming ceramics, glass and metal objects as things that are indifferent to the impact of illumination.

The above remarks on light lead me to return to the issue of the architecture of the Acropolis Museum, as it violates all the established principles of museum lighting.[14] The oft-mentioned glass panels dematerialize walls in the Athenian museum. The light coming through them is natural and intense and floods in from the side rather than from above. Shaped by the presence of huge windows, the exhibition breaks with traditional recommendations for illuminating museums.[15] Diverse artefacts – sculptures, ceramics and metal and glass pieces – are bathed in natural light, while only occasionally being additionally illuminated by spotlights in cabinets or by photographic reflectors. The "archaeological pavilion", a term used to describe Tschumi's deconstruction of the museum through architecture, is a place where light is uncontrolled as it moves across the matter of artefacts in accordance with the time of day, creating reflections and flares of light. Tschumi abandons sacred standards for museums, namely dark rooms that feel like cathedrals or tombs, in favour of an architectural pavilion where light can roam freely. Opening up the museum to light, something that for Le Corbusier was central to understanding the architect as a choreographer or director of an "event" (after Steane 2011: 12), again points back to "movement" and "events", the leitmotifs of Tschumi's architectural practices. What constitutes the "event" is the possibility of transforming sculptures and reconstructing their past contexts. Objects once located on the Acropolis hill were bathed in natural light there, a light that shifted throughout the day. In realizing his design for an archaeological reconstruction, Tschumi created a substitute for experiencing sculptures in their original light.

In deciding to incorporate huge plate glass windows through which light can attack the artefacts, the architect was almost certainly aware of the phototropic effect that guides the eye towards a light source. Tschumi made a conscious decision to give visitors a reference point outside the museum galleries displaying objects: the Acropolis, the very place that the artefacts came from. It can be seen from every point in the exhibition (Jakobsen 2012; Rask 2017; Lending 2018).

Architecture positions visitors in relation to the Acropolis by manipulating the sense of sight through the use of light, the design of the exhibition space and through the artefacts themselves. Starting with the crowning glory of the museum, the Parthenon Gallery, Tschumi performed spatial procedures on the museum by orienting it in reference to the hill. The Parthenon Gallery is positioned at an angle to the lower levels, correlating with the angle of the Parthenon in relation to the Acropolis. The gallery at the top of the museum creates a dialogue with the temple of Athena Parthenos at the level of its construction, with the arrangement of the interiors mirroring exactly the layout of the Parthenon. The space is arranged in such a way that it becomes an ideal reproduction of the design and structure of the temple, with an opportunity provided to constantly verify it against the ancient structure visible through the expansive windows. The gallery is designed to stand in mimetic relation to the temple, with visitors offered the chance to experience kinaesthetically the ancient construction that is not open to visitors today. Such a reading is supported by Graham Harman's recent reworking of the concept of mimesis where the emphasis is no longer on the production of copies of existing things but on the performative becoming of new things (Harman 2019). In this sense, exhibits imitating the spatial arrangement of temples are not only reconstructions and copies of interiors, but within the framework of performative and kinaesthetic experience become fully fledged architecture in their own right.

Reconstruction creates the possibility for a metaphorical translocation back into the times when the temple was in use. This is achieved not only through spatial devices and procedures, such as recreating the outline and leading visitors through a closed and darkened naos, but also through a reconstructive approach to Phidias' famous, and famously contested, Parthenon sculptures. In contrast to the British Museum, where metopes and fragments of tympana are positioned at eye-level and thus presented as sanctified works of art, in the Acropolis Museum, important objects are fixed at the level they would have functioned at in the Parthenon. Visitors can thus view the frieze as if through the eyes of an Ancient Greek. The natural light filling the gallery plays a role in constructing this experience. Just like in ancient times, the Athenian sunshine wanders across Phidias' sculptural oeuvre, its path changing with the time of day and highlighting the contours of what is depicted or the texture of the Pentelic marble. As a result, the reconstruction becomes whole; the metopes hanging in the "original" position they were exhibited in are not only archaeological data serving to recreate the entire temple, but also works of art presented in such a way so as to bring forth their traits to the maximum possible extent: the same traits that were admired by Pericles' contemporaries in Athens. The sculptural contours of the metopes, which are carved more deeply in the upper sections, were initially intended for viewing "from below".

It is also worth drawing attention to the ways in which plaster cast decorations were introduced in place of those that are currently in the British Museum.[16] This procedure, which seems to function as a non-invasive realization of narratives while filling the empty spaces, has a symbolic dimension within the political and ethical arguments relating to restitution. It is worth mentioning the significance for debates on originals and copies that the presentation of inauthentic objects in this particular exhibition has acquired. In their research on eyeball movements, Helen Saunderson, Alice Cruickshank and Eugene McSorley demonstrated that it is not awareness of whether they are originals that alone influences the reception of objects but the entire context and surroundings (Saunderson et al. 2010), with the presentation style adopted in the Acropolis Museum being deeply rooted in authentic pieces. While copies do sit alongside original metopes, the most important factor is that through the windows a view extends across the authentic ruins of the Parthenon, to which visitors' eyes will automatically be drawn as their gaze is attracted to the brightest point.

The Parthenon Gallery, the crowning glory of the museum, is not the only full-scale exhibit that enables visitors to experience a place kinaesthetically, meaning that they perceive movements that are reproduced in space. A similar approach was adopted to the arrangement of objects from the smaller Temple of Nike and the rather unusual Erechtheion. The Temple of Nike is a particular case in point. According to the theories of Michel de Certeau, walking and movement enable us to settle (de Certeau 1988), thus reflecting the kinaesthetic potential of the body. In the case of the archaeological reconstruction of a present object (the Temple of Nike is still standing by the Propylaea) that cannot, however, be accessed by the practice of walking (the Temple of Nike is not accessible – indeed, it is not possible to get closer than ten metres to it, let alone cross its threshold), the museum offers a chance to experience it (James 2009: 1146). The practice of walking creates a relationship between different places: the real but inaccessible ruin of the ancient temple, on the one hand, and the symbolic, accessible "copy" and reconstruction, on the other. The possibility of constantly conducting a verification of the place thanks to the 1:1 scale outline of the foundations on the floor, which is marked out with some original remnants from the small temple, guarantees visitors an experience otherwise unattainable on the actual archaeological site while ensuring that they experience the archaeological reconstruction of a real place more fully.

Christopher Tilley has offered a convincing description of the corporeal experience of an archaeological site. In his phenomenology of landscape (Tilley 1994, 2004), it is first and foremost bodily engagement that has epistemic value (Tilley 2004: 10). It is through physical engagement that objects are discovered, making it possible to see them from multiple perspectives (by moving and positioning ourselves in relation to the object). Like de Certeau, Tilley places significant emphasis on the experiential process having the potential to position us vis-à-vis an object. Kinaesthesis enables us not only to move but also to position our bodies in scale. Tilley reminds us of the key role of experiencing scale and dimensions in bodily experiences of space and landscape. As archaeologists come closer to or distance themselves from research objects, they consider which aspects of the size and shape of the thing under investigation are illusory. Tilley's response, grounded in Maurice Merleau-Ponty's phenomenology, is that "the true size and shape of an object is when it is in reach (and can be measured). Knowledge of a thing is grounded in our bodily relationship with it. The experience of things, each with its own definite size and shape, is given in our bodies" (Tilley 2004: 11). As in the methodologies of sensory geographies, the body serves as a research tool. The human scale and kinaesthetic potential enable us to locate ourselves in a place, building or landscape. Understanding an object, not by viewing models, photographs or maps, but through kinaesthetic practice – walking, positioning oneself in a given environment – extends our experience not only of the place but also of the objects that are participants in the arrangement. It is objects, I would argue, that ensure that the arrangements in the Acropolis Museum become something more than the easily categorizable spatial substitutes of the kind that museum multimedia or other visual representations based on spatial data would be.

The experimental arrangements in the Acropolis Museum are constructed of space and authentic objects – fragments taken from the reconstructed buildings of the Parthenon, the Temple of Nike and the Erechtheion. The complexity of the reconstruction, which is based on the idea that there will be engagement and play between the space and the artefacts, allows us to consider to what extent the elements reproduce the character of the reconstructed space that itself is at the same time a building (MacCormack 2010: 208). In the case of the kinaesthetic experiences derived from the exhibition format of the Acropolis Museum, the artefacts assist the transduction of the experience of museum galleries into a real, yet unattainable, encounter with the reconstructed space of the archaeological site. Following Tim Ingold, then, I would describe the role of artefacts as transducers (Ingold 2013: 102) of visitors' kinaesthetic experiences. Material artefacts, marked by the passage of time, shape the arrangement of the exhibition and through their forms, authenticity and provenance make experiences more genuine.

The exhibition form, particularly the spatial arrangements, fulfils the ideas of an archaeology of the senses that seeks to expand the experience of the past, of sites and objects.[17] The kinaesthetic mobilization of visitors guarantees a more memorable experience while at the same time enabling the verification of representations against both material and reconstructed materials. The presentation of canvases and architecture on slides, in albums or online, even where the human scale is taken into account, provides only virtual images that cannot be verified until they are juxtaposed with reality (Tilley 2004: 11). The Temple of Nike and the Parthenon are viewed from a distance at the archaeological site as they cannot be entered, meaning their scale and form cannot be experienced directly. Even though the experience of reaching the site includes non-visual factors, such as climbing the slope of the hill or feeling the hot Greek sun on the exposed hilltop, the objects are not directly present-at-hand or accessible. The experience of the place is thus incomplete. It is supplemented by the museum arrangements that when compiled with the limited experience of the archaeological site together offer an almost complete experience of the buildings in both their original and recreated locations (Lending 2018: 812). The proximity of the archaeological site and the architectural opening out of the museum onto the ancient ruins is of great significance for the epistemological process. The Acropolis Museum is a place that is subordinate to the rules of sensuous geographies, meaning that, following Rodaway, any approach to it

> cannot just describe the experience of the senses and their role in the constitution of geographical experience, it must also consider more

fundamental questions about the nature of person-environment relationships and what constitutes a geographical reality for a given society
(or culture) at a given moment in time and space.

(Rodaway 1994: 6)

The theory of sensuous geography has been completely absent from archaeology (Hill 2014), yet it enables us to understand the Acropolis Museum as
a space whose exhibition form establishes and determines visitors' relationship with the Acropolis.

Conclusion

The Acropolis Museum, with its archaeological prostheses and kinaesthetic
substitutes, guarantees and supplements that which cannot be rediscovered
in the reality of the archaeological site. The compensatory dimension of
the exhibition set out new relations between the institution of the museum
and the archaeological site. A visit to the museum takes on the character of
a compensatory substitute in the context of the experiences on offer at the
Acropolis, namely encounters with fragmentary artefacts and viewing from a
distance the fragmentary and unreachable structures that cannot be entered.
Experiences unattainable at the Acropolis – seeing the heritage site as a whole,
in its original form and arrangement, or wandering freely around the monumental temples – are fully accessible at the museum, thus forging new qualities of experiencing the past. The introduction to the exhibition narrative of
conservational, technological, spatial and light-based elements, serves, in my
view, to redefine what an archaeological museum can be. Such museums thus
enter the realm of contemporary archaeological theory and its findings, while
the incorporation of non-visual senses transcends the nineteenth-century
paradigm of museum practices (Classen and Howes 2006: 208).

The redefinition of what a museum can be in the galleries of the Acropolis
Museum opens up the artefact-as-exhibit to new meanings: archaeological fragments are divorced from the sentimental-Romantic narratives and
instead serve as illustrations of conservation practices. At the same time,
the traditional meaning of the artefact-as-exhibit is expanded to include
an aspect that is rarely explored beyond specialist discourses. Presented
alongside technological aids, the artefact-as-exhibit therefore shows just
how deep the insights into the ontology of artefacts enabled through digital
and virtual tools can be. Finally, when arranged alongside other objects,
artefacts form a spatial assemblage. As exhibits that recreate the material
impression of a space, artefacts become more than symbols of that space;
they are instead their active transducers, suggestively reconstructing access
to other inaccessible buildings. Like Kate Rask, I also find that artefacts
are central to this museum (Rask 2017: 452), although I would disagree
with her argument that this is a reason to criticize it. I see the centrality of

artefacts as a well-conceived and deliberate device that results from taking an important and difficult decision to give voice to the objects rather than to text or histories.[18]

Notes

1. Critiques of the new institution have been presented in: James (2009); Cohen (2010); Plantzos (2011); Hamilakis (2011); Marshall (2012); Beresford (2015, 2016); Skeates (2017c); Rask (2017). A positive commentary on the Acropolis Museum was presented in: Caskey (2011). As Anthony Snodgrass has rightly noted, "Most of the opposition directed at the new Acropolis Museum [...] has turned out to be politically motivated, mainly from the Left in Greece, mainly from the Right in Britain" (Snodgrass 2011: 625).
2. The Acropolis Museum has been discussed extensively by researchers. For more on the political background, including the question of restitution, see Marstine (2006b); Hitchens (2008); Jenkins (2016). On the politics of visuality: Hamilakis (2013: 70–73); Beresford (2015). These works include extensive bibliographies.
3. For more on the protests, see Filippopoulou (2017); Gravari-Barbas (2020). An analysis of the protests as part of heritage activism is presented by Fouseki and Shehade (2017).
4. Dimitris Plantzos used the phrase "the new Acropolis Museum appears as an alien creature landed in the heart of Athens, determined to fight for its vital space" (Plantzos 2011: 617; see also Carassava 2009).
5. Prizes include the 2011 European Union Prize for Contemporary Architecture and an award organized by the influential architecture website ArchDaily, where the museum was declared one of the top 20 in the world.
6. The concept of the parergon is often introduced in museum studies, particularly with reference to the institutions' "framings": architecture, lighting, guides and infrastructure; see Marstine (2006a: 4a).
7. Examples include The Work of Angels at the British Museum (1989) and Anatomie des chefs-d'œuvre at Museum Quai Branly (2015).
8. Accusations of an "overly archaeological" presentation are evident in Marshall (2012: 42), while claims that the exhibition is "overly aesthetic" appear in Plantzos (2011); Rask (2017: 452); see also James (2009).
9. Miriam Caskey has presented a similar take on the exhibition, noting that the museum presents care and conservation: Caskey (2011: 2).
10. The concept of the prosthesis has been used by, among others, Bjørnar Olsen, Michael Shanks, Timothy Webmoor and Christopher Witmore in relation to the representations of archaeology, which they argue have a prosthetic dimension; see Olsen et al. (2012: 81). Grahame Earl, meanwhile, has used the term "digital prosthesis": Earl (2013).
11. It is worth pointing out here the rather unfortunate conservation efforts applied to the Parthenon marbles by the British Museum in the 1930s. The authorities there were convinced that the beige coating of the marbles was a patina but as it turned out, it was actually the remnant of polychrome, which was thus removed as the marbles were cleaned.
12. The belief that destruction is inherent to archaeology has been discussed extensively in recent years; see for example Olsen et al. (2012: 80).
13. Visitors can also use a personalized app when viewing the exhibition; see Pujol et al. (2013).

14. James M. Beresford shows that light in the Acropolis Museum is primarily of political significance (Beresford 2015).
15. Robin Skeates is critical of the lighting in the Acropolis Museum, claiming that the modernist [sic!] architecture and the plate glass windows typical of it determine that the artefacts are displayed as if they were works of art; see Skeates (2017c: 19).
16. They constitute a *de facto* commentary on the Elgin Marbles. Its subtlety and ability to distance the museum from the controversy has been noted by Miriam Caskey (Caskey 2011: 7).
17. In his critique of the museum, Hamilakis, who conceived the idea of the archaeology of the senses, highlights above all the museum's visual policies (in 2016, when I was investigating the museum, the ban on taking photographs applied only on the first floor), see: Hamilakis (2011, 2013: 35).
18. This does not mean, of course, that the histories of the Acropolis outlined by, among others, Kate Rask (2017), Dimitrios Plantzos (2011) and Yannis Hamilakis (2011) are not noteworthy; however, a website, mobile app or information boards at the archaeological site could be used to present them instead. Indeed, alternative modes of storytelling are available in the museum; see Pujol et al. (2013).

5   Museo dell'Ara Pacis

Artefacts between Research and Art

The Altar of Augustan Peace, *Ara Pacis Augustae*, or Peace Altar, is a marble altar erected by Caesar Augustus (Octavian), in the first-century BCE to commemorate the battles in Hispania and Gaul that put an end to long-lasting internal conflicts and resulted in the *Pax Romana* or the Roman Peace. The altar was consecrated in a ceremony on 30 January, 9 BCE, on the Campus Martius in Rome where it formed an element of a larger commemorative site founded by Augustus, the first Roman Emperor. It is sculpted in valuable Luna marble and entirely covered in reliefs depicting a procession in honour of the peace, botanical motifs, Roman gods and symbols of prosperity and success. The altar depicts a propagandistic image of the peace that was to take hold in the Empire thanks to the wise rule of Caesar Augustus.

This exceptional Augustinian-era monument has a special place on the map of museums in today's Rome. The *Ara Pacis* is located in a museum dedicated to the object, the Museo dell'Ara Pacis (the Peace Altar Museum). The small-scale nature of this institution in the context of the wealth of heritage in the Eternal City means that the Museo dell'Ara Pacis is somewhat off the beaten track, thus not one of the city's top tourist destinations.

In the study that follows, I emphasize the meaning of exhibits presented at the Museo dell'Ara Pacis that visibly contribute to transcending the prevailing narratives of largely traditional Roman archaeological museums. I argue that the museum offers visitors wide-ranging and unusual insights into archaeology and the objects that it studies.

The history of the museum

The Museo dell'Ara Pacis is located on the eastern bank of the Tiber and on the western side of Piazza Augusto Imperatore. The museum building (Figure 5.1) was designed by the US-American architect Richard Meier, who is also responsible for many other museum projects, including the Museum of Contemporary Art of Barcelona (MACBA) and the Getty Center in Los Angeles. The building in Rome opened in 2006. Meier's "white architecture" is typified by simplicity of form, most often achieved by combining concrete and glass. The Museo dell'Ara Pacis does not differ from Meier's usual style,

DOI: 10.4324/9781003327851-8

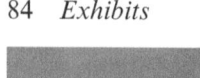

Figure 5.1 Museo dell'Ara Pacis, front facade, architect: Richard Meier, photo: Monika Stobiecka, 2022, © Roma, Sovrintendente Capitolino ai Beni Culturali.

as it is conceived as a regular, rectangular pavilion in concrete with white rendering, with glass and local travertine. In front of the simple museum building is a square featuring monumental stairs and a fountain. The museum blends in with Rome's architectural heritage, which is not disturbed in any way by the institution's small scale. Nevertheless, Meier's museum did not meet with universal approval in Rome, with some declaring it a characterless building that resembled a petrol station (Wilkins 2005: 64).

The comparison with a soulless petrol station requires us to tell the full history of the Ara Pacis Museum. Meier's building, which has its fans as well as zealous opponents, replaced an earlier museum that was founded in 1937. Meier's architectural structure was supposed to ensure better conditions for exhibiting the Ara Pacis while increasing the amount of space available for an educational exhibition and also enabling the introduction of infrastructure that belongs in a modern museum complex. The decision to establish a new museum should not be understood solely as an outcome of pragmatic concerns. Meier's building replaced one designed by the architect Vittorio Ballio Morpurgo, who was commissioned by Benito Mussolini. The contemporary *damnatio memoriae*, a Roman ritual of effacing memory, is indicative of the intention that Meier's transparent architecture would "lift the curse" hanging over the previous location where the Ara Pacis was displayed, one marked by Italy's Fascist era.

The previous museum building was designed by the leading architect of the Fascist period, with the concrete and glass modernist structure, covered in Augustinian-style inscriptions, part of the broader urban development project, the Piazza Augusto Imperatore (Kallis 2000: 830). Alongside new avenues in the centre of Rome, the Via dell'Impero, Via del Mare and Via della Conciliazione (Kallis 2012: 46), and the monumental EUR district, the Piazza Augusto Imperatore was part of the large-scale urban remodelling planned by Mussolini. The references to Caesar Augustus were not limited to naming a square after him. Since the 1930s, Mussolini had consciously pursued cultural policy in which Augustus was the central figure, the *primus inter pares*, or first among equals.

Mussolini's cultural policy was marked by aesthetic pluralism (Adamson 2001: 231). In architecture, Modernism prevailed, while painting was dominated by Futurism into the 1930s before being superseded by *Aeropittura* (Adamson 2001: 238, 240). References to Antiquity went beyond style and were primarily ideological, being communicated subliminally through inscriptions on modernist buildings that resembled ancient epigraphy (Benton 2000). There were literal citations of the heritage of ancient Rome including as part of a series of exhibitions and celebrations marking the "bi-millennia", or two thousandth anniversaries, of the birth of famous Romans (Kallis 2000). Mussolini incorporated the heritage of the Roman Empire into his cultural policy, initially proclaiming himself heir to the legacies of Julius Caesar (Wilkins 2005: 54), before seeing himself as successor to Caesar Augustus from the 1930s. Seeking to revive the idea of the Third Rome, *Il Duce* referred to Augustus' ideologically and visually abundant propaganda programme (for more on the art of the Augustinian period: Zanker 2002).

In order to revive the memory of the first Roman Emperor, Mussolini devised an ambitious scheme covering urban planning and archaeology. In the 1930s, he ordered work to begin on excavations to be conducted around the most important sites relating to the Augustinian age: the mausoleum, the Ara Pacis and the Horologium. It was not uncommon for damage and destruction to form part of the efforts to restore Augustus' memory: medieval and modern structures were knocked down in order to find the Augustinian heritage. As Aristotle Kallis, a specialist on the cultural policy of the Italian Fascists, highlights, destruction was inscribed into the "powerful symbolic liturgy of creation" (Kallis 2012: 41) of this twentieth-century period. Ultimately, the creation of new *lieux de memoire*, or sites of memory, was an element of efforts to legitimize Fascist rule (Kallis 2000: 823). In resurrecting the idea of *Romanità* through a series of propaganda exhibitions and events, *Il Duce* revived the memory of the Great Rome and at the same time struck a blow against the Papal dominance of the Eternal City (Cannistraro 1972: 126–127; Kallis 2000; Adamson 2001). Appropriating fragments of heritage and bringing them to the fore in Rome's urban fabric, Mussolini legitimized propagandistic values and created a new symbolic repertoire that his supporters could identify with.

Augustus played a key role in this process. In the 1930s, when Mussolini began describing himself as successor to Augustus and the first among equals, planning began for the bi-millennial celebration of the emperor's birth. Mussolini had planned to mark the occasion by unveiling and opening to the public the most important monuments associated with the Roman Emperor. One of the sites that was made accessible to visitors was the Ara Pacis. Excavation work to uncover the famous propagandistic memorial was exceptionally challenging. The Altar was located beneath the Palazzo Fiano which was to be preserved from destruction. The monument was removed using a technique involving surrounding it with freezing water to prevent the building above it from collapsing during excavation work (Kallis 2000: 819–820).

Mussolini rejected proposals to display fragments of the Altar in an existing museum or, alternatively, to put it on display in the Baths of Caracalla. His demand was for a fully reconstructed Ara Pacis to be exhibited in a dedicated building. In the modernist pavilion at Piazza Augusto Imperatore, the Altar became an active agent in policies to revive the past, rather than just one of many exhibits on show in the sterile environment of a traditional museum (Kallis 2000: 827). The Museum was opened on 28 September 1938 as part of the year-long celebrations titled *Bimillenario Augusteo*.

Following World War II, Morpurgo's pavilion was subjected to a withering criticism as an element of Fascist urban planning. The modernist structure that had evoked Roman simplicity was now associated exclusively with Mussolini's rule. It is difficult today to assess its destruction and give an opinion on the ambivalent nature of the current museum building. What is undeniable, however, is that the Museo dell'Ara Pacis continues to be a source of heated political controversy. In 2008, the then mayor of Rome, Gianno Alemanno, won favour among the Italian right when he announced plans to raze Meier's building (Garrone 2012). Thus, the new building became as an important actor in cultural policy as the Ara Pacis and the heritage of the Augustinian period that was first excavated and examined in the 1930s.[1]

Description of the exhibition

The exhibition at the modest Museo dell'Ara Pacis is dedicated entirely to the monumental Peace Altar located at the heart of the museum. Objects referring to this highly important piece of heritage from the Augustinian era are discreetly dotted around it without disturbing the reception of this famous archaeological artefact.

Visitors reach the exhibition through an entrance area with ticket offices and a museum shop. The massive doors divide this functional zone from the exhibition space, creating a buffer isolating the main exhibition from the sound of the nearby street. As soon as visitors pass through the threshold of the museum, they have before their eyes the majestic Ara Pacis. The exhibition narrative does not impose a route on visitors, although locating exhibits close to the doors offers a suggestive indication that they should be considered the starting point.

To the left of the entrance is a model depicting a reconstruction of the Campus Martius where the Ara Pacis and Mausoleum of Augustus, who commissioned the altar, had originally been located. Next to this model, along a wall made of carefully carved stone blocks, there is a row of pedestals displaying white marble busts of members of the Julio-Claudian dynasty that Augustus belonged to. In the background there is a simple and elegant family tree of the dynasty. Thanks to these exhibits, visitors can position the Ara Pacis on the map and temporal axis of ancient Rome.

Opposite, on the right-hand side, a narrative relating to selected aspects of the Ara Pacis develops. Against a backdrop of smooth, white stone partitioning walls, a highly diverse set of exhibits is on display. How they are ordered along the exhibition route seems to be arbitrary. Visitors could also begin their tour by entering a white cube-style space showing a film telling the story of the Altar of Augustan Peace. The story begins in the year 13 CE when Rome was transformed into a marble city and the Ara Pacis was commissioned. A high-quality, three-dimensional reconstruction enables visitors to position the altar within the realities of the urban landscape and topography, while also making them familiar with the object's colour scheme, as it was entirely covered in polychrome. The first chapter of the history of the altar is accompanied by an outline of Augustus' significance in the ancient world, the meaning of his title and the extent of the Roman Empire during his rule. The film also presents the religious and symbolic motifs inscribed into the history of the Ara Pacis: the *Pax Deorum*[2] introduced by Augustus in parallel with religious reform and the political reasons for funding this famous monument. Its architecture and location, especially the mathematical ideals that the planning of the Campus Martius was based on, are another theme addressed in the film that also features a wealth of illustration featuring ancient iconographical material. The narrative also presents the subsequent fate of the Peace Altar during the medieval period of decline as ancient Rome fell into oblivion before the Renaissance came and revived interest in it. It was during this time that individual fragments of the altar were gradually discovered. The film depicts how small fragments circulated around European courts and collections between the fifteenth and nineteenth centuries. The final part of the story presents the Ara Pacis in the contemporary era, from its rediscovery in 1903, through the techniques applied during excavation and conservation in the 1930s, to its political exploitation by Mussolini. Opposite the film projection, there are panels spread across the wall describing the very same, engaging history of the altar. It is worth emphasizing that the curators decided to introduce two media formats telling the same story. Visitors who

Figure 5.2 Museo dell'Ara Pacis, exhibit presenting flora depicted on the Peace Altar, photo: Monika Stobiecka, 2022, © Roma, Sovrintendente Capitolino ai Beni Culturali.

prefer reading written information can skip the film, while those who opt to dedicate a few minutes to some interesting educational material can avoid reading the rather extensive texts on the panels.

Subsequent exhibits bring forth the archaeological reconstructions. In one marble display case, damaged fragments of ornaments stemming from the altar's friezes are positioned against a backdrop of colourful reconstructions, giving the impression of the riot of colours that adorned this once polychrome object. A larger exhibit treated the altar in a similar fashion, namely a reconstructive drawing of one of the walls of the altar featuring some of the floral decorations (Figure 5.2). The exhibit is accompanied by information on the role that observing nature played in ancient Rome as well as by photographs of the contemporary varieties of the plants appearing on the relief sculptures on the altar wall. Small fragments located within the reconstructive narrative also appear as elements of an exhibit telling the story of the lost frieze on the stone topping an altar within the Ara Pacis. The objects are positioned on a form of "matrix" inscribed with dimensions that give an idea of the scale of the original frieze.

The exhibition also features one multimedia tablet that is deserving of extensive attention because of its complex approach to the theme of reconstruction. Animations on the tablet address the design of the Peace Altar, the history of its rediscovery, suggestions for reconstruction and its place in the landscape. In the section focusing on its design, there is information on who and what is depicted on the altar, as well as on its current state. There are also older photographic materials, press cuttings referring to the monument and museum, as well as an option to browse online the contents of the museum library. The history of its rediscovery offers visitors a fascinating journey through the ages, indicating when particular pieces of the altar were discovered, what their history is and who ensured they were put back together. Likewise presented chronologically, the suggestions for reconstruction are depicted through colourful, three-dimensional pictures and historical sketches that seem to provide an overview of the entire monument. These materials offer insight not only into research on the Ara Pacis but also how knowledge about it and visualizations of it developed, while at the same time indicating the highly subjective nature of one of the objectives of archaeology, namely reconstruction. In the section on the landscape, visitors can trace the location of the altar through another chronological framing that proceeds from its monumental position in ancient times to its gradual fall into oblivion in the medieval period when the altar was covered by subsequent layers.

The exhibition also features a small number of fragments of sculptures and reliefs, some from the altar itself, others from the period when the Peace Altar was constructed.

Just beyond the centrally positioned Ara Pacis, on the opposite side to the exhibits described thus far, in a narrow gallery corridor positioned across from the wall panel behind which there extends a view of the Tiber, there hangs a contemporary art piece: a mosaic *Ara Pacis* by Mimmo Paladino (Figure 5.3). Against the golden backdrop of the substantial three-dimensional mosaic, there are synthetic displays of plant motifs and geometric patterns featuring human hand and heads, a lamb head, a bird, fish, plants, a boat and goblets. The composition is abstract in style, evoking to some extent the works of Joan Miró. The dreamy, oneiric form of the work, together with the symbolic and contoured depictions of the motifs, are intended to constitute a particular Roman *imaginarium*.[3] Commissioned for the opening of the museum, the work makes full use of the potential for dialogue with the ancient object in the centre of the building.

All the objects described above either tell a story about or relate to the Peace Altar located in the centre of the exhibition space. The monument is illuminated with natural light, meaning that visitors can reconstruct the original context of the object that stood in the open space of the Campus Martius. They can decide whether to move away from the altar, enter it using the monumental stairs or sit on a bench and admire it. They can also encounter it by situating themselves in relation to it, by walking or performing aesthetically focused observation. Since 2016, the experience of the Ara Pacis has been supplemented by virtual elements based on MR, or mixed reality, which involves VR (virtual reality) combined with AR (augmented reality) on the same device as part of the project *Ara com'era* (The Ara as it was)

Figure 5.3 Museo dell'Ara Pacis, *Ara Pacis* mosaic by Mimmo Paladino (fragment), photo: Monika Stobiecka, 2022, © Roma, Sovrintendente Capitolino ai Beni Culturali.

(Trunfio and Campana 2020; Trunfio et al. 2020). Visitors are given headsets that enable them to see, for example, the colourful polychrome of the Peace Altar, with only the sense of sight being directed towards the monument.

Thanks to the diverse exhibits and special virtual formats, guests have the opportunity to apply the information acquired or the reflections and emotions evoked by the museum to the genuine, original architectural object from the age of Augustus.

From culture to nature: Archaeology as a life science

One of the exhibits at Museo dell'Ara Pacis is a panel featuring a partial reconstructive drawing of the floral decoration of the Peace Altar (Figure 5.2). It features fragments of botanical ornaments, while next to it there are descriptions relating to the symbolism of plants in Antiquity, as well as photographs of contemporary varieties of the flora identified on the altar. The panel is an outcome of the research by the Italian botanist and ecologist Giulia Caneva, who conducted in-depth, interdisciplinary studies into the symbolism of the plants featured on the Ara Pacis. As a visualization of archaeobotanical research, the work is one of very few museum exhibits of this kind. Focusing on this piece, I indicate the potential for archaeology to transcend established dichotomies, including the binary of culture and nature and the binary of the humanities and natural sciences. I will show that archaeology, both as the "study of old things" and as "a discipline seeking to reconstruct the lives of people in the past", contributes to a horizontal model of knowledge.

Contemporary archaeology shows great interest in interdisciplinary research, as is evident in projects conducted around the world. Researchers are seeking to develop as far as possible full-scale knowledge of the lives of people in the past by means of complex reconstructions of cultural land-scapes. In doing so, they use tools drawing on the full spectrum of possibil-ities offered by archaeometry.[4] Methods from chemistry, physics, biology and physiochemistry provide the foundations of archaeometry and they enable researchers to conduct in-depth analysis of material culture. Despite its growing popularity, and booming development, archaeometry and the relations between archaeology and the natural sciences are rarely consid-ered within theoretical debates (Hodder 2012: 14), a situation that results in a number of accusations being levelled against archaeology's "scientific turn" (Lidén and Eriksson 2013; Pollard and Bray 2014; Sørensen 2017).

In one of the earlier works of this kind, Andrew Jones drew attention to the two languages spoken by contemporary archaeologists – one theoreti-cal, the other that of "archaeological science" (Jones 2002, 2004; see also Lidén and Eriksson 2013; Fossheim 2017; Lidén 2017). Jones believes that this situation is a result of the legacy Cartesian division of objects and sub-jects that continue to shape Western tradition (Jones 2004: 237). The con-stant and stable objects that appear to promise objectivity are what interests the natural sciences, while subjects are what artists and humanities scholars study. An exception, according to Jones, is material culture, as it constitutes an ironic marriage of what interests the natural sciences and the human-ities (see also Hodder 2012: 13–14). Culture is what archaeologists in the humanities study, while matter is addressed by archaeologists representing the natural sciences. At the same time, material culture constitutes an area of interest for archaeologists applying vastly differing research approaches. Jones hypothesizes and wishes for the integration of approaches to material culture, which would ensure the development of the field of archaeology while expanding the skills of both "species" of archaeologist.[5]

A similar idea, albeit a more precise version of it, permeates Mark Pollard and Peter Bray's article, "A Bicycle Made for Two? The Integration of Scientific Techniques into Archaeological Interpretation" (Pollard and Bray 2007). Their study sought to demonstrate the research, developmen-tal and educational potential of interdisciplinary endeavours. They offered a repost to stringent critics of interdisciplinary research whose analysis focused exclusively on how such approaches apparently multiply the errors of researchers. Pollard and Bray instead reflected on the nature of interdis-ciplinarity in fieldwork, the application of new technologies, the adaption of analytic tools drawn from the natural sciences, the posing of new research questions and the development of education, leading to their proposal that archaeology could become more objective were it to build closer relations with the natural sciences. In contrast to Jones, they focused on the nature of contemporary archaeology rather than on internal differences among archaeologists. Finding that the boundaries between laboratory research and philosophy were becoming increasingly blurred, they emphasized how today the differences between natural scientists and humanities scholars are disappearing. Another crucial factor were the essential conditions outlined by the authors for conducting successful interdisciplinary research. They stressed the essential importance of finding a common aim and language, as well as showing mutual respect, something that archaeologists in particular find difficult to attain owing to clichéd perceptions of the field and even the scholarly belief in the "non-scientific" nature of archaeology (Pollard and Bray 2007: 255; see also Olsen et al. 2012: 15, 27).

The question of language also resonated in the debate that appeared in *Norwegian Archaeological Review* in 2017, starting with an important article by Tim Flohr Sørensen. He rightly highlighted three challenges that archaeology faced in the age of the scientific turn or, as he put it, in the face of "new empiricism" (Sørensen 2017: 101–102). The first is "a growing suspicion towards interpretations that cannot be scientifically proven or quantified objectively" (Sørensen 2017: 102). This leads to a second challenge, or even threat, namely the fetishization of data and the uncritical belief that data can speak for itself. Thirdly, the scientific turn, he argued, has led to an unthinking application of scientific methods, which distorts the idea of interdisciplinarity in archaeology. However critical it might be, Sørensen's article constitutes a crucial contribution to debates. For me, his key argument revolves around the issues of how to frame research questions and present interpretation in archaeometric studies.

Conducting interdisciplinary research in the field of archaeometry requires, first and foremost, skilful setting of research questions, which is something that Pollard and Bray also draw attention to in another text, this time from 2014, where they criticized how methods from the natural sciences seem to be applied "more to tick boxes than actually to answer real questions" (Pollard and Bray 2014).[6] What interdisciplinary archaeology requires, including the branch that turns to digital technologies, is first and foremost posing effective research questions and developing insightful interpretations.

Giulia Caneva's research (Caneva 2010), which resulted in the exhibit in Museo dell'Ara Pacis, is something that fulfils the demands of genuinely interdisciplinary research, of the kind outlined by the above-mentioned authors. The clue lies less in the methods that are applied but rather in the interpretations that emerge. While maintaining the rigour of the natural sciences, Caneva presented her research findings in a book that uses language that is comprehensible for humanities scholars. She noted in the introduction already that she remained disciplined in her approach to research as a result of gaps in her archaeological knowledge. The studies she presents, however, are not marked by any gaps or lack as her work is complex, transcending the boundaries of academic disciplines. Caneva's research sought, first and foremost, to answer the question: are the plants presented on the Peace Altar a realistic image or a product of the artistic imagination? She also posed a series of questions relating to botanical symbolism. Compiling research tools drawn from archaeology, history, geography, biology and ecology, she presented a convincing interpretation in which she showed that the flora carved in marble served not only as decoration but also as something communicating essential meanings while revealing an awareness of biodiversity in the world of Antiquity.

Caneva identified flowers, fruits and leaves among the flora, describing their moment of vegetation while also identifying the environments that they came from.[7] She groups the plants according to botanical standards and then outlines the symbolic significance of each group. Furthermore, Caneva examines whether the way in which plants are presented in the frieze matches natural reality, including whether the species depicted next to each other also coexist in nature. Her in-depth studies provide the basis for a highly interesting interpretation of the floral elements of the Ara Pacis, arguing from the outset of her study that they should not be dismissed as ordinary decoration. The plants and the vegetative cycles identified are intended to correlate with the ideas represented by the gods and historical figures carved on the altar, namely that Caesar Augustus' policies would bring Rome prosperity, development and peace. The period of prosperity is indicated by the blooming acanthus and mallows that turn into spiky thistles, indicative of the difficult beginnings of the "new" era under the first Emperor, while the palms suggest further imperial conquests. All the plants are depicted during their growth phase, which is also indicative of Augustus' political ambitions. The addressees of the altar, the Roman people, were expected to understand the message being communicated. Caneva's interpretation of the ways in which botanical symbolism was part and parcel of the essential content of this propagandistic monument, reveals an image of the Romans as being in close contact with nature and aware of biodiversity. The panel developed on the basis of her research is not only significant as an object presenting the outcome of multi-level research. Since it is displayed in the museum, it communicates an important message to contemporary visitors, namely that biodiversity is one of the key pillars of European civilization, thus something that can be traced back to ancient times, as is evident within the broader framework of current debates on the Anthropocene, climate change and ecological catastrophes.

The narrative presented by just one single exhibit at the same time breaks down the boundaries between the approaches employed with respect to artefacts in the natural sciences and humanities. The marble fragments, usually displayed in an aesthetic context, acquire new and fascinating meanings that are exceptionally relevant to us today. At the same time, the format in which the research findings are presented shows that interdisciplinary projects employing the methods of both the natural sciences and the humanities can not only be visualized in exhibitions but also significantly enrich museum narratives. What is striking, however, is a certain form of disproportion in museums: while there is exponential growth in archaeometric publications, there is not even a hint in archaeological museums of illustrations of such approaches. Here I would again turn to Sørensen's remarks to emphasize the role of interpretation in research employing tools drawn from the natural sciences. I would argue that raw data lacks the potential to provide the inspiration for exhibits, but archaeological museums, as institutions demanding interpretation, could provide a site for testing the validity of interdisciplinary methods and the findings they generate. I agree with David Killick, who stresses the role of narrative and interpretation in interdisciplinary projects, arguing:

> Telling stories about the past is an essential part of the craft of archaeology. Without narratives archaeological reports would simply be catalogues of finds and their classifications. Narratives convey our more or less expert interpretations of our findings [...]. They animate the past and stimulate discussion among experts and interest in archaeology among the wider public.
>
> (Killick 2014: 161)

I can see the potential and possibilities in important shifts, particularly where exhibitions of Classical archaeology are concerned, as it was here that exhibits were traditionally presented as works of art. Transcending the ways of thinking about artefacts as mere artistic objects and instead also seeing in them scientific potential, as Caneva has done with the decorations on the Ara Pacis, is an important step towards overcoming the reductionism typical of many archaeological museums.

   I believe that archaeological exhibitions that would present exhibits as the outcome of interdisciplinary projects that demand great research sensibility and care from archaeologists, as well as creativity in constructing interpretations, could become a crucial way of testing the validity of contemporary archaeology that tends towards the natural sciences. Until now, this potential has been completely underestimated.

Artistic mediations: Contemporary art and archaeology

Prevalent in the Museo dell'Ara Pacis are exhibits that intentionally target the sense of sight. This deep entanglement with narratives of visuality is expressed through film presentations, reconstructions and the content of the multimedia tablet. Using visual tools, the museum positions itself within the modern yet conventional order of archaeological exhibitions. The absence of long display cabinets with typologically arranged objects is not, in my view, the same as transcending knowledge based on visual perception. Nevertheless, the revision of traditional exhibition forms offers visitors a less obvious image of Rome that encourages further reflection. The metaphorical composition by the Italian artist Mimmo Paladino offers a crucial counterpoint in discussions on the nature of contemporary archaeological exhibitions and ways of mediating the past. Taking my cue from Andrew Jones and Paul Bonaventura's view that the history of art and archaeology "are concerned with making past synoptically visible, so that it may function upon the present" (Jones and Bonaventura 2011a: 6), I will attempt to demonstrate the extent to which contemporary art can help negotiate the meanings that we ascribe today to objects, phenomena and landscapes from the past.

Mimmo Paladino's work is titled *Ara Pacis* (Figure 5.3). Paladino created the work, measuring 7 × 8 m, between 2000 and 2006. The composition is the work of Paladino, while the mosaic was created by Costantino Aureliano Buccolieri. The artists placed their signatures on the lower part of the work using the Latin abbreviations *pinxit* (painted [by]) and *fecit* (made [by]). The mosaic takes the form of a relief, while the base of the composition is not flat but made of 20 raised triangles bearing stone tesserae in gold, ochre, emerald, yellow and a reddish colour. The coloured contours are made of glass paste and enamel. The relief composition of the polyhedron depicts symbols that are associated with both Christian and Roman tradition, such as lambs, cups, hands, laurel wreaths, birds and graffiti. The form of the work is inspired by mosaics from Ravenna, while the composition evokes the style of works by Joan Miró and Paul Klee, as well as the abstract tradition of Wassily Kandinsky. The approach to figures and symbols, meanwhile, resembles primitivism.

The symbolic *imaginarium* presented by Paladino was not supposed to correlate with the metaphors of either the Augustinian period or the Ara Pacis. Formally, the work was conceived as a counterpart to Richard Meier's architecture: the polyhedron relief allows light to wander freely across it, creating a counterbalance to the static straight lines produced by the US-American architect. In terms of content, meanwhile, Paladino planned the mosaic as an open work possessing symbolism that is equally open to interpretation (Bucci 2006). The entangled Christian and Roman symbols position the work in an ambivalent realm. The late Antique stylization and the lightly primitivized form of the work tend to speak to what came "after the Altar" rather than correspond with its content and form.

The renowned art critic and curator Achille Bonito Oliva has described Paladino's mosaic as the artist's dream within a dream, a collision of two co-constitutive elements forming it: the past culture and contemporary culture that shapes Paladino's artistic sensibilities.[8] Oliva points towards how the central forces at work in the composition are signs and matter that traverse antagonisms (warm/cool, compact/dispersed) by means of the calibration of colours. All the signs, Oliva argued, are intended to signify the idea of the fragment, thus referring to absence and incompleteness. At the same time, the signs are positioned within the horizon of Paladino's artistic interests. His art often takes up the themes of compensation, supplementation and completing what is absent. His dream-like feast of symbols was accompanied at its vernissage with music by Brian Eno. The creation of a transsculptural, transpainterly work with an accompanying soundscape inspired by Oriental music and the work of John Cage was what led Oliva to term this artistic situation the *Ara Artis*, the Art Altar.

Oliva's influential review features strands linked to materiality and time. In a conversation with the artist, Federica Pirani often refers to memory and time.[9] Another curator, James Putnam, argued in a review that was more focused on the coherence of three elements – Meier's architecture, Paladino's mosaic and Eno's music – that the central and indeed most inspiring element of the work is its inherent connection to the aesthetic perception of the fragment.[10] Oscillating between matter, time, memory and fragment, Paladino's work offers an unusual mode of mediating the narrative of this archaeological museum.

Rodney Harrison and John Schofield, following Colin Renfrew, state that contemporary art can assist archaeologists in understanding the past, researching relations between people and the environment, and analysing material culture in unconventional ways (Harrison and Schofield 2010: 109; see also Harrison 2011). They offer a brief outline of three key trajectories in artistic-archaeological research. First, they suggest treating works of art as an archaeological record. They illustrate in an analysis of Anselm Kiefer's *Nigredo* (1984) and his *La Ribaute* project (begun in 1992) how works of art can be studied from the perspective of archaeology. They suggest that a literal exploration of artworks as archaeological sites and documenting the results of excavations in order to better understand the structure of paintings has the potential to create common ground between archaeologists and art historians interested in finding alternative ways of conducting research.

A second method involves studying archaeological investigation as a performance, thus drawing attention to the dimensions of archaeology as art. This idea is illustrated by the projects of Mark Dion, who has reconstructed the working conditions of archaeologists in his pieces *Tate Thames Dig* and *New England Dig*.

The third approach proposed by Harrison and Schofield reflects the strategy of treating art as an interpretation, narrative and characterization. Here they juxtapose Lucy Orta's *All In One Basket* (1997) and *Hortirecycling* (1999) with the Tucson Garbage Project that was led by William Rathje in the 1980s (Rathje and Murphy 1992; Rathje 2012). Demonstrating the common values and ideas in Orta's works and in Rathje's research findings, namely wastefulness and intensive consumption, Harrison and Schofield show how the subject matter of archaeologists and artists permeate each other and can indeed supplement each other.

For the purposes of the case study presented here, I intend to apply a third research model in which art can assist the construction of interpretations, narratives and characteristics. The path proposed by Harrison and Schofield is regularly mentioned in the context of public archaeology as a means of engaging and educating society through artistic interventions (Harrison and Schofield 2010: 118; see also Tully 2007: 174). Artistic representations have today become the main reason why artists are increasingly often invited onto archaeological sites.[11] Any creative potential enabling interactions with the past significantly expands our sensitivity to the past and deepens reflection (Harrison and Schofield 2010: 118). Contemporary artworks can produce interventions at those points where archaeological tools prove insufficient or they can, as Mimmo Paladino's mosaic showed, build a bridge between the past and present. Artistic efforts tending towards archaeology can help penetrate those areas that often seem impossible to study because they demand immersion in a reality that has long since passed. Finally, they help us to train the archaeological imagination because we rarely have the opportunity to put it into practice, even though we operate within a culture of artistic imagination.

I treat Mimmo Paladino's mosaic as an intervention and therefore I would like to take the path marked out by Harrison and Schofield, which means seeing the artwork through the lens of art-as-archaeology. The materiality of the work – its relief, almost sculpture-like, three-dimensional form – demands reflection on matter. The meandering light, a deliberate element introduced by the architect of the museum where the mosaic is displayed, gives the composition dynamism and sets the material in motion. On the formal level, the work offers pointers towards the notion of vital materialism, according to which objects are understood as active, agentic and unstable. These traits are indeed inherent to archaeological matter, which changes and transforms. The subject matter of the work oscillates metaphorically between time, memory and fragments. The compositional form, which draws on the traditions of contemporary art, reveals Mimmo Paladino's artistic sensibilities. The inspiration stemming from prominent artistic trends collides in the mosaic with Antique-style symbolism and formal references to the famous frieze decorations of Ravenna. As a result, the work transcends the boundaries of time, which is central to the theoretical focus of contemporary archaeology (Lucas 2005). The work's temporality, something that has often been underlined in interviews with the artist, indicates how contemporary art could become engaged in debates on time, something that could be highly valuable to archaeologists. By building a bridge between the past and present, Paladino highlights the survival of traditions and the ways in which elements of the past are entangled with the present. As is the case in archaeology, too, it is through artefacts that the past continues in the present and remains open. Roman symbolism encounters references to Christianity in the form of signs that are considered lasting and stable within contemporary religious traditions. At the same time, Paladino compresses the cultural distance separating contemporary audiences from ancient Rome. Particularly important in this, too, is the mode of composing signs.

The aesthetic role of fragments, something that is fundamental to archaeological practice and thus resonates throughout the entire history of archaeology, plays a crucial role in the *Ara Pacis*. The fragmentary signs, suspended in timelessness, tend to take the form of information that we "receive" from Antiquity through material culture or texts. Paladino's interest in lack, absence and incompleteness correlates perfectly with reflections presented by numerous archaeological theorists. The impossibility of either building a perfect reconstruction or totalizing the image of the past does not acquire nostalgic dimensions in Paladino's mosaic. The apparently chaotic composition allows us to discover the interpretive potential contained in randomly juxtaposed fragments. At the same time, the composition points towards the compensatory value of art in studying the past as interventions from the realm of contemporary art make it possible to expand understanding, reconstruct what is missing and deepen reflections on where the limits of scientific access to the past are. I would thus understand Mimmo Paladino's mosaic as a deep reflection on the idea of archaeological records in Roman culture, according to which objects are temporal, dynamic and transforming, both materially and in terms of their meaning, while being deeply embedded in resonant traditions, fragmented and therefore at the same time inviting us to project and design our own subjective visions of the past.

Subjective interpretation of works on display in archaeological museums enables visitors to become engaged in the spectacle of creating meanings. Responses to a piece of contemporary art, whether enthusiastic, critical or negative, form each visitor's personal baggage, so to speak, which guides them towards reflection and posing questions. While the relations of art and archaeology are often (though perhaps not often enough from the perspective of the theory of art) taken up in archaeological debates, the presence of works of contemporary art at archaeological sites or in archaeological museums nevertheless remains limited. There are also few interpretations of works of contemporary art written by archaeologists in relation to their practices or research material (but see Bailey 2017a, 2017b, 2018). It seems that the relationship between archaeology and art remains heavily burdened by the tradition of a common ancestor, namely Johann Joachim Winckelmann. A common element in this relationship is that aesthetic values are projected onto archaeological material (Russell 2011: 174), which is also something that Michael Shanks and Christopher Tilley rightly commented on in the 1990s. Writing in 1992, they compared archaeological museums to the presentation of ikons in Russia, noting that their curator is the Romantic *homo artifex*, who seeks art in places where it cannot always be found (Shanks and Tilley 1992: 72). They showed that the reduction of finds to the role of artistic objects in fact leads to their fetishization. Continuing along these lines, I would argue, perhaps provocatively, that the juxtaposition of artefacts and works of art enables differentiation, meaning that artefacts are thought of in terms of archaeology rather than art.

Conclusion

In the Museo dell'Ara Pacis, a contemporary version of the gesture of *damnation memoriae* is taking place, one that involves cutting off the Peace Altar from Italy's Fascist past and Mussolini's propaganda. While the historical relations of politics and archaeology are of great interest for a number of people (Murray and Evans 2008), in Italy, where there is still work to do on working through the Fascist past (Mosse 1996: 245), alternative modes of constructing museum narratives are being sought. The modest museum in Rome, now housed in an architecturally neutral building that has been compared to a Texas petrol station, seems to be trying to escape history, and instead offer attractive and alternative ways of presenting a monument that is burdened by legacies of Fascism. The Ara Pacis, displayed in a transparent space, opens itself up to new themes and histories, casting into oblivion things that are uncomfortable for some Italians.

When seen through the lens of archaeobotanical studies, centuries-long traditions of reconstruction or contemporary art, the monument acquires new meanings. What becomes evident, first and foremost, are the new exhibition frameworks that are aligned with the image of contemporary archaeology. The artefact-as-exhibit in the Museo dell'Ara Pacis is an object that points towards a horizonal model of research conducted by archaeologists. It demonstrates and illustrates how archaeology transcends the limits of the humanities, producing knowledge relating to a broad vision of human and non-human life, including plants, animals and the environment. Drawing on the latest research on constructing exhibits, the museum in Rome shows just how radically the image of mundane, rather unspectacular fragments can be transformed, as long as the ways in which they are narrativized employ an interesting theory positioned within the scope of the most pressing current issues that are not only of academic but also social relevance.

Revisions of the traditional archaeological museum narrative are performed in parallel at the Museo dell'Ara Pacis through efforts to open up artefacts-as-exhibits to subjective impressions generated by their juxtaposition with works of contemporary art. The museum refers to the relations between archaeology and art, albeit by posing an alternative that treats artefacts not as works of art but rather as timeless sources of inspiration for contemporary recipients, including artists. Contemporary art becomes, on the contrary, a matrix for differentiating artefacts. It provides a means of challenging reductionist approaches to artefacts-as-works-of-art.

The revision of the exhibition form goes far beyond the artefact, as it also touches upon modes of interdisciplinary research and contemporary art, expands epistemic potential and influences how we can open up to perspectives for perceiving archaeological monuments as dynamic objects positioned at the intersection of culture and nature, time and space, science and art.

Notes

1. Historians' sober opinions were very important to this debate as they emphasized that perceptions of the Augustinian era were shaped primarily by Fascists in the 1930s. At the same time, historians stressed that the current state of knowledge on Augustus and his age owes an undeniable debt to the large-scale archaeological research commissioned by Mussolini (Wilkins 2005: 64; see also Zanker 2002).
2. *Pax Deorum*, or the principle of divine peace, stated that a Roman citizen would be rewarded by the gods if he acted according to divine rules.
3. Pirani, F., [no date] *Conversazione con Mimmo Paladino*. Available from: http://www.arapacis.it/mostre_ed_eventi/mostre/opera_per_l_ara_pacis_mimmo_paladino_brian_eno/conversazione_con_mimmo_paladino [Accessed 1 August 2017].
4. The findings from archaeometric studies are presented in the highly esteemed journals *Archaeometry* and *The Journal of Archaeological Science*. Those publications provide further bibliographic references.
5. Despite its promising hypothesis and numerous illustrative examples, Jones' text has not found much approval among archaeologists. He has been criticized by researchers working in the field of theoretical archaeology; see Lucas (2012: 162–163).
6. I have described a similar phenomenon in the field of digital archaeology: Stobiecka (2019).
7. The plants identified suggests flora typical of meadows and grazing landscapes (Caneva 2010: 44).
8. Oliva, A. B., [no date] *Ara Artis*. Available from: http://en.arapacis.it/mostre_ed_eventi/mostre/opera_per_l_ara_pacis_mimmo_paladino_brian_eno/ara_artis [Accessed 1 August 2017].
9. Pirani, F., [no date] *Conversazione con Mimmo Paladino*. Available from: http://www.arapacis.it/mostre_ed_eventi/mostre/opera_per_l_ara_pacis_mimmo_paladino_brian_eno/conversazione_con_mimmo_paladino [Accessed 1 August 2017].
10. Putnam, J., [no date] *Paladino/Eno at Ara Pacis*. Available from: http://en.arapacis.it/mostre_ed_eventi/mostre/opera_per_l_ara_pacis_mimmo_paladino_brian_eno/paladino_eno_all_ara_pacis [Accessed 1 August 2017].
11. Examples of this include performances and interventions, as well as large exhibitions. See, for example, the exhibition organized to mark the 25th anniversary of the archaeological excavations led by Ian Hodder in Çatalhöyük, which also featured the contemporary artists Refik Anadol and Nazlı Gürlek; the artistic intervention by Frances Gill at a site in Sandby Borg, Sweden: Gill (2015); and the collective exhibition of contemporary Italian artists in Roman fora: Artribune Redazione (2013). See also Cass et al. (2020).

Part III

Artefacts as Exhibits

In the preceding chapters, I presented a bottom-up proposition for (re)defining archaeological artefacts, analysing their place and role as exhibits in museum spaces. My reflections on both artefacts and exhibits lead me to understand artefact-exhibits as palimpsests full of meaning and as multi-layered malleable objects that are inherently inscribed with facets that are either emphasized or rendered withdrawn in museum exhibitions. The juxtaposition of artefacts and exhibits allowed me to demonstrate how far removed artefacts-as-exhibits positioned in museums are from excavation work. Although my selected case studies are exceptional and certainly diverge from the established visions of traditional archaeological museums, I nevertheless believe that they offer a convincing illustration of the transformation of artefacts into exhibits and the diversity involved in giving meaning to museum exhibits.

In this chapter, I will consider the process of modelling artefacts-as-exhibits and problematize the issue of **how artefacts are exhibits**. I will look to answer the questions: how do artefacts undergo metamorphosis and what is the relationship between artefacts-as-exhibits, on the one hand, and contemporary theories and socially desirable interpretations, on the other? In my approach, I am inspired by the work of researchers from the University of Leicester. The publications of Eilean Hooper-Greenhill, Susan M. Pearce and Sandra H. Dudley represent a continuation and advancement of the central theses of New Museology. I argue that their works remain of fundamental significance when thinking about the processes of (re)constructing the state of knowledge in archaeological museums.

In her 1992 publication *Museums and the Shaping of Knowledge*, Hooper-Greenhill presents her particular vision of "museum archaeology" (Hooper-Greenhill 2002). Drawing on the Foucauldian concept of the episteme, she successfully attempted to construct a history of museology from the perspective of an effective history. This allowed her to reveal important connections between exhibits and knowledge, as well as social, economic and political imperatives. Pointing towards a whole series of museum-based entanglements, she shed new light on canonical collections and museums. Discussing the Medici collections, Baroque *Kunstkammern* and the modern,

DOI: 10.4324/9781003327851-9

Enlightenment-era institution of the museum, Hooper-Greenhill dedicated significant attention to the issue of the representation of knowledge. She highlighted that the genealogy of the modern museum has contributed to today's faith in the "objective truth" of such institutions (Hooper-Greenhill 2002: 165–166, 201). She held uncritical acceptance of historical legacies responsible for the fact that traditional exhibition narratives are being reinscribed still today, thus preventing us from thinking about the future of museums (Hooper-Greenhill 2002: 22).

Museums and the Interpretation of Visual Culture, published in 2000, continued the theoretical arguments familiar from *Museums and the Shaping of Knowledge*. Hooper-Greenhill examined the institution of the modern museum, tracing the genealogy of the contemporary "post-museum", something that had started to emerge in the 1970s. She showed that exhibits are arbitrary, fluid and polysemic, and the reason for this lies in their materiality (Hooper-Greenhill 2005: 10, 151–160). Drawing on the return to things that started to gain popularity in the 1990s, Hooper-Greenhill initiated a debate relating to museums and the issue of materiality.

This line of argument was taken up at the same time by the previously cited archaeologist and museum studies scholar Susan M. Pearce and then continued by Sandra H. Dudley. From the late 1990s, Pearce proposed a biographical approach to museums (see also Alberti 2005), one that would view objects as transmitters of knowledge about the past (Pearce 2006b, 2006c, 2006d). Dudley, in turn, focused on what goes missing from museums when the materiality of exhibits is overlooked. Emphasizing the role of form, scale, texture, colour and even the smell of exhibits, Dudley showed that it is indeed such traits that are constitutive of the museum experience because they engage visitors, forcing them into action and produce effects (Dudley 2010ba: 6–7; see also Dudley 2012).

The influence of the three above-mentioned researchers on museum studies, and in particular the issue of the representation and visualization of academic knowledge in museums, has been immense. Hooper-Greenhill's "museum archaeology" offered insight into the relations that exist between museums, academia and audiences. This is something that Bjørnar Olsen and Asgeir Svestad also showed in relation to archaeological museums, employing various concepts from Foucault, including "disciplinary technology" (Olsen and Svestad 1994). Stephanie Moser has also drawn attention to the relationship between academia and archaeological museums. A specialist in representations in and of archaeology, she has described archaeological museums as documents of the history of the discipline (Moser 2010, 2012).

The way narratives are constructed, how artefacts are positioned in relation to each other, and the emphasis on selected facets while others are camouflaged, all influence which vision of archaeology shapes a particular museum. These public institutions are legally obliged to disseminate knowledge by presenting their collections. It is not specialist publications, journals or excavation reports that create the public image of archaeology, but rather archaeological museums, whose doors are open to all (Pearce 1990; Swain 2007; Nash and O'Malley 2012). In continental Europe, museums are recognized in legislation and by society as having a duty to educate the general population. They are thus responsible for the broader image of the discipline and communicating the current state of knowledge in the field.[1]

Following the path carved out by the researchers mentioned above, who have addressed important issues related to illustrating museum-based knowledge and the materiality of museum exhibits, in this part of the book, written from the perspective of an archaeologist and art historian, I will view artefacts as actors entering into temporary relations with researchers, discourses and visions of archaeology projected by society. I will, furthermore, enquire into the meanings given to artefact-exhibits. What information do they provide on the state of the discipline? To what extent do they correspond to the actual state of knowledge in the field? I will call into question the instrumentalization of artefact-exhibits, pointing instead to their agency and theory-making potential, arguing that they are part of a two-way exchange of information between academia and museums.

This part of the book is structured around a differentiation of three strategies employed in contemporary archaeological museums that then refer back to the case studies in Part II. Recognizing the importance of Eilean Hooper-Greenhill's remark on building the future of museums, I have selected certain hyperframes (Bal 1996) operating in museums that not only correlate with the latest trends in archaeological theory but are also, in my view, directed towards the future of archaeological museums. In what follows in this part of the book, I bring forth certain strands presented in the previous chapters and link them together with exhibits from museums that are located far away. In doing so, I differentiate three leading, future-oriented strategies: prosthetic archaeology, the preposterous art of archaeology and the archaeology of all (living) things. I present these selected modes of visualizing current archaeological knowledge in relation to the dominant scientific paradigms in an order that is determined by the extent to which they are evident. In addressing each strategy, I also present supplementary research questions. This model of argumentation will allow me to answer the central question: to what extent can new scientific theories generate new narrative forms and new perspectives for exhibiting artefacts?

Note

1. This is a result of funding models. The situation is somewhat different in British and US-American museums, whose work dominates literature in the field. In large parts of Europe, museums are funded through taxes and regional or central government subsidies.

6 Prosthetic Archaeology

Digital exhibition is a ubiquitous trend in archaeological museums, reflecting the tensions between academia, on the one hand, and modes of disseminating and visualizing specialist knowledge, on the other. The museums that I referred to in the previous section use digital exhibits. The narrative in the Acropolis Museum is co-created by a series of multimedia supplements, including films and digital reconstructions. The Museo dell'Ara Pacis offers a multimedia tablet equipped with all kinds of educational materials, shows films featuring digital reconstructions and offers mixed reality shows. The museums I focused my analytical case studies on introduce digital aids in a balanced fashion and ensure in-depth insight is provided into the essence of artefacts as incomplete objects that in the age of prosthetic technologies acquire new, totalizing dimensions.

Given that digitalization in museums is a global phenomenon, I have opted to focus on analysing exhibitions that are fairly safe and unspectacular in terms of their use of digital media. This was a conscious and deliberate choice. Here I comment on this global museal trend with reference in particular to museums that have opted to introduce into their exhibition spaces simulations, virtual and augmented reality, scans and three-dimensional print outs, and virtual reconstructions. Prosthetic archaeology is understood here as a practice that aims at producing non-invasive reconstructions of material from the past by digitally supplementing fragmentary artefacts and other incomplete archaeological objects. Using this concept, I am able to develop the following research questions: what image of the discipline is presented by museums that apply digital strategies? What stance do the museums adopt towards the academic trend? Do they offer a new type of museum narrative? Do they revise traditional perspectives and do they generate alternative modes of presenting artefacts? Do digital media constitute the only strategy that is directed so clearly towards the future of archaeological museums? Do they offer an in-depth or merely superficial transformation of the artefact-as-exhibit? In answering these questions, I undertake a critical evaluation of

DOI: 10.4324/9781003327851-10

the last decade or two of digital displays while at the same time justifying why in this book I have focused on examples featuring fairly subtle use of multimedia within museum narratives.

The digital turn in archaeology

The digital turn is evident today at every stage of archaeological work, bringing about far-reaching transformations in the analysis of artefacts and interpretations of the past (Edgeworth 2015). Implementing modern methods that make use of solutions provided by IT, mathematics and visual design begins already at the point of archaeological prospection, while it also affects processes of documentation, analysis and interpretation, enters museums and shapes new forms of education and outreach. The ubiquity of digital tools means that methods such as photogrammetry, three-dimensional scanning, and digital imagining and modelling have become standard practices in many archaeological expeditions (Berggren et al. 2015). Archaeological databases created at every stage of research have opened up access to diverse forms of information, speeding up analytical processes and interpretation, as well as moving the nature of archaeological practices away from spade-work and towards screen-work, to use Matthew Edgeworth's terms (Edgeworth 2015). The emergence of subdisciplines such as virtual archaeology (Reilly 1991) and cyber-archaeology (Forte 2010, 2014) offers a clear illustration of the shift away from analogue modes of archaeology towards a virtual or even cybernetic mode (Roosevelt et al. 2015). Generating new types of research objects beyond material and "stable" artefacts, i.e. those that could take the form of malleable, easily transformed data, has opened up the field to new epistemic modes, including digital reflexive archaeology (Morgan 2009) and new modes of outreach, such as digital public archaeology (Richardson 2013; Griffiths et al. 2015).

Digital archaeological practices have also transcended the boundaries between the mechanical registration of artefacts and the generation of Big Data, and in doing so become political tools as they are seen as remedies for contemporary terrorist threats, the spectre of ruination, natural disasters and trading stolen goods (Levy et al. 2012; Lercari et al. 2016; Stanco et al. 2017, but see Ireland and Bell 2021: 150). Despite the profound role that digital methods can play in the work of archaeologists, it is still – unfortunately – the case that their use is dictated by technological instrumentalization, unthinking technophilia and their "cool factor" (Olsen et al. 2012: 88; Shanks and Webmoor 2012; Huggett 2015a). The unreflective application of the latest technologies becomes evident at conferences, in publications and in outreach work, revealing a tendency to treat multimedia as lures both for funding organizations and for tourists or museum visitors (Dallas 2015; Perry 2018; Caraher 2019). The impression prevails that the implementation of any kind of new technology in service of archaeology should be seen as evidence of a radical breakthrough and innovative research, even if the scientific value is doubtful or even treated as being of marginal significance, with research aims instead limited to applying a given method in the field or in relation to a selected group of artefacts (Garstki 2016: 4).[1]

The trivialization of digital archaeology results first and foremost from its radical character. Drawing on the work of the sciences, including mathematics, information science and medicine, digital archaeology is positioned beyond the realm of the "soft" humanities because it is founded upon disciplines that are traditionally perceived as objective, their methods apparently offering incontrovertible findings. I emphasize this aspect because it is of crucial significance for my further discussion of the role of digital and prosthetic archaeology in museums. This mode of interdisciplinary archaeology distances itself from "uncertain" interpretations based in the disparate matter of artefacts and has thus acquired a reputation as novel and revolutionary to an extent that is unprecedented in the history of archaeology. The digital turn has transformed archaeology into an intellectual practice that is performed in front of a computer screen rather than in the field, in direct contact with matter. The so-called "discipline of things" has been cured of its inferiority complex rooted in the Cartesian perception of matter as passive and inert in relation to active thought (Olsen et al. 2012: 19, 27, 61). Some might like to claim that these easily modelled and malleable data that have replaced material objects (Cameron 2007: 53) have ultimately overcome the "failings" of academic archaeology. The physical, haptic and material dimensions of the discipline appear anachronistic and out of date alongside the digital data that archaeologists currently work with.

What has been revised is not only the tangible dimension of research objects but also the very nature of archaeology as a discipline (Huggett 2015a, 2015b). Once perceived as a destructive practice (Schnapp 1996: 18), it is now increasingly seen as a practice of preservation and conservation[2] thanks to the boom in cyber-archaeology projects, which involved dynamic, interactive, complex and autopoietic work with data rather than with material artefacts (Forte 2010: 10). The urge to collect Big Data and commit archaeological objects to memory without turning to invasive fieldwork is indicative of the radical transformation that the digital turn has brought to archaeology. This boom also has far-reaching implications for the realm of representation, as digital reconstructions, simulations, and virtual and augmented reality mean that archaeology not only reproduces but also creates the past, preparing us for the impending brave, new technological reality.

Digital archaeology in museums

The digital turn has had a deep impact on archaeological museum practices. New exhibitions produced using digital technologies have disrupted existing museum typologies, creating alternative models of archaeological museum practices that seem to have little in common with traditional exhibitions of artefacts. Nevertheless, it is worth examining this turn's apparently radical nature closely and seek to weigh up digital exhibitions critically. Highlighting the pros and cons of digital archaeology in museums, I will outline to what extent it has addressed the problems with traditional exhibitions and to what extent it presents new hazards for the process of translating specialist knowledge (Stobiecka 2019).

The first undoubted advantage of multimedia exhibitions is that they are inclusive and participatory. By engaging the senses, visits to such exhibits are not limited to purely intellectual experiences (Brown 2007) and as such guarantee democratic access to knowledge (Brown 2007; Witcomb 2007: 35; Kidd 2014: 71–86). Another advantage stems directly from the nature of cyber-archaeology, which, when understood as a process of generating data, renders digital heritage dynamic and autopoietic (Champion and Dave 2007; Forte 2007, 2014). What this means in practice is that museums can continuously update their exhibits, which is particularly important in accounting for the changing state of knowledge. Another irrefutable advantage is the possibility of framing the "impossible", meaning that access can be granted to distant times and places that are difficult to imagine, let alone understand (Favro 2012; Shanks and Webmoor 2012; Earl 2013; Earl et al. 2013). By constructing a particular museal sensescape using exhibits that recreate smells, sounds and haptic experiences, the distant past feels a lot closer, more tangible and engaging. Artefacts possessing functions that for most ordinary visitors are undefined or unintelligible instead become part of holistic reconstructions and guarantee an immersive experience (Forte 2007: 400–404). Thanks to their diverse modes of illustrating and reconstructing both material objects and the immaterial traits of the environment or landscape, digital exhibitions guarantee visitors more than just an image of the past; instead, they offer the means to "feel" it through the senses. The aesthetics of multimedia exhibitions are also important. They demand special lighting and dark rooms to create a mysterious and enigmatic atmosphere that intrigues and engages the audiences following the narrative. Aside from the spatial configuration of exhibitions and their lighting, the changes in approaches to exhibition aesthetics are also highlighted by well-designed apps, digital exhibits and visualizations that then create a counterweight to established exhibition models that are familiar from traditional archaeological museums (Stobiecka 2020a).

Despite their numerous, undoubtable advantages, multimedia exhibitions also face a series of serious problems that affect visitors' perceptions. By generating a rather specific form of knowledge about the past, they impact the way that archaeology is viewed generally. One certainly important question in discussions on multimedia exhibitions, as well as in academic debates over digital archaeology, concerns the issue of the uncritical and unreflective use of multimedia elements in museum spaces. The "pursuit of the latest trends" is evident first and foremost in the implementation of technological features that either do not fit in with the rest of the exhibition or whose meaning in relation to the broader exhibition narrative remains unclear.

Many archaeological museums have opted to introduce, for example, interactive tablets or panels with information, or games, without considering the fact that devices become damaged, especially when subjected to unconsidered clicking by impatient visitors (Kidd 2014: 87–102). Such situations are commonplace, as is evident in the number of exhibits bearing out-of-order notices in museums. Some multimedia exhibits are constantly susceptible to damage precisely because the objects are treated as gadgets (Kidd 2014: 100).

Another serious hazard posed by multimedia exhibitions, in my view, results from their particular facets, namely the ability to process data dynamically, thus enabling constant mutation and aestheticization. The total, immersive reality that they can offer often has little in common with what can be derived from archaeological data. This mode of presentation could engender the overwriting of history by modelling it according to particular agendas that are not always interested in displaying polyphony. Data manipulation, whether by exhibition designers, graphic designers, curators or IT specialists, that aims at presenting a subjective image of "a beautiful past", is the most serious criticism that can be levelled at multimedia exhibits and museums. The attractive and engaging digitally generated visions of the past could nevertheless potentially dematerialize original and authentic artefacts. The lack of clear points of reference between the spectacular representations of the past and the fragmentary, rather impenetrable artefacts, can mean that visitors to a museum are often more interested in playing games on a tablet or scrolling their way through richly illustrated information than in the objects that the technological supplements were supposed to address. Technology-based exhibitions can thus result in ignorance of artefacts or even in disappointment as visitors do not even come into contact with them (Merriman 2017: 549). It thus becomes difficult to perceive in broken and ruined architectural elements any semblance of a monumental temple or to spot in a rather inconspicuous forest landscape a prehistoric settlement. Consequently, poorly conceived digital exhibitions could offer unrealistic journeys into a colourful, fascinating past stripped of grey, material evidence.

Digital escapism and the museum of the here-and-now

My analysis of multimedia exhibitions and the boom in such formats, evident likewise in Polish historical and archaeological museums (Stobiecka 2020a), enquires into why museums are abandoning material reality. In order to answer this question, I draw on the concept of digital escapism (Stobiecka 2019), which brings together epistemological and ontological issues, while also proving useful in predicting the future of archaeological museums.

Digital escapism can be understood, firstly, as a move towards rejecting artefacts as objects of scientific interest and instead turning to the methods of digital, virtual and cybernetic archaeology in order to create an immersive yet fictitious past. Such a concept of escapism is analogous to the abandonment of matter in favour of a consciously designed vision of a past landscape, society or past events. The grey, fragmentary tissue of artefacts is absorbed by digital tools and drawn into magical, colourful simulations of the past. The dissonance between the faded, dull originals and the artificially generated auratic vision of curators, graphic designers and/or archaeologists encourages us to engage in critical reflections on the issue of representation and the relations between technology and the objects of archaeological research. I also suggest a second way of reading the concept of digital escapism, this time in the context of archaeologists' growing interest in Big Data, database systems and digital repositories (Huggett 2015a, 2015b). This is of huge significance in the context of academic archaeology, as it represents another attempt to link archaeology and the natural sciences, while loosening the bonds with the "soft" humanities and social sciences, with which few archaeologists demonstrate significant affinities. In this sense, digital escapism marks a direction in the study of material culture that seeks to secure data that can facilitate the identification of relations and connections between objects, establish models relating to their agency, and offer possibilities for further research, archiving, transmission, visualization and presentation. While it is difficult to object to such efforts in academia, they might, though, be a source of certain problems in the realm of exhibitions.

As regards my initial reading of digital escapism, I would suggest that the vision of the past presented by archaeological museums that make use of multimedia is indeed attractive, as it is immersive, surprising, engaging and fascinating. As such, this vision has the potential to awaken interest in the past, thus attracting audiences to museums. However, as far as the second interpretation of the concept is concerned, I would argue that digitally generated images might, on the one hand, appear an all-too-real, thus gaining uncritical acceptance as the objective "truth". On the other hand, they might appear too artificial and unreal, as the methods used to create them, given their association with games and simulations, might exert a paradoxical influence on perceptions of the "impossibility" of archaeological visions. If the implementation of digital methods, whether in academia or museums, lacks critical reflection and a clear aim, this will lead only to further trivialization of the image of the discipline. This is because, in the first case, digital representations simplify archaeologists' efforts by giving audiences realistic and deliberately engaging "specimens", while in the second case, distant and incomprehensible relics become even more enigmatic when placed alongside digital supplements.

These tensions in museums offer an illustration of what is happening in academic archaeology, while researchers' difficulties at the same time become evident in exhibitions. As Juan Barceló warned during the 2018 Computer Applications in Archaeology Conference, held in Tübingen, "digital archaeology has gone over to the dark side" (Barceló 2018). The tendency towards "praising methods" and becoming engrossed by digital tools has led to the current situation, whereby archaeologists increasingly return to lines of argument familiar from processual archaeology, namely building models, generalization and "counting in archaeology" (see Sørensen 2017). In seeking objectivity, academic archaeology is again abandoning tangible matter, with the focus of its interests returning to theories resembling those developed in the 1960s. Latour's statement that "we have never been modern" seems all too accurate in this context. But have archaeological museums ever been modern? Have the methods, whose values were supposed to provide the basis for a new image of archaeology, attract mass audiences, guarantee unforgettable experiences and inspire fascination with the past, actually worked?

In answering this question, I will refer back to another one posed in the introduction to this section. Are modern technologies in museums actually modern? Do they generate new and alternative ways of presenting artefacts? Observing immersive simulations, listening to the array of sounds and participating in museum spectacles might all give the impression that a radical change has occurred, that dusty old galleries with glass cabinets full of faded artefacts have long since been cast into oblivion. Yet it is worth highlighting just what kind of narratives multimedia museums construct. Tara Copplestone and Daniel Dunne showed in the 2017 research that was based on several case studies that digital museums, even the world-famous ones, offer visitors little more than a "refreshed version" of traditional archaeological narratives (Copplestone and Dunne 2017). Digital methods, they argue, have been overlaid onto analogue models and thus, firstly, again reduce archaeological museums to oculocentric institutions that are in thrall to visualization; secondly, they fail to exploit the potential of digital technologies in museum practices; thirdly, they fail to enable visitors to create their own, subjective vision of the past because such museums present "paradigmatic" knowledge or even, as I mentioned above, supposedly objective knowledge.

Heidi Geismar has also drawn attention to this genealogy of digital expositions in her book *Museum Object Lessons for the Digital Age* (2018), linking them to Aby Warburg's visual project, the Mnemosyne Atlas, and to André Malraux's idea of the "museum of the imagination". Geismar, a pioneer of research on digital objects in museums, confirmed the continuation of oculocentric tradition. Emphasizing the continuum between the analogue and the digital, she argued that digital poetics hinder alternative ways of shedding light on the materiality or historicity of artefacts (but see Arvanitis and Zuanni 2021; Ireland and Bell 2021; Kenderdine et al. 2021). In her work, Geismar posed an important research question, namely: how do digital objects produce knowledge and meaning in the contemporary world (Geismar 2018: XIX)?

The concept of digital escapism serves to underline Geismar's findings and is also significant for reflections on museal archaeological narratives, revealing the "cult of methods" that, despite its progressive nature, failed to engender the emergence of radically new narratives. Is it thus possible to argue that digital archaeological museums indeed have a future? Despite the prevailing techno-optimism, expressing faith in the continued development of such methods that, in the case of archaeological museums, will enable the creation of further hyper-realistic structures, I nevertheless do not perceive digital archaeological museums as future-oriented. I would argue instead that they are museums of the present, or even of the here-and-now, enabling visualization using methods that are available now but within five years will appear old-fashioned, coming to resemble technological artefacts. This poses another problem that is rarely discussed in the context of the multimedia museum boom: the increasing tempo of the ageing of technological aids that accompanies the exponential growth of such devices. Museums of the here-and-now are thus not oriented towards the future. What is important in such institutions is that they appear to revolutionize exhibitions by introducing attractive, fashionable technologies. This, in turn, enables them to realize short-term objectives, namely attracting more visitors to generate a profit for the institution. Focusing on the here-and-now in museums' digital policy is a move that aims at achieving short-term but spectacular effects, with the sheer number of "digital toys" overshadowing the past, rather than contributing to the conceptualization of well thought out, balanced museum narratives. Such a strategy can, though, have fatal financial consequences for a museum, with the costs of modernizing devices, updating and servicing tablets, not to mention the complete exchange of technological aids, posing a serious burden to cultural institutions.[3]

Such critical reflections lead directly on to questions relating to artefacts-as-exhibits. What is an archaeological object that has been augmented by a digital supplement? What form does its virtual representation take, given that these are now prevalent in multimedia museums and often transformed even further into simulations, virtual reconstructions and augmented reality? Here I would like to differentiate archaeological prostheses – material objects augmented with virtual elements of the kind I described in my analysis of the Acropolis Museum in Athens – and digital representations, which do not constitute supplements of the material structure of an artefact. Museums construct immersive visions of the past, most often making use of a second kind of exhibit, namely representations of artefacts. Their status as artefacts-as-exhibits offers a highly insightful perspective for analysing the digital turn in museums.

Digital representations usually entail recording the details of an object using contemporary methods of documentation, such as photogrammetry or three-dimensional scans. In this form, artefacts become exact digital reproductions of themselves in a given time and place. Having undergone modelling, it is possible to rotate it freely and zoom and out on it. Should it be supplemented by polychrome or missing parts then it becomes a reconstruction. If made on a 3D printer, it becomes a reproduced material copy of itself. Should it be animated, it can become part of a virtual simulation. What occurs in the course of such processes is material reduction – the tangible object with real traits is pared back to become a simulacrum, something that in turn raises important questions about establishing the status of archaeological artefacts in the context of the digital turn. The first such question is: what happens to the original archaeological artefact? The authentic artefact disappears: either it is not part of the exhibition at all (as illustrated by the growing trend for artefact-free exhibitions), or it is completely overshadowed by various forms of digital imaging. Digital technologies contribute to a situation whereby the belief in engaging, virtual visions of the past means that we lose the ability to receive authentic artefacts as attractive and worthy of attention. This can lead to a sense of disappointment with visits to museums or archaeological sites.

Discussions on the status of artefacts in light of the digital turn are usually dominated, however, by another issue, namely that of aura (Witcomb 2007; Jones 2010, 2014, 2017; Garstki 2016; Geismar 2018). Digital objects are stripped of their emotional, material expression that provides the basis for Alois Riegl's idea of age value and Walter Benjamin's aura (but see Zuanni 2021). Many researchers level the accusation that digital copies are illusory and cannot affect views, as this is an outcome of an artefact's material condition (Ouzman 2006; Garstki 2016; but see Jones 2017). Other voices in the debate emphasize that aura is a cultural construct (Holtorf and Schadla-Hall 1999; Jones 2010) and as such cannot shape value-based arguments in the controversy over originals and digital copies. A particularly interesting contribution to these discussions is manifested in the research findings produced by the Manchester-based archaeologists Siân Jones and Stuart Jeffrey. Their archaeological-sociological research is grounded in efforts to include local communities in the documentary work conducted at archaeological sites. Non-specialists learned photogrammetry and how to use 3D scanners, while they were also given the opportunity to select the artefacts to be recorded. Their research findings revealed that aura plays an entirely marginal role in social perceptions of artefacts (Jones 2014; Jeffrey 2015; Jones et al. 2017). The archaeologists emphasized that for the participants in the project, aura and authenticity were not the key reasons shaping the decision to preserve an object. Participants' central motivation for selecting objects to be documented was their social value, so the sense of place they communicated, their contribution to collective memory and entanglement in everyday life (Jones 2014: 25). In the course of the research projects, what emerged was that the people who were involved in selecting and then digitally documenting objects recognized digital representations as being as auratic as the original artefacts. Bruno Latour and Adam Lowe reached similar conclusions a few years earlier in a polemic with the "cult of originals" (Latour and Lowe 2011). They argued that the aura of the original artefact can migrate into copies, with copies themselves acquiring aura over time (see also Ouzman 2006). Analysing reproductions of paintings, they warned that the controversy over aura should not overshadow the ability to differentiate good copies from poor copies. I would argue that the issue of digital archaeology in museums leads us in a similar direction. If they have been prepared meticulously with a clear aim in mind, representations are certainly more than simply subjective images lacking value.

I am also aware of another issue relating to the status of digital arte-facts-as-exhibits, which, while partly connected to Benjamin's concept of aura, also corresponds to my earlier remarks regarding the "museum of the here-and-now". Digital representations are produced in a particular time and a particular place, when the "source object" was in an ideal state[4] and illuminated by special light, thus effectively finding itself under laboratory conditions. During this often time-consuming process, objects undergo petrification. Despite being recorded in "real" time, an object's digital "reduction" is often far-removed from the realities of the material world. Its representation does not foresee changes, metamorphoses or mutations, and as such moves further away from Bennett's idea of vibrant matter while coming closer to resembling a postmodern version of the encyclopaedic illustrations familiar from Enlightenment-era museums. This again reveals the ultimate objective of digital archaeology: stripping the discipline of its embarrassing matter and fixing a stable, objective image of it.

How, then, should we treat artefacts-as-*digital*-exhibits? I would argue that the fairest response, given the undoubted achievements of multimedia museum practices, is to highlight the epistemological potential of this museal hyperframe, which is equal or at least similar to other descriptive and rep-resentational methods applied in archaeology. For now, though, artefacts in digital displays are rendered withdrawn; they do not reveal their ontological traits even within the cosmic and dreamlike mosaic of modern technologies.

The end of matter?

The aim of my "balance sheet" assessing the state of archaeological muse-ums after the digital turn has been to show just how difficult it is to be sim-ply for or against the model of multimedia archaeological museums. Having examined how modern technologies, which exert far-reaching influence on archaeological practices, could also transform artefacts-as-exhibits, I would now like to address and respond to two questions related to why I have chosen to analyse in this book cases featuring such "unspectacular" uses of modern technologies in archaeological museum practices.

The question guiding this subchapter appears to be rhetorical. Guided by a faith in the creative potential and vibrant, vital force of new materialisms, I am convinced that matter, and archaeological matter in particular, will not disappear completely from museums. How, then, can this materiality be brought to the surface? Rather than treating academics' Cartesian com-plexes using modelling and simulations, would it be possible to develop a mode of applying digital and virtual aids that would assist in highlighting the materiality and temporality of artefacts?

I think that I have offered partial answers to these questions in the preced-ing parts of this book. In developing the concept of the archaeological prosthesis, I have attempted to demonstrate that skilled and considered use of multimedia aimed at bringing forth the materiality of objects can guarantee deeper insight into the ontology of artefacts. The case study of the Acropolis Museum in Athens focused on the updating of the reconstructive narrative for the age of modern technologies. The narrative responds to the contemporary Zeitgeist by offering a form supplementation of what is missing together with a mode of recreating what is unimaginable. Archaeological prosthesis does not only refer to the matter, pastness and age value of archaeological artefacts, but also enables us to engage with still relevant political debates and post- and neo-colonial legacies.[5] As such, it becomes a medium that is full of potential and transcends the framework of both archaeology and museums.

An example of this is the *Body can't wait* action, organized in Paris in March 2018, when damaged Antique and neoclassical sculptures were supplemented with prostheses produced on 3D printers (Voon 2018). This action was instigated by Handicap International with the aim of drawing attention to the length of time it takes to wait for prosthetic limbs in conflict zones in Togo, Madagascar and Syria. The Classical statue of Venus de Milo was equipped with two resin prostheses, engendering associations with the figure of the cyborg as proposed by Donna Haraway. The fusion of living organism and machine described by Haraway took the form of a coded device (Haraway 1991: 150). In the case of archaeological prostheses and future cyborgs, coding takes a form that increases our sensitivity towards what is defective, historical and damaged, as well as to things that thanks to technological supplements are revived as augmented originals.

The past and present meet in archaeological prostheses, with the various registers of the temporality of archaeological objects made in the past acquiring presence likewise now. Returning to Heidi Geismar's remarks, I do not believe that digital aids prevent alternative perspectives on the materiality or historicity of artefacts. Noting the vast potential of exhibitions, like those in the Acropolis Museum or in digital installations, such as the projection of mixed reality onto the Peace Altar in the Museo dell'Ara Pacis, I do not reject the idea of new technologies having a role in service of heritage. Having observed how certain features of material are highlighted, thus presenting various periods in the life of an object, and how non-invasive methods supplement the fragile and delicate archaeological fabric, I position myself in favour of a prosthetic archaeology (Stobiecka 2020b) that is located at the intersection of materiality and virtuality. Prosthetic archaeology is not limited to creating digital objects of the kind described by Yuk Hui, i.e. objects that assume their form on monitors or are embedded in computer programmes having been constructed of data and metadata acquired as part of mathematical structures and models (Hui 2016: 1). In other words, prosthetic archaeology is oriented towards objects and materiality, making use of the potential of cyber-archaeology and generating material-digital cyborgs that possess multi-layered cultural, scientific, political and social meaning. Work in digital archaeology heading in this direction is future-oriented because it does not reject out of hand existing achievements in the realm of reconstruction. Instead, it combines these legacies with technological progress and the genuine needs of visitors who are not always seeking immersive journeys into the past but perhaps a space for contemplation anchored in the material fabric of artefacts that make the experience of the past seem authentic.

Notes

1. In this sense, digital archaeology faces similar challenges to archaeometry; see Sørensen (2017).
2. This is the form that, for example, Thomas Levy's project in Petra, Jordan, takes. The archaeological site is scanned regularly and recorded photogrammetrically in order to observe the scale of transformation brought about by climate change. Levy has demonstrated how quickly the erosion of the site is proceeding and he and his team are thus developing long-term strategies to counter this phenomenon in order to preserve heritage; see Levy et al. (2012).
3. Museum experts emphasize the costs involved in maintaining expensive multimedia equipment, as they require servicing while museums lack trained staff. A typical situation described by Polish museum employees is that, for example, tablets are not updated. Devices bought some ten years ago can no longer be updated because software suppliers do not provide new versions for older models. A guiding principle of multimedia museums, according to the director of the Museum of the Future in Nuremberg, is to fully replace exhibitions together with their devices at least every two years, while in the case of traditional museums this occurs every ten years or so.
4. There are exceptions to this rule, though, as objects can be documented before their conservation, a process that can cause damage to the structure of artefacts.
5. This is the nature of projects conducted as part of the digital restitution of heritage. Exceptionally interesting in this regard is the GRAVITATE project led by Sorin Hermon. Researchers involved in the Cyprus Institute initiative sought out digital artefacts that are dispersed around US-American collections. The discovered objects, most often fragments of Cypriot idols, are scanned, matched to fragments located in Cypriot museums and then printed on 3D printers. As Hermon emphasizes, the only remedy for dispersal and destruction of objects today is full digitalization, which also offers a way to avoid battles over restitution of the kind evident in the Acropolis Museum and British Museum; see Phillips et al. (2016); Hermon (2018).

7 The Preposterous Art of Archaeology

In 1968 in the Dwan Gallery in New York, Robert Smithson poured chunks of rock, slate and fragments of mica, all apparently useless rubble, into the form of a steel construction. This installation was accompanied by photographs and maps of the New Jersey area, where the artist had gathered the material. The work was titled *Site/Nonsite* and provided the nucleus of the land art manifesto that was published in *Artforum* as "A Sedimentation of the Mind: Earth Projects". Like many of Smithson's works, this piece gave rise to a series of interesting questions relating to art, archaeology and geology, positioned at the intersection of space and time, matter and thought. So, what did Smithson actually put on display in New York in 1968?

The pioneer of land art exhibited a representation of a specific place that provided the grounding for his theory of *Site/Nonsite* in which rubble is treated as an inherent element of material reality, space and landscape. Matter was supposed to become a substitute for place. But does this really do justice to the artist's intention? Viewing *Site/Nonsite* as an archaeologist, I see a pile of earth that grows each year following the excavation of an archaeological site. Small samples are taken for laboratory analysis, but the vast majority is surplus to requirements, superfluous, useless. The artist shows, however, that this barren earth contains artistic potential and could provide material for art, a form of malleable matter that acquires meaning in the course of the creative process and in institutional settings. I see the *arte-factum* in this context as art-that-has-become, so as something that has emerged from seemingly insignificant rubble, from the material remnants of a place.

In this chapter I enquire into how **artefacts become exhibits** through art. I am interested in the potential for artefacts to become Smithson-like malleable matter, while also considering the genealogy of artefacts as part of the material of art. I will explore the relations between artefacts, contemporary art and aesthetics in order to show the extent to which the possible emergence of a museum that realizes the preposterous art of archaeology could be future-oriented. I will refer to the exhibitions analysed above using two theoretical frameworks – Mieke Bal's project of preposterous history and Frank Ankersmit's reflections on representation and historical experience – to structure my strategy for presenting artefacts mediated through works

DOI: 10.4324/9781003327851-11

of art. While my project here is closer to Ankersmit's idea of a "substitution theory of representation" that prioritizes representation over the thing represented itself (Domańska 2004: 15), I would argue that Bal's remarks, seemingly "anarchistic" in relation to classical approaches to the history of art, could provide an interesting context for my reflections at the boundaries of archaeology and art. In mapping the territory of the preposterous art of archaeology, I will present as broad as possible a perspective for artistic mediations in archaeology that corresponds to the status of contemporary art in relation to the "discipline of things".

Archaeology – art – aesthetics

Research on the contact points between archaeology and art currently addresses questions relating to aesthetics in archaeology, something that is most commonly perceived as involving either reflection on the aesthetic dimension of artefacts in the past (Vickers 1994; Gosden 2001; Currie 2012) or the interpretive potential emerging from the relationship between contemporary art and archaeology (Pearson and Shanks 2001; Jameson et al. 2003; Renfrew 2003; Pollard 2004; Bonaventura and Jones 2011; Danielsson et al. 2012; Shanks 2012; Deshoulières 2014; Russell and Cochrane 2014a; Chittock and Valdez-Tullett 2016a; Bailey 2018). Scholars representing the second of the two strands, focused on theoretical questions, may have different objects of interest but nevertheless highlight similar issues related to negotiating the space between art and archaeology.

In the introduction to the edited volume *Shaping the Past: Sculpture and Archaeology*, Jones and Bonaventura stress that both the history of art and archaeology make the past visible while at the same time showing its impact today (Jones and Bonaventura 2011a: 6). This comparative pointer, I argue, leads to the question of how the past is manifested and materialized in archaeological objects. Does the image of the past correspond to artistic representations of it and what vision of past events do artefacts and works of art offer us today?

In an interesting interpretation of Smithson's piece *Incidents of Mirror-Travel in the Yucatan*, Flora Vilches places it in the context of excavation practices and notes that art has anticipated many of the problems of archaeological theory (Vilches 2011). I would argue that this important trope is particularly significant in the context of representations and visualizations of knowledge. Vilches indicates that Smithson was the first artist to highlight the problem of what lies between the subjective and objective interpretations of the past as constructed by archaeologists. He thus drew attention to the creative potential of artists in constructing or even contesting archaeological representations. Smithson's remarks, like those of other artists, can offer a fresh impulse for formulating new problems in archaeological research.

Colin Renfrew, meanwhile, refers to another land art artist, Richard Long, noting how his artistic imagination closely resembles the archaeological imagination (Renfrew 2014; see also Shanks 2012). Like Michael Shanks, who coined the concept of the archaeological imagination, Renfrew believes in the potential of the archaeological *imaginarium*, which is the repertoire of social visions of archaeology and its historical-Romantic roots that could provide creative inspiration for artists while opening up new interpretive frameworks for archaeologists. A similar argument is taken up by Ylva Sjöstrand, who is convinced that reading archaeological objects as artworks can lead to a re-evaluation of research practices of those working with "things from the past" (Sjöstrand 2017). Her remarks resemble those of Helen Chittock and Joana Valdez-Tullett, who suggest that the return to things and the material turn in the humanities have brought art and archaeology closer together (Chittock and Valdez-Tullett 2016b: VI). Noting the common genealogy of archaeology and the history of art, the authors speak in favour of strengthening the bonds between the disciplines. John Jameson shows that cooperation between the fields of archaeology and art could enable archaeology to transcend dominant Eurocentric cognitive frameworks while also reaching larger audiences effectively by having artists get involved in mediating archaeology (Jameson 2003: 59, 62).

Despite the notable increase in interest in the intersection of art and archaeology, what remains evident is the general disregard for or misconception of projects created in this area. Ylva Sjöstrand, whom I mentioned above, noted this inspiring potential and outlined current research positioned at the boundaries of art and archaeology, but regretted that the majority of publications in this field are overlooked in broader scholarly debates (Sjöstrand 2017: 375). Problems positioned at the intersection of archaeology, art and aesthetics are often dismissed, trivialized and simplified, leading to their marginalization in archaeological theory. The format adopted in research on the reception of Antiquity or Prehistory is often close to classical art history, Erwin Panofsky's iconology, and can even carry traits of art-historical knowledge in the Morellian spirit. Therefore, studying "influenceolgy" is not an attractive proposition for archaeologists, who treat the iconographical or iconological method as just one analytical tool among many. There is even less acceptance of projects located at the intersection of archaeology and aesthetics in which researchers seek – most often – to produce reflections on the aesthetic values of the past. What this leads to, by and large, is the declaration of rather ambitious yet hardly feasible hypotheses that quite often lead to unproductive discussions or are simply ignored because they are too far removed from scholarly norms. Researchers adopting such approaches often turn to the concept of agency, understood in terms of Alfred Gell's anthropological ideas expressed in *Art and Agency* (Gell 2013). However, as Chris Godsen states, archaeologists still tend to lack the tools for a complex analysis of the issue of aesthetics in archaeology (Gosden 2001).

Bonaventura, Cochrane, Jones, Renfrew, Russell, Sjöstrand and Vilches do indeed draw on the tools of the history of art, yet their texts do not offer an entirely coherent vision that might explain the fragmentariness of research at the intersection of archaeology, art and aesthetics. How can research be conducted at this intersection? What methodological tools can be applied? How can the problems explored be conceptualized? How can accusations of being unscientific be avoided? And how can genuinely new perspectives in archaeology be opened up, ones that would involve thinking with archaeology and acting through art?

So far, it is individual projects within the realm of the archaeology of the recent past that have offered an alternative to the above-mentioned paths that possess both evident deficiencies and potential. The strategy proposed by Rodney Harrison and John Schofield, namely "archaeology as art and art as archaeology" (Harrison and Schofield 2010: 105–119), possesses certain methodological potential that could, I argue, bring about revisions of the prevailing approach in the field of archaeology-art-aesthetics, which itself is already a fairly marginal area of research. The research trajectories suggested by Harrison and Schofield encompass three perspectives: art as archaeology, archaeological research as performance and art as an alternative way of analysing and interpreting archaeological objects. At the same time, they demonstrate the array of possible perspectives that could be applied in illustrating the relations between archaeology, on the one hand, and aesthetics and art, on the other, while also encouraging further methodological experiments.

I believe that archaeological museums offer the most fertile ground for considering these problems, precisely because they consciously introduce works of art into exhibition narratives. What they need to do, however, is to develop somewhat different theoretical perspectives that would transcend existing approaches while also posing precise research questions addressing the relationship between archaeology and art, the question of representation, the nature of how the past is experienced, temporality, materiality and, finally, the status of artefacts as exhibits in relation to works of art. A pressing challenge in formulating such questions is presented by exhibitions positioned at the intersection of archaeology and art, as these fields are burdened by the historical legacy of their common genealogy.

What do artefacts want?

The aesthetic order of exhibitions that has for decades dominated archaeological museums around the world has imposed on visitors a particular mode of perceiving archaeological objects as art objects. Even though archaeologists were raising the issue of the excessive aestheticization (understood in terms of a Kantian aesthetics of beauty) of artefacts in the 1990s already, it seems that the exhibition model that renders artefacts as works of art remains prevalent in museums, particularly in local museums of Mediterranean archaeology and in great national galleries, including encyclopaedic museums (Swain 2007: 9). In 1992, Michael Shanks and Christopher Tilley compared archaeological museums to the way ikons are presented in Russia, describing their curators in terms of the Romantic *homo artifex*, who looked for art in places where there was none to be found (Shanks and Tilley 1992: 72). They argued that the reduction of finds to the role of artistic objects *de facto* fetishizes them (Shanks and Tilley 1992: 73). Their highly significant findings seem to have been overlooked in discussions of archaeological museums and in studies located at the intersection of archaeology and art.

Paraphrasing W.J.T. Mitchell's famous question, it is perhaps worth asking: what do artefacts want? Do artefacts in archaeological museums actually want to be works of art? Do they want to free themselves from the institutionally anchored art apparatus? Do they want to escape aesthetic valorization? In his now canonical contribution to the field of visual culture studies, *What Do Pictures Want? The Lives and Loves of Images*, Mitchell brings works of art to life and seeks answers to the question posed in the title (Mitchell 2005). He describes his objectives thus:

> The point, however, is not to install a personification of the work of art as the master term but to put our relation to the work into question, to make the relationality of image and beholder the field of investigation. The idea is to make pictures less scrutable, less transparent; also to turn analysis of pictures toward questions of process, affect, and to put in question the spectator position: what does the picture want from me or from 'us' or from 'them' or from whomever?
>
> (Mitchell 2005: 49)

Any attempt to apply Mitchell's concepts to research on archaeological artefacts would need to conduct a similar study on relations of beholders to artefacts, enquiring into whether artefacts really want to undergo visual reduction, whether they simply want to give museum visitors something nice to look at, or perhaps they seek to transcend such optics and instead tell a story, cause an emotional reaction and bring forth affects?

I think that an answer to these questions could be provided by projects positioned at the intersection of archaeology and art, as they constitute both a form for working through the long-standing relations between the disciplines and their common genealogy, as well as an attempt at transcending dominant ways of thinking about archaeological objects. Particularly interesting in this context are initiatives by the US-American archaeologist Doug Bailey, who conducts research in the realm of art/archaeology (Bailey 2018). Rather than dedicate his efforts to theoretical reflections, as many of the above-mentioned scholars do, Bailey himself creates projects positioned at the intersection of archaeology and art. Drawing inspiration from some of the big names of contemporary art, such as Gordon Matta-Clark, Lucio Fontana and Ai Weiwei, he maps out completely new potential for this subdiscipline. During the American Theoretical Archaeology Group Conference at Syracuse University in 2019, Bailey was inspired by Ai Weiwei's work *Dropping a Han Dynasty Urn* and destroyed an amphora from San Francisco, with the fragments then distributed among the participants of the performance. Bailey's objective was to "liberate" the object, freeing it from the overflowing museum stores while also instigating a certain form of animation of the audience, with each person holding a fragment asked to document its life after being smashed. Similarly, in conducting excavations at the archaeological site in Măgura, Romania, he was inspired primarily by the works of the artists Gordon Matta-Clark and Lucio Fontana. Bailey saw parallels between the excavations at the site and the violation of the surface, which brought about associations with the cuts that he found in the works of Fontana with its motifs of holes, *buchi*, and cuts, *tagli*. Bailey describes his art/archaeology projects in terms of negotiating the limits of art and archaeology, drawing on the tools, methodologies and traditions of both to create works and projects that transcend explanation and interpretation, thus questioning and complicating existing practices.

Perhaps artefacts do indeed want to be understood in this way, as creative, malleable matter that encourages creative practices positioned at the intersection of disciplines. In doing so, they want to inspire the imagination, encourage the construction of individual visions of the past and revitalize interactions with researchers, artists and visitors to museums. Such an approach calls into question the visual paradigm in which archaeological objects are reduced to the status of works of art, with the focus on discovering aesthetic value meaning they remain passive and thus cannot evoke actions, reactions or emotions. I therefore suggest that it is necessary to update archaeology's aesthetic repertoire by turning to the aesthetics of the abject (Kristeva 1982), everyday aesthetics (Saito 2007), the aesthetics of the fragment (Edensor 2005; Olsen and Pétursdóttir 2014) and the aesthetics of the Anthropocene (Davies and Turpin 2015), or simply decentralizing the role of seeking traditional aesthetic values in archaeological objects. Instead, the goal should be finding new potential for reading artefacts involving a certain agency of artefacts that functions in conjunction with inspiration drawn from art.

The increasingly popular format of exhibitions that juxtapose artefacts with contemporary artworks could provide a testbed for such new approaches. One such example is the Museo dell'Ara Pacis, discussed in Chapter 5, where a work of contemporary art functions as a mediator of encounters with the past. It mobilizes subjective feelings and at the same time encourages visitors to compose their own visions of the past.

Here, I have attempted to provide an overview of how exhibitions mediating archaeology, art and aesthetics constitute a museal strategy, recognizing that forms of artistic intervention comprising complex discursive matrixes combining the old and new, the material and ephemeral, the familiar and unfamiliar, are becoming increasingly popular in museums.[1] In my approach, then, I seek to deepen the evident tensions between archaeology and art by drawing on the ideas of Mieke Bal and selected concepts from Frank Ankersmit, as they enable me to formulate a proposal for a preposterous art of archaeology.

Experiencing the past preposterously

The idea of a preposterous history of art was presented by Mieke Bal in her 1999 book *Quoting Caravaggio: Contemporary Art, Preposterous History*, which bore a motto drawn from the poetry of T.S. Eliot: "the past should be altered by the present as much as the present is directed by the past" (Bal 1999: 1). In formulating her theoretical proposal, Bal recognized contemporary art as a "theoretical object" that Old Masters' works should be placed alongside because the mediation between the past and present gives rise to a form of citation that endows the past with new meanings (Bal 1999: 6). Bal illustrates her idea, which recalls earlier findings by other researchers,[2] by exploring relations between Baroque artworks and contemporary art pieces. Her aim is to create tools that would have the potential to help understand works of art. The project of developing a preposterous history of art locates what comes before (the *pre-*) after what comes later (the *post-*). By doing history, incorporating uncertainty and bringing forth the most important elements of the analysis and interpretation of works, it offers a "vision of revision" (Bal 1999: 7). In this sense, the impact of contemporary art on ancient art ensures that it is the latter that is subject to constant negotiation and thus transformed (van Alphen 2007).

I am interested in this constant renegotiation of the past that takes place through contemporary art. However, when taken as a whole, Bal's project seems to be just another call for art historians to take into account their position in the present in their interpretations. Thus, history is less important than temporality. This is why Bal attaches great significance to the fact that recipients of art are positioned in the present and thus carry a particular set of experiences, beliefs and knowledge. What I therefore propose is to shed light on Bal's idea of the preposterous not by using history but by instead turning to Frank Ankersmit's concept of "historical experience". I do so because, firstly, it incorporates recipients in the relations between what is represented and what is representing; secondly, it clearly highlights the linearity of time that is disrupted when perceiving an art object. Historical experience expresses our relationship to the past, moving from the present to the past while at the same time running from the past to the present. This double movement "combines discovery and recovery" (Ankersmit 2004: 47). Historical experience is of an aesthetic nature and gives rise to profundity – a sense of loss and love that emerges from the combination of pain and pleasure in our relationship to the past (Ankersmit 2002). Ankersmit emphasizes that historical experience itself modifies language, a fact that, in my view, does not preclude thinking about art as a language that moulds experience. I believe that it is this form of experience that is familiar to the audiences of archaeological museums. Like archaeologists, visitors can discover the past and recover it, as long as museums offer a space for creating subjective visions of the past. Such a space is offered, I argue, by works of art that comment on, supplement, metaphorize and mobilize the archaeological imagination (Shanks 2012). It is thanks to artworks that archaeological objects are experienced in an aesthetic fashion and thus treated as a trace of what has been lost. At the same time, this mode of experiencing the distant past generates a process of recovery, in the course of which whatever remains is given care and attention. This profound aspect of historical experience resembles the cult of ruins that is also reflected today in practices of protection, in legislation and in doctrines of conservation. Awareness of irredeemable loss as well as the intensified cult of monuments leads to the crystallization of phenomena including heritagization, i.e. the powerful urge to preserve heritage at all costs.

What aspects of our historical experience are changed, then, by works of contemporary art? Pieces that creatively reference ancient histories, events, figures and cultures – such as Mimmo Paladino's *Ara Pacis*, which I analysed in Chapter 5 – constitute subjective representations of the past. Ankersmit formulated a concept that is crucial to my considerations here, the "substitution theory of representation", which gives priority to representation over what is represented. According to Ankersmit, representation acts as a substitute for the past. And for this reason, we should not enquire into how similar the representation is to the actual past but into whether it might function as a substitute for the past. Representation is thus supposed to be of an ontological nature within the framework of historical experience, rather than serve epistemological aims. This is because it is not necessary for there to be any resemblance at all between the object and its artistic representation (Ankersmit 2002). As such, representations are expected to enable historical and aesthetic experiencing of the past. According to this perspective, then, historians appear as artists who represent and present. Mimmo Paladino became exactly this kind of historian, someone creating a space for confrontation between what is familiar (contemporary art) and what is unfamiliar (archaeological objects), with the latter distanced temporally from our current position.

The strategy of a preposterous art of archaeology that I am outlining here is therefore based on creating such conditions for perceiving artefacts that would incorporate other actors into this process – namely works of art and aesthetic spaces. Visitors who had perhaps come with the intention of searching for signs and symbols representing the past in artists' works would now look differently at the archaeological objects displayed alongside the contemporary pieces. Mimmo Paladino's work in the Museo dell'Ara Pacis managed to successfully encourage visitors to revise the *imaginarium* of Antiquity and recognize that the symbols used by the Romans who were alive when the Peace Altar was created were different to those that the Italian artist included in his three-dimensional work. Noting the fragmentary nature of the figures compiled by Paladino, visitors might again turn towards archaeological fragments and perceive in them a certain "whole". The historical experience that visitors acquire at this point is based on an artistic evocation that enables us to think of artefacts in the way that Paladino intended us to, namely as incomplete and damaged, yet at the same time encouraging us to develop our own visions of the past. In this case, Paladino's artwork has the potential to serve as a preposterous reference and as a supplement that liberates the creative imagination. His piece in the museum is representative of the art of archaeology, an idea understood here as a work of art that enables us to rethink archaeology, the past and artefacts.

The tension between preposterousness – where I place the emphasis on the position of the visitor – art and archaeology is also evident in the exhibition at Sir John Soane's Museum in London. This institution is famous for displaying contemporary art within its walls. But what role do the older works displayed there play? I have in mind, for example, Joseph Gandy's *Architectural Ruins – A Vision* (or *A Vision of the Bank of England in Ruins*) (1798), which depicts a ruined rotunda against the background of a cloudy sky. Foregrounded are architectural elements, such as fallen stone blocks, pillars and columns. The interior of the rotunda opens itself up to viewers' gaze to reveal a regular form covered by a dome, only fragments of which survive, while antiquarians work inside using their picks and spades to excavate remnants of the past. The left side of the background is cast in shadow, while the right-hand side is illuminated by a soft light. In the bright part of the composition, the ruins of a sculpturally decorative portico can be seen. The remnants of the architectural construction are covered in lush greenery. The dreamy vision evokes a host of Italian landscapes painted in the nineteenth century by members of the Rovinismo movement, yet it is in fact a travesty of Soane's design for the rotunda of the Bank of England in London. Like Mimmo Paladino's mosaic, this piece sharpens the focus of the lens through which we view the chaotically arranged artefacts in Sir John Soane's Museum. In this case, the audience is given the opportunity to see the fragments collected in the museum in a fresh light as Gandy's watercolour depicts the excavation of artefacts in the late eighteenth century. The material fragments on display in the rooms of the museum are thus made present in the form of painterly representations positioned within the structure of a whole – an ancient ruin being explored meticulously by the first archaeologists. This experience is, again, of an aesthetic nature as it is based on loss and love. Loss because the artefacts are being removed from a ruin that at the time constituted a whole; love because we can still perceive the ruins by **being beside** them. *Architectural Ruins – A Vision* thus becomes another work of archaeology, while when being read by contemporary viewers in a location where it is surrounded by a disorderly collection of artefacts it functions as a "disciplinary document". At the same time, it is a successful preposterous projection of a future ruin whose message is intensified by the presence of unruly material fragments gathered in the Romanticist museum.

The most important facet of the strategy for a preposterous art of archaeology in museums is, in my view, the potential to create a space for subjective and located experiencing of the past. Any museum that marks out such a space by introducing works of art consequently cannot lay claim to having exclusive rights over creating images of the past. I believe that contemporary, critical museums should present multiple perspectives and a host of potential interpretations, rather than imposing on visitors the "one true" vision of the past. I have the impression, as I showed in my analysis of the phenomenon of digital escapism, that what the public is presented with is often an insight into a supposedly objective past that in fact is a subjective projection stemming from the author of a given visualization or reconstruction. Meanwhile, the strategy of a preposterous art of archaeology grants museum visitors an opportunity to refer to their individual experiences, thoughts, existing knowledge and associations as part of constructing their own vision of the past. By incorporating artworks into their narratives, curators and exhibition designers give visitors tools that generate an affective form of experiencing the past. As I showed in my analysis of the Museo dell'Ara Pacis, the exhibition includes both an artwork and a multimedia tablet, with the latter also enabling multiple interpretations as it features a dozen or more ways of reconstructing the Peace Altar. This thus communicates loud and clear that the vision of the past is a construct and it is subject to constant renegotiation. What they see in the ancient relics is up to the visitors themselves. Nevertheless, the means to construct the image of the past are provided by the curators. They are responsible for moderating the relation between the visitors and the past embodied both by the artefacts, and also, in this case, by artworks. Works of art can be of assistance in fostering a more intimate relation to the past precisely because they function on an emotional level. As part of museum narratives, artworks can move, anger, inspire, shock, intrigue or irritate viewers, or indeed leave them indifferent. Still, they usually evoke a response and if it is treated as a preposterous stimulus then it can assist us in revising the image of the past.

What I have proposed above enables me to formulate subsequent research questions: **how do artefacts function as exhibits** in the context of works of art? What new conditions for artefacts does the confrontation with works of art create? What is rendered dormant when artefacts are positioned in an artistic context? Where does the strategy of a preposterous archaeology of art stand in relation to the modes of presenting artefacts that have been familiar throughout the history of museums? Is the project outlined here future-oriented?

Malleable matter

In posing the above questions, I am entering tricky territory that is burdened by the historical legacy of relations between archaeology and art (but see Russell and Cochrane 2014b: 1–2). Positioning artefacts in the realm of art remains a reductive move that strips archaeological objects of their context, original functions and particular microhistory that contains chapters covering the periods of creation, use, deposition and discovery. Nevertheless, I would argue that artefacts can be described using a term drawn from the vocabulary of art history – namely, defining them as malleable matter.

I understand the notion of malleable matter in two ways. First of all, this is what for me defines the potential to mould an object in any possible way through a diverse variety of scientific theories, whether in the course of practical research or in museum spaces. Artefacts thus become malleable matter during interpretation and framing. Writing about artefacts and presenting the multiple facets of archaeological finds, I noted that almost all the objects described in Chapter 2 here could just as well have been given any of the other "labels". Indeed, one artefact tells many stories and refers to multiple narrative strands that are derived from its materiality by researchers and then by museum curators. I also referred to studies conducted in museums, presenting a whole range of modes of exhibiting archaeological objects with the aim of showing just how many options there are for illustrating how artefacts function as exhibits. I will now turn to a specific example I found in both museums explored in the in-depth case studies: stone architectural elements featuring floral decorations. In the Museo dell'Ara Pacis, such pieces served to illustrate that there was awareness of biodiversity in the Ancient world, while in the case of the Acropolis Museum the exhibit "From nature to marble", which I did not discuss in detail in Chapter 4, was supposed to indicate just how immaculately Ancient Greek artists could imitate nature (Figure 7.1). The same kind of artefact was moulded into an exhibit by bringing forth a leading facet, one that was either simply interesting or could be seen as a corresponding to the current state of knowledge and interests in the field. Malleable artefacts thus constitute palimpsests bearing multi-layered meanings that seem to be revealed in the course of excavation. Curators, like archaeologists, select a layer of meaning that is then entangled with other exhibits to create a narrative network. A malleable artefact, then, is also one whose potential as an exhibit is revealed through the process of constructing the formats of dominant knowledge.

On the other hand, the malleability of artefacts leads me to consider the historical-artistic entanglements of archaeology. I will return here to themes that I have already addressed. In the introduction to this book, I highlighted that at the time of its founding archaeology was entangled in the visual paradigm. The original methodological tools, such as typologies and seriation that were used to legitimize academic archaeology, served to give order to unruly matter. Archaeological matter was thus classified, arranged in sequences, series and rows that at the same time provided temporal axes. The evolutionary model for presenting archaeological objects reduced them to the status of signs marking the stages of the birth, development and decline of a particular style or culture. The typological exhibition model that imposed an aestheticizing gaze also made it difficult to delineate the boundaries between material culture and art. Objects that in the past might only have had functional significance were ascribed, first and foremost, aesthetic values. In previous chapters, I have indicated the common genealogy of archaeology and art history, noting that this has given rise to

Figure 7.1 Acropolis Museum, *From nature to marble* – exhibit, photo: Monika Stobiecka, 2016, by courtesy of the Acropolis Museum.

a predilection for presenting archaeological objects as works of art. This is something that resonates, for example, in the aesthetic model of exhibition outlined by Peter Vergo. The negation of the archaeological context and individual histories has given rise to a situation in which archaeological objects are still judged according to the craftsmanship involved in making them. While this might not seem surprising in terms of Attic vases, Egyptian jewellery or Scythian metalwork, applying the same approach to Lusatian ceramics or palaeolithic tools might prove harmful. Researchers studying archaeological aesthetics would probably respond at this juncture by saying that an Acheulean hand-axe has as much right to be considered a work of art as Duchamp's ready-mades or the conceptual works of Sol LeWitt (Currie 2012: 31). Nevertheless, what is often forgotten, I would argue, is that while works of art are created intentionally, their status is awarded institutionally. Duchamp's *Fountain* would have remained an ordinary urinal created by the R. Mutt company had the author not **made** it into a work of art, so an *arte-factum*. Smithson did the same with rubble from New Jersey. The Acheulean hand-axe was not intentionally created as a work of art, or at least we do not know whether it was and cannot establish if it was. In all likelihood, it was created as a tool that, following Leroi-Gourhan, served an extension of the human hand (Leroi-Gourhan 1993).

The typological model thus created a long-standing impasse in archaeological museum practices. Archaeological museums do not display works of art, but rather artefacts that have been stripped of their multivalent potential and archaeological context, as they are arranged in rows and given rather unenlightening labels. Why, then, is it the case that despite being aware of this oppressive museal policy, I nevertheless see an opportunity to refresh archaeological exhibitions through contemporary art?

Both ways of interpreting the malleability of artefacts lead me in the direction of recognizing the strategy of a preposterous art of archaeology as a means of mobilizing the potential contained in including works of contemporary art in archaeological narratives. Firstly, the comparison of artefacts to the malleable material of art and treating archaeology as art seems appropriate to me because it opens up new possibilities for framing and reading archaeological objects. Malleability in this sense means freedom of interpretation and the possibility of moulding a subjective image of the past that emerges through the application of any relevant scientific theories that are then consistently updated either by way of reference to new research findings or by implementing the preposterous association of contemporary art and artefacts. Secondly, the long-standing tradition of presenting artefacts as works of art should be revised and updated. This becomes possible in an age when artists are showing increasing interest in the past, materiality, fragmentariness, ruination and archaeology. What is necessary, then, is to rework the existing relations to the artistic paradigm that are so burdensome and oppressive for artefacts. These relations should be cast in a new light and confronted with the latest artworks, rather than allowing them to be reinscribed on the basis of journeys back into the past, using Renaissance and academicist painting to petrify artefacts within mythological settings.

I would like to emphasize strongly that the perspective outlined here does not intend to suggest a dichotomy of archaeology/art. I am aware, after all, of the new thing-oriented approaches in art, including research on the materiality of objects, and I ascribe great importance to such perspectives as part of efforts to revise the canon of the history of art and its methodologies. I believe that both artefacts and works of art are vibrant matter that transforms and changes. My intensions here are somewhat different in that I am going against traditional analogies of art and archaeology, including attempts to reduce artefacts to works of art on the basis of aesthetic claims that are sometimes difficult to ratify in relation to stone tools, clay vessels and other small everyday objects. What I propose, then, is a revision of precisely such modes of perception that have been built upon the foundations of nineteenth-century museum practices. At the same time, I suggest that archaeology requires interventions that could also come, for example, from the field of ethnography, which has also influenced contextual exhibition models. For obvious reasons, however, I am focusing on art as I argue that the need for engaged art in archaeology has never been more pressing, while the need for contemporary art to think with archaeology has likewise never been greater.

Indeed, such actions are gradually being recognized and applied in bringing archaeological heritage to life in European and US-American museums. In 1999, the artist Mark Dion conducted the project *Thames Dig* with the support and patronage of the Tate Gallery.[3] It involved conducting archaeological excavations on the bank of the River Thames, with the finds displayed in the gallery. The project is located at the intersection of the archaeology of the recent past and the *art&science* movement. By recreating scientific tools, the artist positions himself as an archaeologist, which means that his works can quite easily be described in terms of archaeology as art. In 2013, works by leading Italian contemporary artists were put on display at the forums in Rome (Artribune Redazione 2013). As such, one of the original functions of the forums was restored as they had in the past served as exhibition spaces. The works mediating the past were submerged in ancient heritage, creating ideal conditions for constructing a preposterous experience. Since 2010, Alfred Seiland has been photographing the world's top archaeological sites, revealing the emptiness, passing of time, degradation and financial exploitation that affects them. His photographs were displayed in the Albertina Museum in Vienna in 2018.[4] Since 2015, Sir John Soane's Museum has hosted temporary contemporary art exhibitions (Figure 7.2). The original artefacts provide the backdrop for contemporary pieces, revealing the fragmentary nature of those works.

I have provided this overview in order to illustrate that the number of works positioned at the intersection of archaeology and contemporary art grows each year. What is striking is that in spite of this, there is a lack of in-depth theoretical reflection in the field of archaeological theory. Similarly, the vast majority of archaeological museums remain indifferent towards this promising trend. The introduction of Mimmo Paladino's mosaic into the narrative of the Museo dell'Ara Pacis is exceptional in this respect and constitutes a milestone in the formation of new, revised relations between archaeology and art. My vision of the future archaeological museum is that

Figure 7.2 Marc Quinn, *Drawn from life* – temporary exhibition in Sir John Soane's
Museum, photo: Monika Stobiecka, 2017, by courtesy of the trustees of
Sir John Soane's Museum, London.

of an institution engaged in mediating a past that is inaccessible to visitors,
but doing so by also drawing on the potential of contemporary art. While
we might have familiarized and tamed the artistic imagination as we are in
constant contact with visual culture, we are nevertheless much less fluent in

using the archaeological imagination. Confronting a work of art creates a field for constructing an individual, synoptic vision of the past and sets in motion the creative imagination, a concept that reveals common ground with Shanks' archaeological imagination (2012). This is what archaeological museums can achieve if they incorporate contemporary art into their narratives.

The strategy for a preposterous art of archaeology that I have proposed and outlined here is not a completely new idea. It is rather a revised form of exhibition, one that targets visual and aesthetic experiencing of the past. It offers an alternative insofar as the works that are juxtaposed with artefacts give rise to affect, generate interest, supplement, comment on and metaphorize the experience of the past. Presented alongside works of art, artefacts-as-exhibits become multifarious creative matter that encourages both reflection and efforts to create the past in the future. They could influence the emergence of new research fields within the realm of archaeology and art, while the exhibitions mediating the flow of knowledge between academia and museums could constitute an important step towards providing legitimacy for the, often marginalized, academic research taking place in this area. I believe that with the dynamic growth in artists' interest in archaeology and archaeology-adjacent topoi, contemporary art could, paradoxically, encourage the emergence of new facets of artefacts while opening up new theoretical horizons, just as Robert Smithson's artworks provided archaeology with new perspectives.

Notes

1. See Artribune Redazione (2013); *Sarah Lucas: Power in Woman* (2016). Available from: https://www.soane.org/whats-on/exhibitions/sarah-lucas-power-woman [Accessed 25 July 2018]; *Marc Quinn: Drawn from Life* (2017). Available from: https://www.soane.org/whats-on/exhibitions/marc-quinn-drawn-life [Accessed 25 July 2018]; *Paul Coldwell: Picturing the Invisible* (2019). Available from: https://paulcoldwell.org/portfolio-item/picturing-the-invisible/ [Accessed 12 May 2022].
2. The key terms in Bal's project play on concepts developed by Giovanni Careri, Hubert Damisch and Louis Marin. The preposterous was discussed by Careri (1994). The concept of the "theoretical object", meanwhile, comes from earlier ideas developed by Damisch and Marin.
3. *Mark Dion, Tate Thames Dig 1999* (2000). Available from: https://www.tate.org.uk/art/artworks/dion-tate-thames-dig-t07669 [Accessed 25 July 2018]; see also Vilches (2011: 199–223).
4. *Alfred Seinland* (2018). https://www.albertina.at/en/exhibitions/alfred-seiland/ [Accessed 12 May 2022].

8 The Archaeology of All (Living) Things

A third strategy that I will outline in relation to archaeological museums is based on an aspect of a classical definition of archaeology proposed by Colin Renfrew and Paul Bahn. The authors of the leading textbook for trainee archaeologists write that one vision of archaeology defines its objective as "the reconstruction of the lifeways of the people responsible for the archaeological remains" (Renfrew and Bahn 2012: 17). What interests me above all in this description of the discipline's goals is that it presents archaeology as being a (past) life science.

In the earlier section on artefacts, I have shown that the concept of life should also encompass the non-human actors that are archaeological relics. I presented a diagram, Artefacts: interventions and bottlenecks (Figure 3.1), which outlines a model based on the "life of an artefact" that is inspired by the writings of both archaeologists and philosophers of things. I understand life, in the context of archaeology, to be human and non-human, networked, relational and dynamic, and encompassing the life of artefacts, objects, flora, fauna and remains. Birth, existence and death form a life cycle that applies to humans and non-humans alike. It has become customary to treat archaeology as being closest to the final element because it appears to study graves, burial grounds, pyramids and burial practices, coming into contact with remains that are subjected to a series of specialist anthropological and archaeometric analyses. Certain subdisciplines of archaeology have been founded, such as the archaeology of death or thanatoarchaeolgy (or in French *thanato-archéologie*), as well as newer perspectives that examine death and genocide in the recent past, such as Holocaust archaeologies and forensic archaeology. As Ewa Domańska has argued, death constitutes "one (foundational) life event", meaning that it is a form of life (Domańska 2017: 297). In her book on the ontology of the dead body, Domańska draws on work in archaeology and the above-mentioned subdisciplines, as well as its auxiliary tools, including taphonomy, to present a convincing argument that could be of crucial significance to archaeologists because it restores and revives the seemingly dead object of research, finding value in the posthumous life of matter.

The holistic understanding of life that incorporates recognition of death, as well as decomposition and decay, as a stage of life, leads to a vitalizing and

DOI: 10.4324/9781003327851-12

vibrant conception of the dead body. This has far-reaching consequences for the redefinition of archaeological practices. Such an understanding of life and death, which comes close to the theory of vital materialism, contains the potential to revitalize and animate archaeologists' research objects that for centuries had simply appeared dead (Thomas 2004; Olsen et al. 2012; Hamilakis 2013). The idea of treating death both literally (the death of humans, the death of animals) and metaphorically (for example, going out of use, or deposition treated as "the death of an object") has been part of the discipline since its foundations, with research objects viewed as dead and stable. What archaeology needs, though, is to understand death in the terms proposed by Ewa Domańska. This would lead, first of all, to a revision of what constitutes archaeologists' object of research, moving away from seeing it as something dead and instead towards a vision of it as active, dynamic and constantly changing. Such a move facilitates the correlation of archaeological practice and theory, itself seen as something grounded in the realities of research. As I have argued earlier in this book, archaeological artefacts are in constant motion, with their apparent "death" as a result of deposition in fact being a moment that inaugurates new life. My understanding of life is that it is something independent of human beings that can be seen in terms of material life and coexistence in the environment, which in turn influences and shapes the objects that archaeologists discover. Secondly, Domańska's vitalist conception of death has the potential to create a platform for encounters between cultural-social archaeology and archaeometry. The structure of the argument in her book has much in common with the ways in which archaeological research is conducted. In my analysis of the Museo dell'Ara Pacis, I mentioned the two languages that archaeologists use today: the language of the humanities and that of the natural sciences. As Andrew Jones has noted, these vocabularies are alien to each other (Jones 2004). Ian Hodder, meanwhile, stated that the lack of synergies between the languages is a result of humanities-based archaeology being over theoretical while archaeometric approaches are far-removed from theorizing and lack precise programmatic objectives (Hodder 2012: 14). In Domańska's *Nekros: Ontology of the Dead Body*, these two approaches are brought together, as she demonstrates that it is possible to create a common language with respect to a research object that is also of significant interest to archaeologists.

If we treat life as a systemic category of archaeological research, we can imagine a completely new model for a critical museum. Turning towards life while conducting a re-evaluation of the concept of death can play a key role in conceiving a mode of archaeology that thus comes closer to bringing together the work in humanities-based archaeology and archaeometry, while at the same time treating culture and nature in symmetrical terms. Given the interdisciplinary and transdisciplinary profile of such a reorientation, it has the potential to rethink the archaeological museum. Were this to happen, it would constitute a genuine revolution in archaeological museum practices as such institutions would cease to be focused on dead objects, with vibrant, dynamic artefacts instead becoming central. Artefacts seen in terms of existence and constant transformation would thus possess the potential for an agency that could lead to engaged exhibitions oriented towards the present and future.

In the age of the Anthropocene, with a rapidly heating climate, mass species extinction, migration crises, neo- and post-capitalism, rising nationalisms and increasing environmental destruction, I am convinced that we need an archaeology that would make us aware of planetary threats while offering answers to future-related questions by addressing life in the past (Solli et al. 2011; Harrison 2016). Archaeological museums that could introduce a programme based on a conception of archaeology as a science of life (in the past) understood holistically would become the living embodiment of the idea of a "critical museum". The animation of artefacts and indicating that events and phenomena from the past also possess contemporary significance marks an attempt to escape the prevailing archaeological paradigm. One illustration of this are the debates over the beginnings of the Anthropocene, with teams of archaeologists moving the caesura between epochs back from the age of the industrial revolution to the neolithic revolution (Smith and Zeder 2013) or even to the time of migration by anatomically modern humans (Erlandson and Braje 2014). At the same time, I also point to projects that enable us to draw conclusions based on knowledge of the past while recognizing the value of archaeological research as a contribution to the latest debates on the planetary condition, ecosystems, environments, the present and future. What I am also interested in is the ongoing resonance of artefacts today as a way of questioning the idea that they are located exclusively in the past while instead emphasizing their material grounding in the present, the here-and-now.

My aim in outlining a strategy that I term the archaeology of all (living) things is to show and connect three phenomena that are crucial for contemporary archaeology. I was inspired to take this path by an exhibit in the Museo dell'Ara Pacis that resulted from research conducted by Giulia Caneva, who sought to produce a reconstruction of Ancient Roman consciousness of biodiversity. In presenting this strategy, I want to first of all draw attention to the fact that archaeology, even if divided into a humanities-based version and a natural science one, is a life science that reflects a horizontal model of knowledge; secondly, it has the potential to generate symmetry between human and non-human lives; thirdly, what emerges from such promising perspectives can provide subject matter for a new type of archaeological museum: a museum of life. At the same time, as I shall show, the museum of life as a location for the archaeology of all (living) things can operate on two registers: the epistemological, where life as a systemic category refers to the existence of problems and phenomena in reality, and the ontological, where the category of life refers to the essence and existence of things. In proposing these two possible modes of reading the archaeology of (living) things, I will refer to debates in the field of archaeological theory. I shall return to reflections on archaeology and archaeometry, while also referring to the project of symmetrical archaeology. My aim, though, is not to connect these distant discussions but rather to indicate their potential in building both epistemological (archaeology and archaeometry) and ontological (symmetrical archaeology) foundations for a life-oriented archaeological museum.

Life as an epistemological category: Archaeology and archaeometry

I supplemented my analysis of the archaeobotanical exhibit from the Museo dell'Ara Pacis with several remarks relating to archaeology's internal methodological schism. I showed how representatives of humanities-based archaeology and archaeological science, including archaeometry, approach material culture. What is the reason for the existence of these two different languages? Why is their conscious, theoretically grounded, integration not always possible? In response to these questions, I would like to outline a potential way out of this impasse while also indicating a limit condition for the emergence of archaeological museums that would be museums of life.

Arkadiusz Marciniak, a Polish archaeologist who has successfully integrated both approaches, noted that the schism within archaeology results first and foremost from ontological and epistemological historical legacies. He highlights that the goal of archaeologists identifying with the processual paradigm that has played a leading role in shaping archaeology since the 1960s was to give the discipline a status similar to that of the natural sciences:

> accepting the rules of these disciplines assumes that it is possible to apply procedures of explanation and that consequently it will be possible to create laws, rules and generalizations; in a word, this marks a path towards the nomothetization of archaeology.
>
> (Marciniak 1996: 24)

The critique of processual archaeology came from post-processual archaeologists who ruled out the possibility of mathematicizing research objects. Their approach was closely bound up with the humanities. Stressing the individual nature of sites and cultures, they rejected the processualists' positivist approach, promoting instead contextual analysis in place of building models and generalizations.

Beyond the theoretical-historical consistency that has given rise not only to two species of archaeologist but also to the two languages they employ, I would also stress the lack of mutual respect that is often manifested in arrogance within the archaeological community (Lidén and Eriksson 2013;

Lidén 2017). Pollard and Bray write of the widespread myth that "it is eas-
ier to teach a chemist or physicist enough archaeology to understand the
issues than it is to teach an archaeologist to understand chemistry or physics" (Pollard and Bray 2007: 255). Though rather depressing, this remark is
highly accurate and it leads me to consider a completely different issue. It
is difficult to assume that a recent archaeology graduate, or indeed even an
experienced archaeologist, would be equipped to conduct at the same time
sophisticated theoretical experiments, biological and physical analyses, and
identification of animal and human remains, while also finding associations
with all the strands of landscape archaeology. There is no need for archaeologists to be both chemists and humanities scholars. They can pick one path
or the other but should remain aware of the gaps in and insufficiencies of
their knowledge with respect to other areas of a discipline that is "a nexus
of the humanities, social science and natural science" (Edgeworth 2012: 76).
They can join research teams, turn towards specialist expertise or commis-
sion analyses and reports. What is most essential, however, is to become
aware of the essence of archaeological research, acquiring competence in
methods and knowledge of what the "other species" of archaeologist is
doing, thus combatting ignorance und unfamiliarity.

Adopting this ethos as an archaeologist is the limit condition for conducting research on life – broadly conceived – in the past. It should not be
forgotten that archaeological practice is always a collective endeavour, with
archaeologists working on excavations as a team. Not only interhuman but
also interdisciplinary integration as part of a team of specialists is essential
to the success of complex research while providing the only way of avoiding
reductionism. Without such a conception of collaboration, I see no way for
a united, coherent and at the same time transdisciplinary archaeology, of
the kind that is currently favoured by funding bodies (Sørensen 2017), to
emerge. Only such a mode of archaeology, based on mutual respect, consciousness and integration, stands a chance of meeting the challenges of
innovative research questions (Pollard and Bray 2007: 253).

The multisided analysis of artefacts by humanities archaeologists and
archaeological scientists collaborating within complex studies of the environment and landscape or the holistic study of lifeways, technologies, gen-
ders, and social roles and structures makes archaeology a discipline that is
fascinating, and not only to archaeologists but in its social resonance, too.
Its reception by society is shaped, as I have stressed repeatedly, first and foremost by museums. These institutions are not necessarily interested, though,
in reprofiling their exhibitions with respect to offering an illustration of interdisciplinary archaeology. This is why I found the archaeobotanical exhibit
in the Museo dell'Ara Pacis so interesting. It offers the first step towards the
construction of an archaeological museum positioned at the intersection of
disciplines, meaning that it would not display artefacts exclusively as the
research objects of humanities scholars but would also draw attention to how
their meanings are shaped through interdisciplinary research. A museum

actively engaged in visualizing current prevailing paradigms would present an opportunity to re-evaluate the socially and historically conditioned image of archaeological museums as art galleries.

The contemporary profile of archaeology as a discipline that is developing in the humanities, social sciences and natural sciences provides the basis for an important finding within my project that works towards remaking archaeological museums as museums of life. This finding relates to the nature of exhibits on display. Whatever their profile, archaeological museums collect and display highly diverse finds, ranging from tools and everyday equipment from the past, through human and animal remains, to architectural elements, decorations, ritual objects and art. They are viewed through the lenses of the methods of both the humanities and natural sciences. The object of archaeological research is per se nature-culture. Nevertheless, exhibition narratives in archaeological museums are primarily directed towards bringing forth the cultural qualities of museum objects. This is partly a result of historical legacies related both to the specialist nineteenth-century museums traditionally divided into art historical and natural history institutions, as well as to the traits of archaeology's earliest methodological tools that meant the discipline was positioned closer to the former type of museums.

I believe that transcending this classical model and instead highlighting the interdisciplinary nature of contemporary archaeology to reveal the status of archaeological objects as nature-culture right now offers a significant opportunity for a radical revolution in archaeological museum practices. The reasons for this are, I argue, numerous. From the perspective of the particular economy of museums, presenting the interdisciplinary nature of archaeology would have the potential to attract broader audiences, so not only those interested in history and culture but also those fascinated by the environment, its past and transformations. Moving through the field of life – of humans, animals and ecosystems – archaeological museums could create a broader narrative horizon that would be conducive to addressing current problems with exhibitions. In museums with such a profile, there would also be a certain revision of archaeology's role as "an auxiliary science of history" that could perhaps lead to a re-evaluation of the prevailing image of the discipline. Updating the epistemological dimensions of archaeological museums along these lines could present a significant opportunity, in my view, to outline and test many of the promising theoretical directions that archaeology is heading in. The new theoretical developments are transforming fundamentally our thinking about not only the past but also the present and future. Taking into account the current prioritization of inter- and transdisciplinary research in archaeology and by public funding bodies, it is important to ensure that its findings are both presented and challenged in museums. For Kristian Kristiansen, archaeology is currently entering a "post-paradigmatic" age that is disrupting the

hegemony of post-processualism in favour of an interdisciplinary archaeology that applies Big Data and conducts advanced research on aDNA
(ancient DNA), a fact that illustrates, he argues, how the discipline is
at the cusp of a third science revolution. In his article, "Towards a New
Paradigm? The Third Science Revolution and its Possible Consequences in
Archaeology", Kristiansen issues a forewarning, calling upon us to prepare
for a revolution that could, by developing further the natural science perspective in archaeology, lead to us viewing archaeological phenomena and
objects through a deterministic lens (Kristiansen 2014: 26). He argues that
the impending changes demand from archaeologists, above all, full social
engagement, as the familiar and widely implemented forms of disseminating archaeological knowledge, like public archaeology and community
archaeology, will prove insufficient. In light of the coming revolution, what
archaeology needs, Kristiansen argues, is critical debate and new modes of
public outreach that would address crucial issues on the local, global and
glocal scales relating to minority histories, migration histories and histories of gender and sexuality. While these approaches have been applied
and the themes addressed in the past already, they nevertheless remain
pertinent to us today. These challenges can be met by the new strategy for
archaeological museums that I am outlining here.

I understand the museal archaeology of all (living) things here as a means
of narrativizing and visualizing archaeology based on the results of interdisciplinary research that contribute to a broad outline of life in the past. What
I am interested in is the way exhibitions produce knowledge. Structured as
they are around the category of "life", exhibitions refer to continuously relevant themes, motifs and problems that have been studied in the past, still
resonate today and will shape the future.

Life and the essence of things: Symmetrical archaeology

There can be no archaeology or innovative inter- and transdisciplinary
research without things. Often it is those mundane, fragile and fragmentary
things that are crucial. What I propose, then, is another method of reading
the archaeology of (all) living things, one that is closer to the central challenge of this book, namely: promoting an ontological approach to artefacts.
Particularly instructive in this sense, then, is Bjørnar Olsen and Christopher
Witmore's project of symmetrical archaeology. This idea has inspired my
attempt to conceive of museum artefacts and exhibits as living things (Olsen
2012a, 2012b, 2013: 84–88, 98–101; Witmore 2014; Olsen and Witmore 2015,
2021). I consider this perspective to be important for several reasons. It fos-
ters the democratization of the objects of archaeological research (as small
artefacts are no less significant than impressive temples), which gives rise to
another of its advantages: it is not reductionist. The equal treatment of each
kind of find, whether human or non-human, also makes it possible to evade

the trap of anthropocentrism. Finally, this approach fits broader discussions in the humanities relating to a new approach to things. As Olsen writes,

> this new materialism actually puts archaeologists in a unique position not only to make their skills relevant and to contribute significantly on the intellectual scene, but also to realize the full potential of the archaeological project.
>
> (Olsen 2012b: 20)

Like Olsen, I believe that archaeology as the "study of old things" currently occupies a privileged position to mark out directions that reflections on the subject of things could take, sensibilizing us to their existence and indicating what we might learn from them.

The project of symmetrical archaeology, which above all gives voice to the actors being studied, regardless of whether they were once humans, animals, plants or tools, was introduced by Bjørnar Olsen partly with the aim of giving recognition to less spectacular and less sensational finds, so to mundane objects (Olsen 2013: 2–3, 18–19). The Norwegian archaeologist has opposed reading artefacts in terms of metaphorical, representative or embodied meanings, highlighting how interpretation has necessarily pushed objects to the margins while positioning humans centrally as creators or users. By putting symmetrical archaeology into practice, Olsen sought to find a remedy for the archaeological condition which has left "people without things" (Olsen 2013: 133–134). His project has, however, shifted the vector of interest not only towards things but also other non-human actors entangled in mutual relations and being-in-the-world. Olsen perceived his theoretical proposal not as something belonging to the realm of non-anthropocentric humanities but as an element of the political-ethical "return to things" that follows Latour in doing justice to the role of things in creating reality. Such approaches thus perceive society as something that emerges from the interactions of humans and non-humans, organic and non-organic beings and the nature-culture fusion. The symmetry Olsen proposes means, in this context, viewing the difference between entities (humans, plants, animals and things) not in terms of oppressive binary categories and negations, but as exchange, interaction, relations, collaboration and coexistence (Olsen 2013: 138–139). As I see it, the perspectives outlined here are explicitly political because, as Olsen shows, they sensitize people to the actors surrounding them and to human–non-human being in the world. Creating a symmetry of relations between people, things, animals and plants in the past and highlighting how the dichotomy of culture and nature is ancillary to how, for example, these concepts were treated in Ancient times.[1] This encourages, I believe, reflection on our current position in the world while strengthening the narratives pursued in environmental humanities and also in bio- and eco- approaches in the social sciences and cultural studies.

Christopher Witmore has connected this way of understanding symmetrical archaeology to new materialism. He outlined three limit conditions for symmetrical archaeology: (1) focusing on entities rather than processes; (2) understanding "the past-as-it-was" not as a starting point but as an outcome of the work of interpretation and of relations between the entities studied; (3) conceiving the world of things as indelibly linked to humans (correlationism) (Witmore 2014: 11). Following the new materialists, Witmore defines as entities everything that emphasizes the division of human and non-human, or ecofacts and artefacts. Drawing on Karen Barad and Graham Harman, he writes that "objects are never finite" but "always infinite" and therefore cannot be treated reductively (Witmore 2014: 8, 18). These remarks bring him close to collapsing the classical definition of archaeology suggested by Renfrew and Bahn mentioned at the outset of this chapter. Witmore also seems to recognize that the discipline of archaeology can thrive in connection with the latest symmetrical and non-reductionist approaches to things (Witmore 2014: 21). While I fully agree with him, I will continue to maintain that archaeology is the discipline of old things while emphasizing my attachment to the concept of "life" that I have "extracted" from the traditional definition of archaeology that I seek to contest.

I am encouraged in this endeavour by the project of everyday aesthetics, developed by the Japanese philosopher Yuriko Saito, which could be attractive for archaeological museums. She understands aesthetics as something based not on a traditional honorific and contemplative approach to objects, phenomena or activities, but rather on active deeds of an aesthetic nature. Reflecting on the dusty objects that we clean and the broken ones we repair, Saito highlights the forms of care that are shaped in the course of everyday contact with things. Furthermore, she sensitizes us to the fact that many of our everyday experiences of things have an ethical dimension reflected in respect, considerateness, sensitivity and care (Saito 2007: 222). In this sense, her project calling for an everyday aesthetics draws attention to, or perhaps even strengthens, Olsen and Witmore's arguments relating to the political-ethical return to things and the concomitant symmetrical archaeology. Being-in-the-world always was and remains a being-with-things towards which we cannot be indifferent. Regardless of whether we are able to exhaust their sensory properties or, on the contrary, never manage to encounter and explore their infinite nature, we nevertheless live with things and treat them in a special way.

As places whose remit is above all caring for things by collecting, storing and conserving them, museums should be institutions that support an ethical approach to things, as encouraged by Olsen and Witmore in the field of archaeology, while drawing on the ethos described by Saito. Things demand action, they move us, intrigue us and encourage us to think or act. In the age of post-capitalist accumulation of things whose relevance to archaeology is convincingly outlined by Alfredo González-Ruibal (2019), what is necessary is particular sensitivity and care towards things. I am calling neither for anthropomorphizing things nor for the dehumanization of people through contact with things, but rather for a recognition of the symmetry that is connected to and produces greater respect for and greater considerateness towards the material world. Our everyday life is being-with-things. This is as true today as it was 1,000 or 2,000 years ago.

Vibrant matter and living things

Thinking about artefacts in terms of being, existence, change and continuity, granting them traits of life rather than rendering them as dead objects that have gone out of use and become "detritus", mobilizes completely new potential for exhibitions. Guided by the distinction of epistemological and ontological conceptions of life, as outlined at the start of this chapter, I will now demonstrate how artefacts can be relevant exhibits for discussions relating to future life and the current ethos towards things.

Something that was fundamental in inspiring the discussions in this chapter was an exhibit in the Museo dell'Ara Pacis in Rome. Telling a story about biodiversity, the exhibit encouraged enquiry into how our approach to ancient plants has changed. How does our knowledge and recognition of flora differ from ancient Romans' approaches? What do we know about flora? Offering an illustration of the significant botanical consciousness that was present in Ancient society, the exhibit highlights three crucial issues; firstly, it provides powerful evidence of how people in Antiquity could serve as role models for us and how much we could learn from them; secondly, it signals subtly yet clearly that today there has been a decline in sensitivity towards the world of nature and that we know relatively little about it; thirdly, and finally, the exhibit provoked questions about our current relationship to nature and what shapes it. In this way, the artefacts presented in one exhibit became involved in serious debates on our current relationship to the environment and its mindless exploitation. It is worth noting at this juncture that the same type of exhibit that I described in the previous chapter is also evident in the Acropolis Museum in Athens. Here, however, the stone plants were not narrativized in such a way that would enable them to address current problems and encourage visitors to pose crucial questions.

The pioneering exhibit in the Museo dell'Ara Pacis would not have been exhibited in such a form were it not for the interdisciplinary research conducted by Giulia Caneva. This leads me to the conclusion that the construction of engaged exhibits demands multi-level, interdisciplinary research. The exhibits familiar to us from typological arrangements could be displayed in a completely different fashion were the findings of interdisciplinary research to be applied to them. Lipid analysis of vessels could provide information on the diet of ancient populations, enabling the verification of ancient cookery books. Petrographic analysis of the material used for sculptures could offer insight into the routes that it had traversed in the past. Jewellery decorated with animal motifs could tell the history of which animals were known in particular geographical regions. Tracing popular archaeological texts in the daily press, reading short reports and analysing archaeological posts on social media has affirmed my conviction that such approaches could provide microhistories of archaeological objects and it is this kind of material that indeed interests broad audiences. Such microhistories could also form part of museum narratives. Building bridges between us and our ancestors, touching upon areas that form our everyday lives in past and present, is the stuff of the future of museums.

Rather than speaking about the archaeology of migration, animal archaeology, the archaeology illness or medical archaeology, why do museums insist on addressing themes that interest only a small group of recipients? Indeed, archaeology is now dealing with those areas that are marginalized by museums. What archaeological museums need therefore are narratives that could construct a new sensitivity towards the past, understood as being the life of humans in the past together with their relations to the environment and non-human entities that continue to resonate into the present. What could we learn from archaeological museums about our current age? What can archaeology teach us about the challenges we are seeking to address today? How could museums illustrate contemporary planetary threats? First and foremost, they could achieve this by abandoning a purely cultural paradigm and instead including in their narratives exhibits that evoke reflections in visitors, giving rise to questions and revisions to existing relations with the environment. Suited to such a role are exhibits that illustrate interdisciplinary research, like the graphic archaeobotanical reproduction displayed in the Museo dell'Ara Pacis that I have analysed here. By including zooarchaeolgical exhibits into museum narratives, shedding new light on remains (by, for example, presenting research relating to the causes of death) and recreating primeval landscapes that have little in common with our contemporary surroundings, archaeological museums could become critical institutions. By placing emphasis on what we can learn from the past and how this can influence the formation of contemporary reality, museums position themselves as engaged, active participants in shaping our everyday lives. There is no shortage of fascinating research that has contributed to getting audiences engaged with planetary problems, encouraged reflection and made people aware of how to combat a global crisis.

William Rathje's visionary research conducted at the University of Arizona in 1970s had exactly such a dimension. Rathje employed archaeological analogies as part of the Tucson Garbage Project, which explored the extent of degradation at rubbish dumps in the context of cultural consumerism (Rathje and Murphy 1992; Rathje 2012). Rathje showed, among other things, that paper degrades slowly and is therefore not as environmentally friendly as often claimed. The "garbology" that he founded constitutes, I would argue, the best evidence for value of seeing archaeology as a life science, with research in this field liberating an engaged attitude, thus potentially leading to a transformation of ways of thinking while encouraging a sense of greater responsibility for the planet.

Despite interdisciplinary archaeology increasingly offering answers to many questions that are of interest to contemporary audiences – ranging from those concerning human-animal relations through those addressing migrations and the reasons for them to those examining when cancerous cells evolved – the material basis enabling us to pose universally significant questions is, in the case of archaeology, almost always material remnants and traces of life in the past. I thus understand life in the context of artefacts-as-exhibits in two ways: on the one hand, it constitutes a potential theme for framing artefacts within discussions about what is socially significant, as outlined above; on the other hand, however, I perceive in them an ontological pathway that makes it possible to give voice to agency, biologism and the existence of things. This is what I will turn to below.

An example of an exhibition that reveals vibrant artefacts is evident in part of the prehistorical section of the Neues Museum in Berlin (Figure 8.1). The artefacts on show there are fragmented, damaged and displayed in the same mass amounts that they are found in at archaeological sites, hence they are presented simply gathered up in piles or in the course of conservation. They are thus indicative of the materialist approach to exhibits, offering a perfect summary of archaeology as the science of old things. The "uncomfortable", troubling matter, burdened by historical legacies, that for many decades discouraged archaeologists from engaging in research on mundane objects, is used in the Neues Museum to provide a forceful revelation of the object of archaeological research. Usually, it is only in their final stage that studies provide an impression of a "complete", totalized whole, i.e. a reconstruction of the past. The mass of mundane, everyday objects from the past, including even damaged vessels undergoing conservation, lead us behind the scenes, lifting the veil on archaeologists' tools to tell us about the discovery of mysterious, unstable objects that change before our eyes. Museums shape a particular "truth of matter" that to a large extent relies on making objects dynamic, showing them "as they are" and pointing out to visitors a series of processes taking place either on the material level of an artefact that are independent of human interventions or within the framework of the mechanisms, controlled by conservators, that give voice to the agency of matter. The objects on display in the Neues Museum are liberated; they are not treated reductively but are shown "as they are", fully entitled to transform, fully entitled to their own life. Stressing this active, dynamic and – to use Jane Bennett's term – vibrant matter restores things' inherent agency and underlines the transformative forces that were denied objects within the Cartesian paradigm.

Conducting research inspired by symmetrical archaeology and new materialism with the aim of grasping the ontology of artefacts and exhibits, I often considered whether it is at all possible to transfer the postulates of

Figure 8.1 Neues Museum, permanent exhibition, fragment depicting conservational work on artefacts, © Staatliche Museen zu Berlin, Museum für Vor- und Frühgeschichte, photo: Achim Kleuker.

theories oriented towards things and materiality to museums. Encounters with the objects on display led me to revise my ideas repeatedly. Nevertheless, I have returned here to reflect on the Neues Museum, which I visited in 2016 and 2019, with the intention of offering an answer to the question of how to capture the ontology of things as part of exhibits. My proposed strategy involves demonstrating the effects that artefacts have on their surroundings as living, vibrant, unstable objects. One result could be conservational narratives of the kind that emerged in the Acropolis Museum: spectacular archaeological prostheses used to uphold the fragile material of an object; another could be presentation formats similar to those in the Neues Museum, with damaged everyday objects being tended to by museum curators. The ontology of artefacts-as-exhibits is revealed by *doing*: by describing, analysing, conserving or by other procedures forming part of archaeologists' everyday lives. Deeds motivated by their duty of care towards the ongoing lives of things provide us with a vital lesson: they teach us respect, care and sensitivity towards the material reality that we inhabit.

Note

1. This is illustrated perfectly by Philippe Descola in his brief chapter, "The Roman Landscape, the Hercynian Forest, and Romantic Nature" (Descola 2013: 53–56).

Conclusion
Towards a Critical Archaeological Museum

The focus of this book has been on tracing the transformation of artefacts into exhibits within museum spaces. The aim of the investigations presented here was to demonstrate the flows occurring between institutions housing exhibitions and theories generated in academia. Starting with reflections on the ontology of artefacts and exhibits, before then analysing two selected exhibitions, I have shown how exhibition frameworks based upon theories that are currently enjoying popularity in archaeology can endow finds with dynamism and animate them, transforming, discovering and expanding their meanings. I have recognized that theories play a central and formative role in constructing the multivalent nature of artefacts-as-exhibits. By juxtaposing the prevailing paradigms of a methodologically and theoretically rich archaeology, I have demonstrated how the same kind of artefact can serve as malleable material that is open to multiple interpretations and theoretical multiplicity. Outlining three strategies archaeological museums could adopt – prosthetic archaeology, the preposterous art of archaeology and the archaeology of (all) living things – I have underlined at the same time how the mediation of archaeology is to a significant extent dependent both upon socially desirable interpretations and upon the available and popular methods of presenting, in both senses of the word, the past. My reflections on the current state of practices in archaeological museums and my attempts to point to affirmative and "good" exhibition practices as alternatives to those that "kill" artefacts by placing them in cabinets led me to the conclusion that given today's theoretical diversity in archaeology, the spatial organization of museums demands particular vision and imagination. Taking inspiration from various theories and approaches, museums should ensure exhibitions correspond to the current state of the discipline and also be more courageous in putting new perspectives to the test. There can be no critical museum without archaeological imagination.

The ideas developed in this book together with my proposal for a critical archaeological museum and a museum of life emerge from and contribute to discussions on challenges currently facing archaeology and

DOI: 10.4324/9781003327851-13

heritage studies. It is possible to highlight three limit conditions, necessary for such a museum to come into existence:

- the application of the latest theories;
- attempting to create sensibilizing narratives that are relevant to our age;
- engaging the archaeological imagination.[1]

The correlation of exhibition theory and practice as proposed by the late Polish art historian, art critic and director of the National Museum in Warsaw Piotr Piotrowski, is something that stems from the findings of research conducted in New Museology in the 1990s and 2000s. As numerous other researchers have shown, museums have functioned and continue to function as mirrors that visually reflect disciplinary realities as well as what is deemed socially significant. Museums are the calling card of archaeology, justifying its social usefulness. Archaeological museums should not be heritage parks that present (and petrify) models developed in the nineteenth century, but should instead offer a space for new theories and research methods that provide a focus for vibrant discussions, while at the same time addressing current challenges facing archaeologists. This demand results from, among other things, the need to provide a justification for the social usefulness and importance of the discipline, raise awareness of the research conducted in the field and demonstrate how public funds are being used in archaeological studies. In continental Europe at least, archaeology is a discipline maintained by European Union, national and regional funding that is generated from tax revenue.[2] Bearing in mind these funding models, archaeologists have a particular responsibility to present their discipline publicly in a way that reflects their actual research practices, rather than according to the anachronistic nineteenth-century model that has little in common with current realities. On the other hand, representing theory in exhibitions creates an opportunity to renegotiate research methods or even attempt to secure their legitimacy as prevailing paradigms. The history of exhibitions being dominated by the typological model can teach us many lessons. Facing up to the legacies of this exhibition model poses a challenge that could certainly be met by new theories that would thus demonstrate their attractiveness and legitimacy.

Referring to Marshall McLuhan's prophetic phrase, "the medium is the message" (McLuhan 2003 [1964]), I would like to stress that the contemporary tendency towards exhibition media, tools and multimedia leads to the content (or message) of exhibitions losing significance. Outlining my idea of prosthetic archaeology, I placed particular emphasis on museums' prevailing technophilia, something that often leads to the original artefacts becoming lost along with the fascinating histories that they contain. The problem, then, is not "how" archaeology is put on display but "what" is exhibited. This is indeed an ontological question, one that is fundamental both to what I address in this book and to the critical archaeological museum. Archaeological museums do not necessarily need to employ the tools of the digital turn or use contemporary art, two forms that I have examined in this book, in order to engage with questions that are relevant to our contemporary situation and which sensitize us to the problems of our world. They could instead use countless other media to frame artefacts, drawing out the objects' important histories and, above all, engage visitors. In order to meet this challenge and become critical institutions, archaeological museums need to activate the archaeological imagination. While we do demonstrate sensitivity to art, what we lack is archaeological imagination. And it is museums that should provide spaces to train it.

The final limit condition draws inspiration from a study by Michael Shanks, with his ideas permeating this book throughout. Shanks defines the archaeological imagination as the creative impulse that is at the core of archaeology and inspires efforts to "recreate the world behind the ruin, to reanimate the people behind the sherd of antique pottery", with this impulse inscribed into the "discourses and institutions commonly associated with modernity", such as museums, academia, legislation and conservation (Shanks 2012: 25). The archaeological imagination is, he argues, "rooted in a sensibility, a pervasive set of attitudes towards traces and remains, towards memory, time and temporality, the fabric of history" (Shanks 2012: 65). Shanks emphasizes that it demands constant effort, curiosity, doubt and patience in encounters with material traces and remains, as it continues to influence how we represent the past (Shanks 2012: 65). If we do need to search for a crisis of archaeology (Swain 2007: 8; Bintliff and Pearce 2011), then it is to be found, in my view, in the crisis of the imagination that paralyses not only some institutions responsible for public engagement and outreach but also archaeologists themselves as they conduct their research and seek to develop narratives.

Does this mean, then, that the archaeological imagination is fading, with the past shrinking accordingly? Are we no longer capable of approaching the past with fantasy? Have we lost our sensibility towards fragments, ruins and traces? I believe that the pursuit of objectivity that results from archaeology being transferred into the realm of the natural sciences bears some responsibility for the disregard for "telling stories" and constructing narratives that sensitize us to things from the past and their lasting presence. Although the idea of aura might be deemed old-fashioned and imagination is perceived as an expression of scientific incompetence, I nevertheless believe that they hold some promise. As André Malraux noted when writing about the museum of the imagination, such an institution constitutes a museum of transformation that in a rather banal yet inexorable fashion completely changes the past and present. Following this line, in my project for a critical museum of archaeology I favour the kind of representation that is based on the archaeological imagination and offers insight into change. Such changes might be understood as theoretical negotiations, updates and revisions of opinions that emerge, as Malraux also stresses, from the changing state of knowledge. The archaeological imagination promotes an idea of theories as flows rather than as fixed dogmas.

The transformations that are the focus of this book are set in motion by permitting the imagination to enter archaeological discourse. Such a move is encouraged by the archaeologists Elisabeth S. Greene and Justin Leidwanger, who presented a critical analysis of an artwork created by the British contemporary artist and celebrity Damien Hirst (Greene and Leidwanger 2017). In 2017, in parallel to the Venice Biennale, Hirst put on an exhibition called *Treasures from the Wreck of the Unbelievable* in two huge halls, the Punta della Dogana and Palazzo Grassi. On display were artefacts supposedly discovered on the wreckage of a Roman ship that sank in the Indian Ocean and was owned by the freed Antiochian slave Amotanius. His collection included countless treasures and wealth, including Egyptian, Greek and Roman sculptures, Maya and Chinese artefacts, as well a statue of Mickey Mouse and the *Jungle Book* characters Mowgli and Baloo. Hirst undertook the painstaking work of conserving the objects apparently discovered by underwater archaeologists. Still, many of the objects on display bear traces of damage, are covered in sea flora and are marked by patina. The exhibition was accompanied by a huge catalogue of artefacts (Hirst et al. 2017), archaeological documentation from the excavation and recovery, photographs and drawings identifying various types and analogies.

The wonderfully conceived history of the slave Amotanius, who does not appear in any historical record but was modelled on a figure in Cicero's speeches aimed against the Sicilian governor and collector Verres, is perhaps the most spectacular display of archaeological imagination. The eccentric Hirst spent ten years preparing a project that combines pop-cultural motifs drawn from Indiana Jones and Titanic (Greene and Leidwanger 2017: 2). According to Greene and Leidwanger, the work demonstrates the significant need for attractive archaeological stories that transcend the dimensions of the discovery and commodification of artefacts. While archaeologists have criticized Hirst for a work in which they perceive expressions of imperialist and neo-colonialist tendencies as well as a reduction of artefacts to the role of works of art and commodities subject to the rules of the market, I would rather focus on what archaeologists might learn from this piece. It is quite simply a work to inspire the archaeological imagination.

Greene and Leidwanger believe that Hirst's project perpetuates an anachronistic approach to archaeology, maintaining an image of archaeologists as people who exploit heritage objects to sell on the open market. They thus compare Hirst to Arthur Evans, the famous discoverer of Knossos who was accused, most notably, of a rather "free" and therefore certainly non-scientific "reconstruction" of the mythical King Minos' heritage. It is difficult to deny the aptness of this analogy given Hirst's description of the history of the *Unbelievable* ship and the likewise rather incredible artefacts. At the same time, the critics overlook what archaeology owes to researchers such as Evans. Without them, there would be none of the fascination and excitement that Hirst managed to recreate with his exhibition in Venice. For the eccentric artist, the possibilities are boundless. And this applies all the more so to archaeology and its narratives that are inspired by the archaeological imagination, sensitivity towards the past and curiosity.

Crossing fantasy with reality could become a strength of a critical museum of archaeology, something that is a political project, too, because it is based on a symmetry of the role of objects in creating history and visions of the past while at the same time offering a response to the challenges of the present and future. Encounters between the archaeological imagination, on the one hand, and the realities of practice and current theories, as well as current challenges sensitizing us to the here-and-now of narratives, on the other, can help affirm the status of archaeology as a universally important discipline that is not simply oriented towards the past but rather draws on findings from the past and orients them towards the future. Archaeology involves visionary work on material objects from the past that in turn enable us to understand the present and anticipate the future.

Notes

1. I am aware of the similarities between my proposition and those suggested in the 1990s already by Michael Shanks and Christopher Tilley (1992). The reflections inspired by current research thus draw attention to the fact that not much has changed in archaeological museum practices over the past three decades.
2. This important aspect is not often discussed in research on archaeological museums conducted primarily in the US and UK (Kristiansen 2014: 13).

References

Adamson, W. L., 2001. Avant-garde Modernism and Italian Fascism: Cultural Politics in the Era of Mussolini. *Journal of Modern Italian Studies*, 6(2), 230–248.

Alberti, S. J. J. M., 2005. Objects and the Museum. *Isis*, 4, 559–571.

Alfred Seinland, 2018. Available from: https://www.albertina.at/en/exhibitions/alfred-seiland/ [Accessed 29 June 2022].

Allison, P. M. (ed.), 1999. *The Archaeology of Household Activities*, London – New York: Routledge.

Andersson, D. T., 2014. Trusted Vagueness. The Language of Things and the Order of Incompleteness, in *Ruin Memories. Materiality, Aesthetics and the Archaeology of the Recent Past*, eds. B. Olsen & Þ Pétursdóttir, London – New York: Routledge, 33–40.

Ankersmit, F., 2002. *Historical Representation*, Stanford: Stanford University Press.

Ankersmit, F., 2004. *Wprowadzenie do wydania polskiego*, trans. E. Domańska, in *Narracja, reprezentacja, doświadczenie. Studia z teorii historiografii*, ed. E. Domańska, Kraków: Universitas, 29–54.

Artribune Redazione, 2013. *Arte contemporanea ai Fori Romani. Tutte le foto in anteprima della mostra Post-classici, il video-speach con il curatore. E un appello al Ministro Bray*. Available from: http://www.artribune.com/tribnews/2013/05/arte-contemporanea-ai-fori-romani-tutte-le-foto-in-anteprima-della-mostra-post-classici-il-video-speach-con-il-curatore-e-un-appello-al-ministro-bray/ [Accessed 1 August 2017].

Arvanitis, K. & C. Zuanni, 2021. Editorial: Digital (and) Materiality in Museums. *Museum & Society*, 19(2), 143–148.

Bailey, D., 2017a. Art/Archaeology: What Value Artistic-Archaeological Collaboration? *Journal of Contemporary Archaeology*, 4(2), 246–256.

Bailey, D., 2017b. Disarticulate–Repurpose–Disrupt: Art/Archaeology. *Cambridge Archaeological Journal*, 27(4), 691–701.

Bailey, D., 2018. *Breaking the Surface. An Art/Archaeology of Prehistoric Architecture*, Oxford: Oxford University Press.

Bal, M., 1996. The Discourse of the Museum, in *Thinking about Exhibitions*, eds. B. W. Ferguson, R. Greenberg & S. Nairne, New York: Routledge, 201–218.

Bal, M., 1999. *Quoting Caravaggio: Contemporary Art, Preposterous History*, Chicago – London: University of Chicago Press.

Barad, K., 2007. *Meeting the Universe Halfway. Quantum Physics and the Entanglement of Matter and Meaning*, Durham – London: Duke University Press.

Barceló, J., 2018. *The Dark Side of Digital Archaeology.* Presentation delivered at the 46. Conference of Computer Applications and Quantitative Methods in Archaeology (CAA 2018).

Barkan, L., 1999. *Unearthing the Past: Archaeology and Aesthetics in the Making of Renaissance Culture*, New Haven – London: Yale University Press.

Benjamin, W., 1979. On Language as Such and on the Language of Man, in *One-Way Street, and Other Writings*, eds. E. Jephcott & K. Shorter, London: NLB, 107–123.

Bennett, J., 2010. *Vibrant Matter: A Political Ecology of Things*, Durham – London: Duke University Press.

Bennett, T., 1998. Speaking to the Eyes: Museums, Legibility and the Social Order, in *The Politics of Display. Museums, Science, Culture*, ed. S. Macdonald, London – New York: Routledge, 22–30.

Benton, T., 2000. Epigraphy and Fascism. *Bulletin of the Institute of Classical Studies. Supplement*, 75, 163–192.

Beresford, J. M., 2015. Museum of Light: The New Acropolis Museum and the Campaign to Repatriate the Elgin Marbles. *Architecture MPS*, 7(1), 1, 1–34.

Beresford, J. M., 2016. The Caryatids in the New Acropolis Museum: Out of Sight, Out of Light, Out of Mind. *Journal of Conservation and Museum Studies*, 14(1), 3–16.

Berggren, Å, N. Dell'Unto, M. Forte, S. Haddow, I. Hodder, J. Issavi, N. Lercari, C. Mazzucato, A. Mickel & J. S. Taylor, 2015. Revisiting Reflexive Archaeology at Çatalhöyük: Integrating Digital and 3D Technologies at the Trowel's Edge. *Antiquity*, 89(344), 433–448.

Bergson, H., 1991. *Matter and Memory*, trans. N. M. Paul & W. S. Palmer, New York: Zone Books.

Bernard Tschumi Architects, 2011a. *Acropolis Museum.* Available from: http://www.tschumi.com/projects/2/ [Accessed 19 January 2017].

Bernard Tschumi Architects, 2011b. *Architectural Fact Sheet.* Available from: http://www.theacropolismuseum.gr/en/content/museum-history [Accessed 19 January 2017].

Bille, M. & T. F. Sørensen, 2007. An Anthropology of Luminosity. The Agency of Light. *Journal of Material Culture*, 12(3), 263–284.

Binford, L., 1962. Archaeology as Anthropology. *American Antiquity*, 28(2), 217–225.

Bintliff, J. & M. Pearce (eds.), 2011. *The Death of Archaeological Theory?* Oxford: Oxbow.

Bonaventura, P. & A. Jones (eds.), 2011. *Sculpture and Archaeology*, Surrey – Burlington: Routledge.

Brenna, B., 2013. The Frames of Specimens: Glass Cases in Bergen Museum around 1900, in *Animals on Display, The Creaturely in Museums, Zoos, and Natural History*, eds. L. E. Thorsen, K. A. Rader & A. Dodd, Pennsylvania: Pennsylvania State University Press, 37–57.

Brown, D., 2007. Te Ahu Hiko: Digital Cultural Heritage and Indigenous Objects, People, and Environments, in *Theorizing Digital Cultural Heritage. A Critical Discourse*, eds. F. Cameron & S. Kenderdine, Cambridge: The MIT Press, 77–92.

Bucci, C. A., 2006. *Il mio mosaico su piani sfalsati bagno di luce su tessere di pietra.* Available from: http://ricerca.repubblica.it/repubblica/archivio/repubblica/2006/04/22/il-mio-mosaico-su-piani-sfalsati-bagno.html [Accessed 1 August 2017].

Burström, M., 2013. Fragments as Something More: Archaeological Experience and Reflection, in *Reclaiming Archaeology: Beyond the Tropes of Modernity*, ed. A. González-Ruibal, London – New York: Routledge, 311–322.

Cameron, F., 2007. Beyond the Cult of the Replicant – Museums and Historical Digital Objects: Traditional Concerns, New Discourses, in *Theorizing Digital Cultural Heritage. A Critical Discourse*, eds. F. Cameron & S. Kenderdine, Cambridge: The MIT Press, 49–76.

Caneva, G., 2010. *I codice botanico di Augusto. Roma – Ara Pacis. Parlare al Popolo attraverso le immagini della natura/The Augustus Botanical Code. Rome – Ara Pacis. Speaking to the People through the Images of Nature*, Roma: Gangemi Editore.

Cannistraro, P. V., 1972. Mussolini's Cultural Revolution: Fascist or Nationalist? *Journal of Contemporary History*, 7, 3(4), 115–139.

Caraher, W., 2019. Slow Archaeology, Punk Archaeology, and the 'Archaeology of Care'. *European Journal of Archaeology*, 22(3), 372–385.

Carassava, A., 2009. *In Athens Museum Is an Olympian Feat.* Available from: http://www.nytimes.com/2009/06/20/arts/design/20acropolis.html?_r=1 [Accessed 16 August 2016].

Careri, G., 1994. *Bernini. Flights of Love, the War of Devotion*, trans. L. Lappin, Chicago: University of Chicago Press.

Caskey, M., 2011. Perceptions of the New Acropolis Museum. *American Journal of Archaeology*, 15(1). Published online. Available from: https://www.ajaonline.org/online-review-museum/911 [Accessed 17 January 2023].

Cass, N., G. Park & A. Powell (eds.), 2020. *Contemporary Art in Heritage Spaces*, London – New York: Routledge.

Champion, E. & B. Dave, 2007. Dialing Up the Past, in *Theorizing Digital Cultural Heritage. A Critical Discourse*, eds. F. Cameron & S. Kenderdine, Cambridge: The MIT Press, 333–348.

Chan, A. A., 2017. Translating Archaeology for the Public. Empowering and Engaging Museum Goers with Past, in *Museums and Archaeology*, ed. R. Skeates, New York – London: Routledge, 522–541.

Charmaz, K., 2014. *Constructing Grounded Theory*, Los Angeles: SAGE.

Childe, V. G., 1951. *Social Evolution*, London: Watts & Co.

Chittock, H. & J. Valdez-Tullett (eds.), 2016a. *Archaeology with Art*, Oxford: Archaeopress.

Chittock, J. & J. Valdez-Tullett (eds.), 2016b. Archaeology with Art: A Short Introduction to This Book, in *Archaeology with Art*, Oxford: Archaeopress, V–VIII.

Classen, C. & D. Howes, 2006. The Museum as Sensescape: Western Sensibilities and Indigenous Artifacts, in *Sensible Objects. Colonialism, Museums and Material Culture*, eds. C. Gosden, E. Edwards & R. B. Phillips, Oxford – New York: Berg, 199–222.

Cohen, B., 2010. Deconstructing the Acropolis. *American Journal of Archaeology*, 114, 745–753.

Cohen, J., 2015. *Stone. An Ecology of Inhuman*, Minneapolis – London: University of Minnesota Press.

Copplestone, D. & Dunne, 2017. Digital Media, Creativity, Narrative Structure and Heritage. *Internet Archaeology*, 44. Published online. Accessible from: https://intarch.ac.uk/journal/issue44/2/index.html [Accessed 17 January 2023].

Currie, G., 2012. The Master of the Masek Beds: Handaxes, Art, and the Minds of Early Humans, in *The Aesthetic Mind: Philosophy and Psychology*, eds. E. Schellekens & P. Goldie, Oxford – New York: Oxford University Press, 9–31.

Dallas, C., 2015. Curating Archaeological Knowledge in the Digital Continuum: From Practice to Infrastructure. *Open Archaeology*, 1, 176–207.

Danielsson, I.-M. B., F. Fahlander & Y. Sjöstrand (eds.), 2012. Encountering Imagery: Materialities, Perceptions, Relations. *Stockholm Studies in Archaeology 57*, Stockholm: Stockholm University.

Davies, H. & E. Turpin (eds.), 2015. *Art in the Anthropocene. Encounters among Aesthetics, Politics, Environments and Epistemologies*, London: Open Humanities Press.

de Certeau, M., 1988. *The Practice of Everyday Life*, trans. S. Rendall, Berkeley: University of California Press.

Derrida, J., 1979. The Parergon, trans. C. Owens. *October*, 9, 3–41.

Derrida, J., 2006. *Specters of Marx. The State of the Debt, the Work of Mourning and the New International*, trans. P. Kamuf, New York – London: Routledge.

Descola, P., 2013. *Beyond Nature and Culture*, trans. J. Lloyd, Chicago – London: University of Chicago Press.

Deshoulières, V., 2014. *La voix d'Arkhè: le paradigme archéologique dans la création moderne et contemporaine*, Paris: Hermann.

Diderot, D., 2011. The Salon 1767, in *Ruins*, ed. B. Dillon, London – Cambridge: Whitechapel Gallery, 22.

Domańska, E., 2004. Miejsce Franka Ankersmita w narratywistycznej filozofii historii, in F. Ankersmit, *Narracja, reprezentacja, doświadczenie. Studia z teorii historiografii*, ed. E. Domańska, Kraków: Universitas, 5–28.

Domańska, E., 2017. *Nekros. Wprowadzenie do ontologii martwego ciała*, Warszawa: Wydawnictwo Naukowe PWN.

Domańska, E., 2018. Affirmative Humanities, trans. P. Vickers. *History–Theory–Criticism*, 1, 9–26.

Dornieden, T., A. A. Gorbushina & W. E. Krumbein, 2000. Patina, in *Of Microbes and Art*, eds. O. Ciferri, P. Tiano & G. Mastromei, Boston: Springer, 105–119.

Dudley, S. H. (ed.), 2010a. *Museum Materialities. Objects, Engagements, Interpretations*, London – New York: Routledge.

Dudley, S. H. (ed.), 2010b. Museum Materialities: Objects, Sense and Feeling, in *Museum Materialities. Objects, Engagements, Interpretations*, London – New York: Routledge, 1–18.

Dudley, S. H. (ed.), 2012. *Museum Objects. Experiencing the Properties of Things*, London – New York: Routledge.

Earl, G. 2013. Modelling in Archaeology: Computer Graphic and Other Digital Pasts. *Perspectives on Science*, 21(2), 226–244.

Earl, G., V. Porcelli, C. Papadopoulos, G. Beale, M. Harrison, H. Pagi & S. Keay, 2013. Formal and Informal Analysis of Rendered Space: The Basilica Portuense, in *Computational Approaches to Archaeological Spaces*, eds. A. Bevan & M. Lake, Walnut Creek: Routledge, 265–305.

Edensor, T., 2005. *Industrial Ruins: Spaces, Aesthetics, and Materiality*, Oxford: Berg.

Edgeworth, M., 2012. Follow the Cut, Follow the Rhythm, Follow the Material.... *Norwegian Archaeological Review*, 45, 76–92.

Edgeworth, M., 2013. The Clearing: Archaeology's Way of Opening the World, in *Reclaiming Archaeology: Beyond the Tropes of Modernity*, ed. A. González-Ruibal, London – New York: Routledge, 33–43.

Edgeworth, M., 2015. From Spade-Work to Screen-Work. New Forms of Archaeological Discovery in Digital Space, in *Visualization in the Age of Computerization*, eds. A. Carusi, A. S. Hoel, T. Webmoor & S. Woolgar, New York – Oxon: Routledge, 40–58.

Edgeworth, M., 2016. Grounded Objects: Archaeology and Speculative Realism. *Archaeological Dialogues*, 23(1), 93–113.

Edgeworth, M., J. Benjamin, B. Clarke, Z. Crossland, E. Domańska, A. C. Gorman, P. Graves-Brown, E. C. Harris, M. J. Hudson, J. M. Kelly, V. J. Paz, M. A. Salerno, C. Witmore & A. Zarankin, 2014. Archaeology of the Anthropocene. *Journal of Contemporary Archaeology*, 1(1), 73–132.

Elliott, C., 2017. Bandages, Bitumen, Bodies and Business – Egyptian Mummies as Raw Materials. *Aegyptiaca. Journal of the History of Reception of Ancient Egypt*, 1, 26–47.

Ellis, C., 2004. *The Ethnographic I: A Methodological Novel about Autoethnography*, Walnut Creek: Altamira Press.

Erlandson, J. M. & T. J. Braje Todd, 2014. Archeology and the Anthropocene. *Anthropocene*, 4, 1–7.

Favro, D., 2012. To Be or Not to Be in Past Spaces: Thoughts on Roman Immersive Reconstructions, in *Re-Presenting the Past: Archaeology through Image and Text*, eds. S. Bond & S. Houston, Oxford: Oxbow Books, 151–168.

Filippopoulou, E., 2017. The Acropolis Museum: Contextual Contradictions, Conceptual Complexities. *Museum International*, 69(1–2), 22–3.

Flannery, K. V., 1967. Culture History vs. Cultural Process: A Debate in American Archaeology. *Scientific American*, 217(2), 119–127.

Forte, M., 2007. Ecological Cybernetics, Virtual Reality, and Virtual Heritage, in *Theorizing Digital Cultural Heritage. A Critical Discourse*, eds. F. Cameron & S. Kenderdine, Cambridge: The MIT Press, 389–408.

Forte, M., 2010. Introduction to Cyber-Archaeology, in *Cyber-Archaeology*, Oxford: Archaeopress, 9–14.

Forte, M., 2014. Virtual Reality, Cyberarchaeology, Teleimmersive Archaeology, in *3D Recording and Modelling in Archaeology and Cultural Heritage. Theory and Best Practices*, eds. F. Remondino & S. Campana, Oxford: Archaeopress, 113–127.

Fossheim, H. J., 2017. Science, Scientism, and the Ethics of Archaeology. *Norwegian Archaeological Review*, 50(2), 116–119.

Fouseki, K. & M. Shehade, 2017. Heritage Activism and Cultural Rights: The Case of the New Acropolis Museum, in *Heritage in Action. Making the Past in the Present*, eds. H. Silverman, E. Waterton & S. Watson, Cham: Springer, 137–150.

Gaimster, D. (ed.), 1994. Museum Archaeology in Europe. *Proceedings of a Conference Held at the British Museum, 15–17 October 1992*, Oxford: Oxbow Books.

Gaimster, D. (ed.), 2007. *Making History: Antiquaries in Britain, 1707–2007*, London: Royal Academy of Arts and the Society of Antiquaries of London.

Garrone, L., 2012. *Non si abbatterà il muretto dell'Ara Pacis arriva lo stop della soprintendenza.* Available from: http://roma.corriere.it/roma/notizie/cronaca/12_settembre_1/muretto-ara-pacis-stop-sovrintendenza-2111647965285.shtml?refresh_ce-cp [Accessed 1 August 2017].

Garstki, K., 2016. Virtual Representation: The Production of 3D Digital Artifacts. *Journal of Archaeological Method and Theory*, 1, 1–25.

Geismar, H., 2018. *Museum Object Lessons for the Digital Age*, London: UCL Press.

Gell, A., 2013. *Art and Agency: An Anthropological Theory*, Oxford: Clarendon Press.

Gill, F., 2015. *En dörr på Sandby borg.* Available from: http://experimentelltkulturarv.se/en-dorr-pa-sandby-borg/ [Accessed 1 August 2017].

Glasser, B. G. & A. L. Strauss, 2008. *The Discovery of Grounded Theory: Strategies for Qualitative Research*, New Brunswick – London: Aldine Transaction.

González-Ruibal, A., 2016. Archaeology and the Time of Modernity. *Historical Archaeology*, 50(3), 144–164.

González-Ruibal, A., 2019. *An Archaeology of the Contemporary Era*, Abingdon – Oxon – New York: Routledge.

Gosden, C., 2001. Making Sense: Archaeology and Aesthetics. *World Archaeology*, 33(2), 163–167.

Gosden, C., E. Edwards & R. B. Philips (eds.), 2006. *Sensible Objects. Colonialism, Museums and Material Culture*, Oxford – New York: Berg.

Gould, R. A. & M. B. Schiffer (eds.), 1981. *Modern Material Culture: The Archaeology of Us*, New York: Academic Press.

Gravari-Barbas, M., 2020. The Challenges of Star Architecture in Historic Cities: The Case of the Acropolis Museum in Athens, in *About Star Architecture*, eds. N. Alaily-Mattar, D. Ponzini & A. Thierstein, Cham: Springer, 267–289.

Greene, E. S. & J. Leidwanger, 2017. Damien Hirst's Tale of Shipwreck and Salvaged Treasure. *American Journal of Archaeology*, 122(1), 2–11.

Griffiths, S., C. Bonacchi, G. Moshenska & L.-J. Richardson, 2015. OK Computer? Digital Community Archaeologies in Practice. *Internet Archaeology*, 40. Published online. Accessible from: https://doaj.org/article/17652c206e8e4d75b-769ec3082db3a02 [Accessed 17 January 2023].

Haber, A., 2013. Evestigation, Nomethodology and Deictics, in *Reclaiming Archaeology: Beyond the Tropes of Modernity*, ed. A. González-Ruibal, London – New York: Routledge, 79–88.

Hahn, T., 2002. Lighting, in *The Manual of Museum Exhibitions*, eds. B. Lord & G. D. Lord, Walnut Creek – Lanham – New York – London: Altamira, 167–170.

Hamilakis, Y., 2011. Museums of Oblivion. *Antiquity*, 85, 625–629.

Hamilakis, Y., 2013. *Archaeology and the Senses. Human Experience, Memory, and Affect*, New York: Cambridge University Press.

Haraway, D., 1991. *Simians, Cyborgs and Women. The Reinvention of Nature*, New York: Routledge.

Harman, G., 2011. *The Quadruple Object*, Winchester: Zero Books. [e-book version]

Harman, G., 2019. A New Sense of Mimesis, in *Aesthetics Equals Politics. New Discourses across Art, Architecture, and Philosophy*, eds. M. Foster & M. Shaw, Cambridge – London: The MIT Press, 49–64.

Harrison, R., 2011. Surface Assemblages. Towards an Archaeology in and of the Present. *Archaeological Dialogues*, 18(2), 141–161.

Harrison, R., 2016. Archaeologies of Emergent Presents and Futures. *Historical Archaeology*, 50(3), 165–180.

Harrison, R. & J. Schofield, 2010. *After Modernity. Archaeological Approaches to the Contemporary Past*, Oxford: Oxford University Press.

Heidegger, M., 1970. *What Is a Thing?* trans. W. B. Barton Jr. & V. Deutsch, Chicago: Henry Regner Company.

Heidegger, M., 1977. *The Question Concerning Technology and Other Essays*, trans. W. Lovitt, New York: Harper.

Heidegger, M., 1996. *Being and Time*, trans. J. Stambaugh, Albany: State University of New York Press.

Heidegger, M., 2004. *What Is Called Thinking?* trans. J. G. Gray, New York: Perennial.

Hermon, S., 2018. *Novel Approaches to the Re-Assembly, Re-Association and Re-Unification of Cultural Heritage Collections – The GRAVITATE Project Solution*. Wystąpienie na 46. konferencji Computer Applications and Quantitative Methods in Archaeology (CAA 2018).

Hicks, D. & M. C. Beaudry (eds.), 2010. *The Oxford Handbook of Material Culture Studies*, Oxford: Oxford University Press.

Hill, L. J., 2014. Human Geography and Archaeology: Strange Bedfellows? *Progress in Human Geography*, 39(4), 1–20.

Hirst, D., E. Geuna & A. Corry (eds.), 2017. *Damien Hirst: Treasures from the Wreck of the Unbelievable*, Venezia: Pinault Collection.

Hitchens, C., 2008. *The Parthenon Marbles. The Case for Reunification*, London – New York: Verso.

Hodder, I., 1997. 'Always momentary, fluid and flexible': Towards a Reflexive Excavation Methodology. *Antiquity*, 273(71), 691–700.

Hodder, I., 1999. *The Archaeological Process: An Introduction*, Oxford: Blackwell.

Hodder, I., 2005. *Reading the Past: Current Approaches to Interpretation in Archaeology*, Cambridge: Cambridge University Press.

Hodder, I., 2012. *Entangled. An Archaeology of the Relationships between Humans and Things*, Oxford – Malden – Chichester: Wiley-Blackwell.

Hodder, I., 2016. *Studies in Human-Thing Entanglement*. Available from: http://www.ian-hodder.com/books/studies-human-thing-entanglement [Accessed 16 April 2018].

Holtorf, C., 2006. *Archaeology Is a Brand! The Meaning of Archaeology in Contemporary Popular Culture*, London – New York: Routledge.

Holtorf, C., 2013. On Pastness: A Reconsideration of Materiality in Archaeological Object Authenticity. *Anthropological Quarterly*, 86(2), 427–443.

Holtorf, C., & T. Schadla-Hall, 1999. Age as Artefact: On Archaeological Authenticity. *European Journal of Archaeology*, 2(2), 229–247.

Hooper-Greenhill, E., 2002. *Museums and the Shaping of Knowledge*, London – New York: Taylor & Francis.

Hooper-Greenhill, E., 2005. *Museum and the Interpretation of Visual Culture*, New York: Routledge.

Huggett, J., 2015a. A Manifesto for an Introspective Digital Archaeology. *Open Archaeology*, 1, 86–95.

Huggett, J., 2015b. Digital Haystacks: Open Data and the Transformation of Archaeological Knowledge, in *Open Source Archaeology: Ethics and Practice*, eds. A. T. Wilson & B. Edwards, Warsaw – Berlin: De Gruyter, 6–29.

Hui, Y., 2016. *On the Existence of Digital Objects*, Minneapolis – London: University of Minnesota Press.

Impey, O., & A. MacGregor (eds.), 1987. *The Origins of Museums. The Cabinet of Curiosities in Sixteenth- and Seventeenth-Century Europe*, Oxford: Clarendon Press.

Ingold, T., 2011. *Being Alive. Essays on Movement, Knowledge and Description*, Oxon: Routledge.

Ingold, T., 2013. *Making. Anthropology, Archaeology, Art and Architecture*, London – New York: Routledge.

Ireland, T. & T. Bell, 2021. Chasing Future Feelings: A Practice-led Experiment with Emergent Digital Materialities of Heritage. *Museum & Society*, 19(2), 149–165.

Jakobsen, A. S., 2012. Experience in-between Architecture and Context: The New Acropolis Museum, Athens. *Journal of Aesthetics & Culture*, 4(1). Published online. Accessible from: https://www.tandfonline.com/doi/full/10.3402/jac.v4i0.18158 [Accessed 17 January 2023].

James, N., 2009. The Acropolis and Its New Museum. *Antiquity*, 83, 1144–1151.

Jameson, J. M., 2003. Art and Imagery as Tools for Public Interpretation and Education in Archaeology, in *Ancient Muses: Archaeology and the Art*, eds. J. M. Jameson, J. E. Ehrenhard & C. A. Finn, Tuscaloosa – London: The University of Alabama Press, 57–65.

Jameson, J. M., J. E. Ehrenhard & C. A. Finn (eds.), 2003. *Ancient Muses: Archaeology and the Art*, Tuscaloosa – London: The University of Alabama Press.

Jeffrey, S., 2015. Challenging Heritage Visualisation: Beauty, Aura and Democratisation. *Open Archaeology*, 1, 144–152.

Jenkins, T., 2016. *Keeping Their Marbles. How the Treasures of the Past Ended Up in Museums... and Why They Should Stay There*, Oxford: Oxford University Press.

Jones, A., 2002. *Archaeological Theory and Scientific Practice*, Cambridge: Cambridge University Press.

Jones, A., 2004. Archaeometry and Materiality: Materials-Based Analysis in Theory and Practice. *Archaeometry*, 46(3), 327–338.

Jones, A., 2014. Meeting Pasts Halfway: A Consideration of the Ontology of Material Evidence in Archaeology, in *Material Evidence. Learning from Archaeological Practice*, eds. R. Chapman & A. Wylie, Oxon – New York: Routledge, 324–338.

Jones, S., 2010. Negotiating Authentic Objects and Authentic Selves: Beyond the Deconstruction of Authenticity. *Journal of Material Culture*, 15(2), 181–203.

Jones, S., 2014. Wrestling with the Social Value of Heritage: Problems, Dilemmas and Opportunities. *Journal of Community Archaeology & Heritage*, 4(1), 21–37.

Jones, S., 2017. Unlocking Essences and Exploring Networks: Experiencing Authenticity in Heritage Education Settings, in *Sensitive Pasts: Questioning Heritage in Education. Making Sense of History*, eds. C. Van Boxtel, M. Grever & S. R. E. Klein, Oxford: Berghahn Books, 130–152.

Jones, A. & B. Alberti, 2015. Archaeology after Interpretation, in *Archaeology after Interpretation: Returning Materials to Archaeological Theory*, eds. B. Alberti, A. Jones & J. Pollard, London – New York: Routledge, 15–35.

Jones, A. & P. Bonaventura, 2011a. Shaping the Past: Sculpture and Archaeology, in *Sculpture and Archaeology*, eds. P. Bonaventura & A. Jones, Surrey – Burlington: Routledge, 1–17.

Jones, A. & P. Bonaventura (eds.), 2011b. *Sculpture and Archaeology*, Surrey – Burlington: Routledge.

Jones, S., S. Jeffrey, M. Maxwell, C. Hale & C. Jones, 2017. 3D Heritage Visualisation and the Negotiation of Authenticity: The ACCORD Project. *International Journal of Heritage Studies*, 24(4), 333–353.

Kallis, A., 2000. 'Framing' Romanità: The Celebrations for the Bimillenario Augusteo and the Augusteo – Ara Pacis Project. *Journal of Contemporary History*, 46(4), 809–831.

Kallis, A., 2012. The "Third Rome" of Fascism: Demolitions and the Search for a New Urban Syntax. *The Journal of Modern History*, 84(1), 40–79.

Kenderdine, S., L. Hibberd & J. Shaw, 2021. Radical Intangibles: Materializing the Ephemeral. *Museum & Society*, 19(2), 252–272.

Kidd, J., 2014. *Museums in the New Mediascape. Transmedia, Participation, Ethics*, Surrey – Burlington: Routledge.

Killick, D., 2014. Using Evidence from Natural Sciences in Archaeology, in *Material Evidence. Learning from Archaeological Practice*, eds. R. Chapman & A. Wylie, Oxon – New York: Routledge, 159–172.

Kopytoff, I., 1987. The Cultural Biography of Things: Commoditization as Process, in *The Social Life of Things Commodities in Cultural Perspective*, ed. A. Appadurai, Cambridge: Cambridge University Press, 64–92.

Kristeva, J., 1982. *Powers of Horror. An Essay on Abjection*, trans. L. S. Roudiez, New York: Columbia University Press.

Kristiansen, K., 2014. Towards a New Paradigm? The Third Science Revolution and Its Possible Consequences in Archaeology. *Current Swedish Archaeology*, 22, 11–34.

Lacoue-Labarthe, P. & J.-L. Nancy, 1988. *The Literary Absolute. The Theory of Literature in German Romanticism*, trans. P. Barnard & C. Lester, New York: State University of New York Press.

Latour, B., 1999. *Pandora's Hope: Essays on the Reality of Science Studies*, Cambridge: Harvard University Press.

Latour, B., 2002. *We Have Never Been Modern*, Cambridge: Harvard University Press.

Latour, B., 2005. *Reassembling the Social: An Introduction to Actor-Network-Theory*, Oxford – New York: Oxford University Press.

Latour, B. & A. Lowe, 2011. The Migration of Aura or How to Explore the Original through Its Facsimile, in *Switching Codes*, ed. T. Bartscherer, Chicago: University of Chicago Press, 275–298.

Lea, J., 2017. Teaching the Past in Museums, in *Museums and Archaeology*, ed. R. Skeates, New York – London: Routledge, 473–484.

Lending, M., 2018. Negotiating Absence: Bernard Tschumi's New Acropolis Museum in Athens. *The Journal of Architecture*, 23(5), 797–819.

Lercari, N., J. Shulze, W. Wendrich, B. Porter, M. Burton & T. E. Levy, 2016. *3-D Digital Preservation of At-Risk Global Cultural Heritage*, w: *EURO-GRAPHICS Workshop on Graphics and Cultural Heritage*, eds. C. E. Catalano & L. De Luca. Available from: https://doi.org/10.2312/gch.20161395 [Accessed 16 June 2018].

Leroi-Gourhan, A., 1993. *Gesture and Speech*, trans. A. Bostock Berger, Cambridge – London: MIT Press.

Levy, T., N. G. Smith, M. Najjar, T. A. DeFanti, A. Yu, L. Min & F. Kuester, 2012. *Cyber-Archaeology in the Holy Land. The Future of the Past*, San Diego: Biblical Archaeology Society.

Lidén, K., 2017. A Common Language Is the Basis for Sound Collaboration. *Norwegian Archaeological Review*, 50(2), 124–126.

Lidén, K. & G. Eriksson, 2013. Archaeology vs Archaeological Science. Do We Have a Case? *Current Swedish Archaeology*, 21, 11–21.

Llewelyn, J., 2001. Representation in Language, in *Art and Representation: Contributions to Contemporary Aesthetics*, ed. A. C. Sukla, Westport: Praeger, 29–58.

Lucas, G., 2005. *The Archaeology of Time*, London – New York: Routledge.

Lucas, G., 2008. Time and Archaeological Event. *Cambridge Archaeological Journal*, 18(1), 59–65.

Lucas, G., 2012. *Understanding the Archaeological Record*, New York: Cambridge University Press.

Lucas, G., 2014. Evidence of What? On the Possibilities of Archaeological Interpretation, in *Material Evidence. Learning from Archaeological Practice*, eds. R. Chapman & A. Wylie, Oxon – New York: Routledge, 311–323.

Lucas, G., 2015. Afterword: Archaeology and the Science of New Objects, in *Archaeology after Interpretation: Returning Materials to Archaeological Theory*, eds. B. Alberti, A. M. Jones & J. Pollard, London – New York: Routledge, 369–413.

Lucas, G. & B. Olsen, 2022. The Case Study in Archaeological Theory, *American Antiquity*, https://doi.org/10.1017/aaq.2021.151.

Lynch, M., 1985. *Art and Artifact in Laboratory Science. A Study of Shop Work and Shop Talk in a Research Laboratory*, London: Routledge.

MacCormack, D. P., 2010. Thinking in Transition: The Affirmative Refrain of Experience/Experiment, in *Non-Representational Theories and Geography*, eds. B. Anderson & P. Harrison, Farnham – Burlington: Ashgate, 201–220.

Macdonald, S. & G. Fyfe (eds.), 1999. *Theorizing Museums. Representing Identity and Diversity in a Changing World*, Oxford – Malden: Blackwell Publishers.

Macdonald, S. (ed.), 1998. Exhibitions of Power and Powers of Exhibition: An Introduction to the Politics of Display, in *The Politics of Display. Museums, Science, Culture*, London – New York: Routledge, 1–21.

MacLeod, S., L. H. Hanks & J. Hale (eds.), 2012. *Museum Making. Narratives, Architectures, Exhibitions*, New York: Routledge.

Marc Quinn: Drawn from Life, 2017. Available from: https://www.soane.org/whats-on/exhibitions/marc-quinn-drawn-life [Accessed 25 July 2018].

Marciniak, A., 1996. *Archeologia i jej źródła. Metody faunistyczne w praktyce badawczej archeologii*, Warszawa – Poznań: Wydawnictwo Naukowe PWN.

Mark Dion, Tate Thames Dig 1999, 2000. Available from: https://www.tate.org.uk/art/artworks/dion-tate-thames-dig-t07669 [Accessed 25 July 2018].

Marshall, C. R., 2012. Athens, London or Bilbao? Contested Narratives of Display in the Parthenon Galleries of the British Museum, in *Museum Making. Narratives, Architectures, Exhibitions*, eds. S. MacLeod, L. H. Hanks & J. Hale, New York: Routledge, 34–47.

Marstine, J. (ed.), 2006a. *New Museum. Theory and Practice*, Malden – Oxford – Victoria: Blackwell Publishing.

Marstine, J. (ed.), 2006b. Introduction. What Is New Museum Theory? in *New Museum. Theory and Practice*, Malden – Oxford – Victoria: Blackwell Publishing, 1–37.

McClung, F. E., 1974. Artifact Study: A Proposed Model. *Winterthur Portfolio*, 9, 153–173.

McLuhan, M., 2003. *Understanding Media: The Extensions of Man*, London – New York: Gingko Press.

Merkel, J., 2002. The Museum as Artifact. *The Wilson Quarterly*, 1, 66–79.

Merriman, N., 2017. Involving the Public in Museum Archaeology, in *Museums and Archaeology*, ed. R. Skeates, New York – London: Routledge, 543–563.

Meskell, L., 2013. Dirty, Pretty Things: On Archaeology and Prehistoric Materialities, in *Cultural Histories of the Material World*, ed. P. N. Miller, Ann Arbor: University of Michigan Press, 92–107.

Mickel, A., 2019. Essential Excavation Experts: Alienation and Agency in the History of Archaeological Labor. *Archaeologies: Journal of the World Archaeological Congress*, 15, 181–205.

Miller, P. N. (ed.), 2013. *Cultural Histories of the Material World*, Ann Arbor: University of Michigan Press.

Mitchell, W. J. T., 2005. *What Do Pictures Want? The Lives and Loves of Images*, Chicago: University of Chicago Press.

Morgan, C., 2009. (Re)Building Çatalhöyük: Changing Virtual Reality in Archaeology. *Journal of the World Archaeological Congress*, 5(3), 468–487.

Moser, S., 2010. The Devil Is in the Detail: Museum Displays and the Creation of Knowledge. *Museum Anthropology*, 33(1), 22–33.

Moser, S., 2012. Archaeological Visualization: Early Artifact Illustration and the Birth of the Archaeological Image, in *Archaeological Theory Today*, 2nd edition, ed. I. Hodder, Cambridge – Malden: Polity Press, 292–321.

Mosse, G., 1996. Fascist Aesthetics and Society: Some Consideration. *Journal of Contemporary History*, 31(2), 245–252.

Murray, T. & C. Evans (eds.), 2008. *Histories of Archaeology: A Reader in the History of Archaeology*, Oxford: Oxford University Press.

Nash, S. E. & N. O'Malley, 2012. The Changing Mission of Museums, in *Archaeology in Society. Its Relevance in the Modern World*, eds. M. Rockman & J. Flatman, New York: Springer-Verlag, 97–109.

Nativ, A., G. Lucas, M. Edgeworth, C. Witmore & O. Harris, 2018. On the Object of Archaeology. *Archaeological Dialogues*, 25(1), 1–47.

Newhouse, V., 1998. *Towards a New Museum*, New York: Monacelli Press.

Oliva, A. B. [no date] *Ara Artis*. Available from: http://en.arapacis.it/mostre_ed_eventi/mostre/opera_per_l_ara_pacis_mimmo_paladino_brian_eno/ara_artis [Accessed 1 August 2017].

Olsen, B., 2012a. Symmetrical Archaeology, in *Archaeological Theory Today*, ed. I. Hodder, Cambridge: Polity Press, 208–228.

Olsen, B., 2012b. After Interpretation: Remembering Archaeology. *Current Swedish Archaeology*, 20, 11–35.

Olsen, B., 2013. *In Defense of Things: Archaeology and the Ontology of Objects*, Lanham: AltaMira Press.

Olsen, B. & Þ Pétursdóttir (eds.), 2014. *Ruin Memories. Materiality, Aesthetics and the Archaeology of the Recent Past*, London – New York: Routledge.

Olsen, B., M. Shanks, T. Webmoor & C. Witmore, 2012. *Archaeology. The Discipline of Things*, Berkeley – Los Angeles – London: University of California Press.

Olsen, B. & A. Svestad, 1994. Creating Prehistory: Archaeology Museums and the Discourse of Modernism. *Nordisk Museologi*, 1, 3–20.

Olsen, B. & C. Witmore, 2015. Archaeology, Symmetry and the Ontology of Things. A Response to Critics. *Archaeological Dialogues*, 22(2), 187–197.

Olsen, B. & C. Witmore, 2021. When Defense Is Not Enough: On Things, Archaeological Theory, and the Politics of Misrepresentation. *Forum Kritische Archäologie*, 10, 67–88.

Ouzman, S., 2006. The Beauty of Letting Go: Fragmentary Museums and Archaeologies of Archive, in *Sensible Objects. Colonialism, Museums and Material Culture*, eds. C. Gosden, E. Edwards & R. B. Phillips, Oxford – New York: Berg, 269–301.

Pandermalis, D., S. Eleftheratou & C. Vlassopoulou, 2015. *Acropolis Museum Guide*, ed. S. Eleftheratou, Athens: Acropolis Museum Editions.

Paterson, M., 2009. Haptic Geographies: Ethnography, Haptic Knowledges and Sensuous Dispositions. *Progress in Human Geography*, 33(6), 766–788.

Paul Coldwell: Picturing the Invisible, 2019. Available from: https://paulcoldwell.org/portfolio-item/picturing-the-invisible/ [Accessed 12 May 2022].

Pearce, S. M., 1990. *Archaeological Curatorship*, London: Leicester University Press.

Pearce, S. M. (ed.), 2006a. *Interpreting Objects and Collections*, New York: Routledge.

Pearce, S. M. (ed.), 2006b. Thinking about Things, in *Interpreting Objects and Collections*, New York: Routledge, 125–132.

Pearce, S. M. (ed.), 2006c. Objects as Meaning; or Narrating the Past, in *Interpreting Objects and Collections*, New York: Routledge, 19–29.

Pearce, S. M. (ed.), 2006d. Museum Objects, in *Interpreting Objects and Collections*, New York: Routledge, 9–11.

Pearson, M. & M. Shanks, 2001. *Theatre/Archaeology*, London – New York: Routledge.

Pedeli, C. & S. Pulga, 2013. *Conservation Practices on Archaeological Excavations. Principles and Methods*, trans. E. Risser, Los Angeles: The Getty Conservation Institute.

Peltz, L. & M. Myrone (eds.), 1999. *Producing the Past: Aspects of Antiquarian Culture and Practice, 1700–1850*, Cambridge: Routledge.

Perry, S., 2018. Why Are Heritage Interpreters Voiceless at the Trowel's Edge? A Plea for Rewriting the Archaeological Workflow. *Advances in Archaeological Practice*, 6(3), 212–227.

Pétursdóttir, Þ. & B. Olsen, 2018. Theory Adrift: The Matter of Archaeological Theorizing. *Journal of Social Archaeology*, 18(1), 97–117.

Phillips, D., 2004. *Daylighting. Natural Light in Architecture*, Oxford – Burligton: Taylor and Francis.

Philips, S. C., P. W. Walland, S. Modafferi, L. Dorst, M. Spagnuolo, Ch. E. Catalano, D. Oldman, A. Tal, I. Shimshoni, S. Hermon. 2016. GRAVITATE: Geometric and Semantic Matching for Cultural Heritage Artefacts. in *EUROGRAPHICS Workshop on Graphics and Cultural Heritage*, eds. C. E. Catalano & L. De Luca. Accessible form: http://dx.doi.org/10.2312/gch.20161407 [13 January 2023].

Piotrowski, P., 2011. *Muzeum krytyczne*, Poznań: Rebis.

Pirani, F. [no date] *Conversazione con Mimmo Paladino*. Available from: http://www.arapacis.it/mostre_ed_eventi/mostre/opera_per_l_ara_pacis_mimmo_paladino_brian_eno/conversazione_con_mimmo_paladino [Accessed 1 August 2017].

Plantzos, D., 2011. Behold the Raking Geison: The New Acropolis Museum and Its Context-Free Archaeologies. *Antiquity*, 85, 613–630.

Pollard, J., 2004. The Art of Decay and the Transformation of Substance, in *Substance, Memory, Display: Archaeology and Art*, eds. C. Renfrew, C. Gosden & E. DeMarais, Cambridge: McDonald Institute for Archaeological Research, 47–62.

Pollard, M. & P. Bray, 2007. A Bicycle Made for Two? The Integration of Scientific Techniques into Archaeological Interpretation. *Annual Review of Anthropology*, 36, 245–259.

Pollard, M. & P. Bray, 2014. The Archaeological Bazaar. Scientific Methods for Sale? Or: Putting the "Arch-" Back into Archaeometry, in *Material Evidence. Learning from Archaeological Practice*, eds. R. Chapman & A. Wylie, Oxon – New York: Routledge, 113–127.

Potts, A., 1994. *Flesh and the Ideal: Winckelmann and the Origins of Art History*, New Haven – London: Yale University Press.

Preziosi, D. (ed.), 2009. Introduction, in *The Art of Art History: A Critical Anthology*, Oxford – New York: Oxford University Press, 13–21.

Pujol, L., A. Katifori, M. Vayanou, M. Roussou, M. Karvounis, M. Kyriakidi, S. Eleftheratou & Y. Ioannidis, 2013. From Personalization to Adaptivity: Creating Immersive Visits through Interactive Digital Storytelling at the Acropolis Museum, in *9th International Conference on Intelligent Environments, Athens, Greece, 16–19 July 2013*, eds. J. A. Botía & D. Charitos, 541–554. http://eprints.gla. ac.uk/143500/ [Accessed 28 June 2022].

Putnam, J. [no date] *Paladino/Eno at Ara Pacis*. Available from: http://en.arapacis.it/ mostre_ed_eventi/mostre/opera_per_l_ara_pacis_mimmo_paladino_brian_eno/ paladino_eno_all_ara_pacis [Accessed 1 August 2017].

Pye, E., 2017. Issues in Practice. Conservation Procedures, in *Museums and Archaeology*, ed. R. Skeates, New York – London: Routledge, 109–141.

Rask, K., 2017. The New Acropolis Museum. Where the Visual Feast Trumps Education, in *Museums and Archaeology*, ed. R. Skeates, New York – London: Routledge, 450–455.

Rathje, W., 2012. Appendix: Garbology 101, in *Encyclopedia of Consumption and Waste: The Social Science of Garbage*, 2 [N–Z], eds. C. A. Zimring & W. Rathje, Los Angeles: Sage, 1027–1114.

Rathje, W. & C. Murphy, 1992. *Rubbish! The Archaeology of Garbage*, Stuart: University of Arizona Press.

Reilly, P., 1991. Towards a Virtual Archaeology, in *CAA90. Computer Applications and Quantitative Methods in Archaeology 1990*, British Archaeological Reports International Series 565, eds. S. Rahtz & K. Lockyear, Oxford: Tempus Reparatum, 132–139.

Renfrew, C., 2003. *Figuring It Out. What Are We? Where Do We Come from? The Parallel Visions of Artists and Archaeologists*, London: Thames and Hudson.

Renfrew, C., 2014. Colin Renfrew: A Conversation, in *Art and Archaeology*, eds. I. A. Russell & A. Cochrane, New York – Heidelberg – Dordrecht – London: Routledge, 9–20.

Renfrew, C. & P. Bahn, 2012. *Archaeology: Theories, Methods and Practice*, London: Thames and Hudson.

Rich, S., 2019. *Shipwreck Hauntography. Underwater Ruins and the Uncanny*, Amsterdam: Amsterdam University Press.

Richardson, L., 2013. A Digital Public Archaeology? *Papers from the Institute of Archaeology*, 23(1). Published online. Accessible from: https://discovery.ucl.ac.uk/ id/eprint/1430285/ [Accessed 17 January 2023].

Rodaway, P., 1994. *Sensuous Geographies. Body, Sense and Place*, London: Routledge.

Roosevelt, C. R., P. Cobb, E. Moss, B. R. Olson & S. Ünlüsoy, 2015. Excavation Is Destruction Digitization: Advances in Archaeological Practice. *Journal of Field Archaeology*, 40(3), 325–346.

Rouba, B. J., 2012. The Significance of Research in the Process of Conservation, in *Interdisciplinary Research on the Works of Art*, eds. J. Olszewska-Świetlik, J. M. Arszyńska & B. Szmelter-Fausek, Toruń: Wydawnictwo Naukowe Uniwersytetu Mikołaja Kopernika, 41–50.

Russell, I. A., 2011. Art and Archaeology. A Modern Allegory. *Archaeological Dialogues*, 18(2), 172–176.

Russell, I. A. & A. Cochrane (eds.), 2014a. *Art and Archaeology*, New York – Heidelberg – Dordrecht – London: Routledge.

Russell, I. A. & A. Cochrane (eds.), 2014b. Introduction, in *Art and Archaeology*, New York – Heidelberg – Dordrecht – London: Routledge, 1–8.

Saito, Y., 2007. *Everyday Aesthetics*, Oxford: Oxford University Press.

Sarah Lucas: Power in Woman, 2016. Available from: https://www.soane.org/whats-on/exhibitions/sarah-lucas-power-woman [Accessed 25 July 2018].

Saunderson, H., A. G. Cruickshank & E. McSorley, 2010. The Eyes Have It: Eye Movements and the Debatable Differences between Original Objects and Reproductions, in *Museum Materialities. Objects, Engagements and Interpretations*, ed. S. H. Dudley, Oxon – New York: Routledge, 89–98.

Scheerer, S., O. Ortega-Morales & C. Gaylarde, 2009. Microbial Deterioration of Stone Monuments—An Updated Overview. *Advances in Applied Microbiology*, 66, 97–140.

Schiffer, M., 1976. *Behavioral Archaeology*, New York: Academic Press.

Schnapp, A., 1996. *The Discovery of the Past: The Origins of Archaeology*, trans. I. Kinnes & G. Varndell, London: The British Museum Press.

Scott, M., 2015. Normal and Extraordinary Conservation Knowledge: Towards a Post-Normal Theory of Cultural Materials Conservation. *AICCM Bulletin*, 36(1), 3–12.

Shanks, M., 1998. The Life of an Artifact in an Interpretive Archaeology. *Fennoscandia Archaeologica*, XV, 15–31.

Shanks, M., 2012. *The Archaeological Imagination*, Walnut Creek: Left Coast Press.

Shanks, M. & C. Tilley, 1992. *Re-Constructing Archaeology. Theory and Practice*, London – New York: Routledge.

Shanks, M. & T. Webmoor, 2012. A Political Economy of Visual Media in Archaeology, in *Re-Presenting the Past: Archaeology through Image and Text*, eds. S. Bond & S. Houston, Oxford: Oxbow Books, 85–108.

Shepherd, N., 2013. Ruin Memory: A Hauntology of Cape Town, in *Reclaiming Archaeology. Beyond the Tropes of Modernity*, ed. A. González-Ruibal, London – New York: Routledge, 233–243.

Sirefman, S. 1999. Formed and Forming: Contemporary Museum Architecture. *Daedalus*, 3, 297–320.

Sjöstrand, Y., 2017. The Concept of Art as Archaeologically Applicable. *Cambridge Archaeological Journal*, 27(2), 371–388.

Skeates, R. (ed.), 2017a. *Museums and Archaeology*, London – New York: Routledge.

Skeates, R. (ed.), 2017b. Introduction to Part I, in *Museums and Archaeology*, London – New York: Routledge, 43–45.

Skeates, R. (ed.), 2017c. Museum and Archaeology. Principles, Practice, and Debates, in *Museums and Archaeology*, London – New York: Routledge, 1–40.

Skeates, R. (ed.), 2017d. Speaking for the Past in the Present. Text, Authority, and Learning in Archaeology, in *Museums and Archaeology*, London – New York: Routledge, 346–360.

Smith, B. D. & M. A. Zeder, 2013. The Onset of the Anthropocene. *Anthropocene*, 4, 8–13.

Smithson, R., 1968. A Sedimentation of the Mind: Earth Projects. *Artforum*, 82–91.

Snodgrass, A., 2011. Soft Targets and No-Win Dilemmas: Response to Dimitris Plantzos. *Antiquity*, 85, 625–629.

Solli, B., M. Burström, E. Domańska, M. Edgeworth, A. González-Ruibal, C. Holtorf, G. Lucas, T. Oestigaard, L. Smith & C. Witmore, 2011. Some Reflections on Heritage and Archaeology in the Anthropocene. *Norwegian Archaeological Review*, 44(1), 40–88.

Sørensen, T. F., 2017. The Two Cultures and a World Apart: Archaeology and Science at a New Crossroads. *Norwegian Archaeological Review*, 50(2), 101–115.

Stanco, F., D. Tanasi, D. Allegra, F. L. M. Milotta, G. Lamagna & G. Monterosso, 2017. Virtual Anastylosis of Greek Sculpture as Museum Policy for Public Outreach and Cognitive Accessibility. *Journal of Electronic Imaging*, 26(1), 1–12.

Steane, M. A., 2011. *Architecture of Light. Recent Approaches to Designing with Natural Light*, London: Routledge.

Stewart, K., 2008. Weak Theory in an Unfinished World. *Journal of Folklore Research*, 45(1), 71–82.

Stiegler, B., 1998. *Technics and Time, 1: The Fault of Epimetheus*, trans. R. Beardsworth, & G. Collins, Stanford: Stanford University Press.

Stobiecka, M., 2018. Multifunctionality of Stone Objects – First Remarks on Marble Mortars from Akrai, in *On the Borders of Syracuse. Multidisciplinary Studies on the Ancient Town of Akrai/Acrae, Sicily*, ed. R. Chowaniec, Warszawa: Instytut Archeologii Uniwersytetu Warszawskiego, 389–402.

Stobiecka, M., 2019. Digital Escapism. How Objects Become Deprived of Matter. *Journal of Contemporary Archaeology*, 5(2), 194–212.

Stobiecka, M., 2020a. Farewell to Tradition? Presenting Archaeology after the Digital Turn. *Advances in Archaeological Practice*, 8(3), 313–318.

Stobiecka, M. 2020b. Towards a Prosthetic Archaeology. *Journal of Social Archaeology*, 20(3), 335–352.

Sullivan, L. P. & S. Terry Childs, 2003. *Curating Archaeological Collections: From the Field to the Repository*, Walnut Creek: AltaMira Press.

Swain, H., 2007. *An Introduction to Museum Archaeology*, Cambridge: Cambridge University Press.

Taussig, M., 2006. What Color Is the Sacred? *Critical Inquiry*, 33(1), 28–51.

Thomas, J., 1996. *Time, Culture, and Identity: An Interpretative Archaeology*, London: Routledge and Kegan Paul.

Thomas, J., 2004. *Archaeology and Modernity*, London – New York: Routledge.

Thomas, J., 2015. The Future of Archaeological Theory. *Antiquity*, 89(348), 1287–1296.

Thorsen, L. E., K. A. Rader & A. Dodd (eds.), 2013. *Animals on Display, The Creaturely in Museums, Zoos, and Natural History*, Pennsylvania: Pennsylvania State University Press.

Tilley, C., 1994. *A Phenomenology of Landscape. Places, Paths and Monuments*, Oxford: Berg.

Tilley, C., 2004. *The Materiality of Stone: Explorations in Landscape Phenomenology*, Oxford: Berg.

Ting, W. Y. V., 2010. Dancing Pot and Pregnant Jar? On Ceramics, Metaphors and Creative Labels, in *Museum Materialities. Objects, Engagements, Interpretations*, ed. S. H. Dudley, Oxon – New York: Routledge, 189–203.

Trunfio, M. & S. Campana, 2020. A Visitors' Experience Model for Mixed Reality in the Museum. *Current Issues in Tourism*, 23(9), 1053–1058.

Trunfio, M., S. Campana & A. Magnelli, 2020. Measuring the Impact of Functional and Experiential Mixed Reality Elements on a Museum Visit. *Current Issues in Tourism*, 23(16), 1990–2008.

Tsingarida, A. & D. Kurtz (eds.), 2002. *Appropriating Antiquity/Saisir l'Antique: Collections et Collectioneurs d'antiques en Belgique et en Grande-Bretagne au XIXe siècle*, Bruxelles: Livre Timperman.

Tully, G., 2007. Community Archaeology: General Methods and Standards of Practice. *Public Archaeology*, 6(3), 155–187.

van Alphen, E., 2007. Visual Archives as Preposterous History. *Art History*, 30(3), 364–382.

Vergo, P. (ed.), 1989a. *The New Museology*, London: Reaction Books.

Vergo, P. (ed.), 1989b. Reticent Object, in *The New Museology*, London: Reaction Books, 41–59.

Vickers, M., 1994. Aesthetics in Archaeology. *Cambridge Archaeological Journal*, 4(2), 255–256.

Vilches, F., 2007. The Art of Archaeology. Mark Dion and His Dig Projects. *Journal of Social Archaeology*, 7(2), 199–223.

Vilches, F., 2011. Mirrored Practices: Robert Smithson and Archaeological Fieldwork, in *Sculpture and Archaeology*, eds. P. Bonaventura & A. Jones, Surrey – Burlington: Routledge, 97–112.

Voon, C., 2018. *Classical Sculptures Raise Prosthetic Limbs for Disability Rights*. Available from: https://hyperallergic.com/431449/venus-de-milo-sculpture-3d-printed-prostheses/?utm_source=twitter&utm_medium=social&utm_campaign=sw [Accessed 16 June 2018].

Weker, W., 1998. żelazo archeologiczne – procesy korozji i podstawowe metody doraźnej konserwacji, in *Pierwsza pomoc dla zabytków archeologicznych*, ed. Z. Kobyliński, Warszawa: SNAP – Oddział Warszawski, 47–61.

Wilkins, A. T., 2005. Augustus, Mussolini, and the Parallel Imagery of Empire, in *Donatello among the Blackshirts: History and Modernity in the Visual Culture of Fascist Italy*, eds. C. Lazzaro & R. J. Crum, Ithaca: Cornell University Press, 53–66.

Witcomb, A., 2007. The Materiality of Virtual Technologies: A New Approach to Thinking about the Impact of Multimedia in Museums, in *Theorizing Digital Cultural Heritage. A Critical Discourse*, eds. F. Cameron & S. Kenderdine, Cambridge: The MIT Press, 35–48.

Witmore, C. 2014. Archaeology and New Materialism. *Journal of Contemporary Archaeology*, 1(2), 1–44.

Woodward, S., 2020. *Material Methods. Researching and Thinking with Things*, London – Los Angeles: SAGE Publishing.

Zanker, P., 2002. *The Power of Images in the Age of Augustus*, Ann Arbor: University of Michigan Press.
Zuanni, C., 2021. Theorizing Born Digital Objects: Museums and Contemporary Materialities. *Museum & Society*, 19(2), 184–198.

Editorial note

Some of the findings presented here have also been published in: Stobiecka M., 2019. Digital Escapism. How Objects Become Deprived of Matter. *Journal of Contemporary Archaeology*, 5(2), 194–212 and Stobiecka, M., 2020. *Natura artefaktu, kultura eksponatu. Projekt krytycznego muzeum archeologicznego* [The Nature of Artefacts, the Culture of Exhibits: Towards a critical archaeological museum], Warszawa: Wydawnictwo IBL PAN.

Index